BENEATH
— *the* —
WINTER SYCAMORES

JIM BAHM

TABLE OF CONTENTS

THE INTRODUCTION

In October 1976, Arthur Jones, an inmate at Draper Prison near Montgomery, Alabama, informed writer Jeff Newman that he had spoken to Bruno Richard Hauptmann before he was executed for the murder of Charles Lindbergh's son in 1936. Hauptmann, who had supposedly never admitted anything to anyone regarding the kidnapping, gave Jones a detailed account of that ill-fated night in 1932. Newman's article was published by the National Enquirer and unfortunately was not taken seriously. Critics wanted to know why Jones waited so long before he came forward with this information. The fact is Jones did not wait until 1976, but he was sworn to secrecy until after Bruno Richard Hauptmann died. When Hauptmann was executed in 1936, Jones circulated his story but was still in prison and was unable to get anyone to listen.

Since I was a boy of nine or ten years, I have been intrigued with the Lindbergh Kidnapping. I can remember going to visit the Lindbergh home up in Hopewell, New Jersey with my parents and my uncle. A short drive from my hometown of Trenton; it was a beautiful place—nestled in the hills of the Sourland Mountains. I remember my father driving around those hills, searching for the estate they called Highfields; it seemed like it took hours just to find it. In 1935, the Lindberghs gave the four hundred acre tract of land to the state of New Jersey where it would become a home for troubled boys. I wondered then whether my parents and my uncle were just into history, or if they were trying to show me where I would end up if I failed to perform well in school.

Both of my parents were no more than seven when the little Lindbergh child was stolen from his home on that windswept March night in 1932. My uncle was much older. Before my parents and my uncle passed away in the 1990's, they were still able to recall some of the memories from that historic event in 1932. Most of what they remembered was from their own parents, who talked about it often. In Trenton, there was great skepticism that one man was capable of such an audacious crime. The Lindbergh home was well hidden in those hills. On a moonless winter night, without paved roads and streetlights, just getting there would have proved difficult. It seemed quite amazing that Hauptmann would even attempt such a risky undertaking. Why, and how, one man would attempt to perpetrate a kidnapping of the most famous baby in America alone, by climbing a ladder, snatching the child and spiriting him away in the dark is difficult to comprehend. And why he would ask for only fifty thousand dollars from the child's famous father is vexing. Why would a carpenter make such a crude ladder? And use boards from his attic? Would a German immigrant write ransom notes that sounded so obviously German? Many avenues of doubt have been traveled but everyone who navigates those roads runs into the same dead end. You must prove it otherwise. By using Arthur Jones' testimony, I will not only open and navigate the roads, but also create a believable and viable theory; that Bruno Richard Hauptmann was part of a loosely organized ring that was responsible for the kidnapping of the Lindbergh baby.

It was always interesting to hear my father recall the night they executed Hauptmann at Trenton State Prison for the kidnapping and murder of the Lindbergh baby. The power surge from the electric chair's voltage caused the lights in the neighborhood to flicker on and off. My uncle, who was a real history buff, always had doubts about the outcome of the "Trial of the Century". He thought the trial was a sham and that Hauptmann could not have done it alone. Later on, I found that both my dad and my uncle had reasons for being so interested in the case. For a short time, my dad worked as a guard at Trenton State Prison, referred to by locales and inmates alike as The Wall. While there, he was given a note containing intricate details about the case from a prisoner who had privileged information on the kidnapping. The note was unsigned, its author unknown. My uncle, who happened to know one of the lead detectives on the case, was fortunate to get some confidential information as well. Neither man bothered to do anything about the information to which they were privy.

My father tossed the typed three page single-spaced account of the kidnapping into his dresser drawer in 1950 and left it there until his death in 1999. It lay there in the same spot untouched, but every so often I would go into his room and read it.

I was in my teens when my uncle told me that he knew who the real kidnapper of the Lindbergh baby was. I was astounded. "Really, you know who did it? Tell me, c'mon tell me." He said he couldn't tell me, but that when he died, I could go to his safety deposit box and the name of the kidnapper would be in there. Apparently, my Uncle Jack had been sworn to secrecy as well by the man who gave him this valuable information. One night several years later, I was pressuring him to tell me. We were having a few drinks at one of his favorite watering holes and I think he probably had one too many shots of his favorite Irish whiskey. I'm ashamed to say this but I may have pressured him a wee bit too much, for I was able to get him to tell me the big secret.

Serious about writing a book on the Lindbergh kidnapping, I started reading every possible book I could find on the case, and none had ever presented the theory according to the account given to my dad. More recent books have proposed theories that have gotten close. Initially, I didn't know the identity of the prisoner who wrote the account given to my dad, but I decided to pursue the leads anyway, and see how far I could get, realizing that such an undertaking might fall apart at any time. At times when it looked like that might be the case, I would find some factual information that would keep it together.

Author Jim Fisher, who wrote the book _The Ghosts of Hopewell_, claims that anyone who challenges the verdict is a revisionist, and technically that is correct. But any law scholar would not deny that the trial was improperly conducted. My motivation was not to revise history, but to take one man's account and see if it could work. It is a fact that Arthur Jones spoke with Bruno Richard Hauptmann when the two were on death row together in 1935. In my opinion, his account as supposedly told to him by Hauptmann is better than any other theory, including the prosecution's, despite the verdict.

I first found out about Arthur Jones after reading Fisher's book. In his book, Fisher mentioned the article written for the National Enquirer by Jeff Newman. As he had done previously with anyone who proposed alternate theories, Fisher was extremely critical, but he failed to conduct the proper research to verify if Arthur Jones was indeed on death row with Hauptmann. Immediately, the light bulb went on. I wondered if Jones was the same guy who wrote the account that my dad had sitting in his drawer for so long. I was able to get a copy of the Newman article through Lindbergh archivist Mark Falzini at the New Jersey Police Museum in West Trenton, NJ. After reading the article, I knew we had the author of my dad's account because the information was so similar. Mark had also sent me information on Jones, confirming that they did indeed spend almost six months together in the death house in 1935. My next step was to contact Jeff Newman. I found out that Jeff Newman was an accomplished Boston attorney and was also a successful photojournalist. He covered the Soviet-Afghan War, was one of the first people to interview Charles Manson, and is currently one of the best media attorneys in the country. I e-mailed Newman and he told me that we should talk.

I have spoken with him several times regarding Arthur Jones and he has provided me with excellent insight and information. I was amazed that he could remember such detail thirty years later. Newman told me he really believed that Arthur Jones was telling the truth. He said that Jones was dying from diabetes and had already had one leg amputated, while the other was nothing but a festering wound caused by the effects of the disease. Newman said that despite Jones' poor health, he spoke with great acuity. Jones was very philosophical about his impending death. He wondered how his past behaviors and transgressions would play out when he died. One thing he thought might help him was to get the truth out, and tell what he knew about the Lindbergh Kidnapping. Jones swore that he was telling the truth. He had nothing to gain by coming forward other than to free his mind and he believed this truth could only help him after his death. Hopefully, he was at peace when he died thirteen days later of a massive brain hemorrhage.

I have reconstructed the kidnapping according to the Arthur Jones account. It was not always easy making everything fit exactly as in the written account, because Jones admitted that he could not remember everything exactly as it was told to him. But he swore his basic story was the truth. It seems Arthur Jones was the only person Bruno Richard Hauptmann ever confided in regarding the Lindbergh Kidnapping. So in a sense, the account is Hauptmann's. He and Arthur Jones spoke once a week during shower time, they passed scraps of paper in books and spoke in code when they could. Hauptmann had Jones promise not to say anything until his death. After Hauptmann's execution in 1936, no one was ready to listen to an account of the kidnapping from a convict on death row. Even forty years later in the fall of 1976, people were skeptical. Not only were people skeptical of a National Enquirer article, but they also wondered why some convict would wait forty years to tell his story. Well, I know now that he did not wait. He started circulating that information in 1936 after Hauptmann's execution, again in 1950 when his account ended up in the hands of my dad at Trenton State Prison, and still in 1976, as an old man, he wrote a letter to the National Enquirer and allowed Jeff Newman to interview him.

I hope I can relate the Jones and Hauptmann account, so that people will find out the truth. Do I believe the account? Yes, or I would not have taken the trouble to recreate this scenario. Had Jeff Newman recalled Jones in a different light as a non-credible schemer, I would have abandoned this project. It may not be one hundred percent exact, but I believe it is as close as anyone has ever gotten. Some people will have their doubts, but that is not unusual. I went through and carefully checked every angle before I added more details and dialogue. I am thankful to so many previous authors who painstakingly went through the evidence as they proposed their theories. Lloyd Gardner's book *The Case that Never Dies* is very insightful and a must read for anyone interested in the Lindbergh Kidnapping. I have read just about every book written about the kidnapping and I have analyzed all the details before I applied them to the Jones account. I combined this information with detailed dialogue to make it work. This book is creative non-fiction and should be perceived as such. I am aware that it will be controversial because it is not very flattering toward a national hero. I cannot apologize for that because if Jones was telling the truth as I believe, there should be no apology.

And the person my uncle told me was responsible for the kidnapping of the Lindbergh baby? Charles Lindbergh. Harry Walsh, detective of the Jersey City Police Department and one of the chief investigators on the case, told my uncle many years ago: "They knew it was him, but he was just too big to bring down."

This book is dedicated to "Big Nick" and "Sir John" who put the bug in my ear when I was just a curious kid playing on the streets of Trenton, NJ, and to Arthur Jones who wanted people to listen to his story when he appropriately titled his account of the Lindbergh Kidnapping, "Did Justice Triumph?"

·

For a little boy named
Charlie Lindbergh

"Of all nature's gifts to the human race, what is sweeter to a man than his children?"

CICERO (106-43BC)

CHAPTER ONE
1950/THE NOTE

Nick sat on the bench. He cuffed his sweaty forehead with his right hand, tightened his fingers and massaged his temples. His last day had been a long one. The incessant vulgarities, a near riot and a time clock that wasn't moving had made it difficult. He closed his eyes, raised his chin upward and then leaned his head against the concrete wall. Finally, his shift was over. In fact, his short career as a prison guard was over and he was looking forward to starting a new job with the railroad. At least he wouldn't have to deal with the bullshit any more. All he had to do was wait for this one prisoner; just some guy named Jones who wanted to give him something before he departed. Maybe it was just a goodbye card—he didn't know. He remembered he had helped the man obtain an old Remington typewriter that the prison store was throwing out. The shiny, black beauty barely worked because the metal letters would jam up and stick to each other. After getting the approval from the captain, he delivered it to his cell any way. Christmas had come early—Jones was thrilled to death. Nick smiled at the thought despite keeping his eyes closed. With his body getting more relaxed, he let his mind wonder some more when he heard the prisoner walking down the hall. He opened his eyes to see Arthur Jones heading his way.

Jones took short steps but he had a certain swagger in his gait. He posed no threat and wore no cuffs or shackles. The guards who were supposed to watch him showed little concern. The prisoner paused for a second before he handed Nick a smudged plain white envelope, checking to see if the contents were in order. Nodding to the young guard; he spoke in a typical 'Jersey' accent but softly and in a high tone.

"Nick, take this. It ain't gonna do me no good. If I was on the outside, I'd take it to the *Daily News*, make myself some money and let the truth be known. But I ain't stupid, Nick. I know I ain't never gonna get out. Been here since I was in my twenties—in the wrong place at the wrong time. You know how that goes. But I ain't mad at nobody. You're a good man and I trust you. You take that note and make money off it. What's in there is the truth. And I put it down there as I remembered it."

Nick wasn't sure what Arthur Jones was talking about. He only knew Jonesy a little. Thought he was a good guy, despite being trapped behind The Wall. He had been charged with murder and sentenced to death back in the early thirties. After an appeal, he was given a lighter sentence. That was all Nick could remember about his case. He remembered Jones saying that he had no family. His family had evolved into a handful of prisoners and a few guards at the prison. After bouncing around New Jersey's prison system, The Wall was still his home. Jones was about forty years old, but a receding hairline and some recent health problems had made him look older.

"I thought of you, Nick. You're not like some of these other guards, they're lifers; they'll be in this place forever. You're young and you're getting the hell out of this place. The Wall just ain't no place for a good man like you to be working. There's information in that letter that might make some money for you. Like I said, you take it to the *New York Daily News*. They'll pay you. It's still not too late for the truth to be told."

The young guard's forehead wrinkled beneath his own receding black hairline. He seemed surprised, but he smiled and stuck the envelope in his pocket without even asking what it was. The older prisoner stared at the young guard. His one eye was closed slightly and then he whispered.

"Look, Nick—you're a bright guy and I think you're honest. That information ain't gonna do me no good. You do something with it. I swear to you, it's the truth." For a few seconds neither said anything. "Well anyway, I heard you're leavin', goin' on to pursue other interests, I just want to wish you good luck. I'd like to be leavin' myself, but the only leavin' I'm gonna be doin' will be when I leave this world. I'm gonna miss you Nick. You've been nice to me."

Arthur Jones gave the guard a big smile and winked at him. He was a likeable prisoner, possessed an infectious personality that most of the other criminals didn't. Nick felt sad for him. He could not remember seeing anyone show up to see him on visitation days or holidays. While others got to talk to relatives, Jones sat alone. Nick wondered if he was really guilty of murder. He remembered what Jones told him. He had gotten drunk, tried to rob somebody but couldn't remember killing anyone. But there were no excuses. You dealt with the cards you were given and made the best of it. For some reason the state of New Jersey spared him execution, and Arthur Jones was making Trenton State Prison his home.

He nodded toward the guard, his glasses unable to hide the circles beneath his eyes. "You take care of yourself, Nick." Another guard stepped forward and walked the prisoner down the corridor towards the main building.

A nostalgic blend of old wood mixed with linseed oil and turpentine permeated the air as the pair walked off. They continued down another dusty hall while another guard followed both of them. Before they got too far, Nick raised his voice slightly.

"Take care, Arthur, good luck to you." He tried to make sure that he wasn't too friendly for he didn't want anyone there at the prison to think that he and Jones were more than just prisoner and prison guard, or that there was any violation in his professional responsibility. It didn't matter to him that he was leaving the job after only a short time, but he did have a soft spot for the man. Arthur Jones wasn't like the others and the incarceration at The Wall was taking its toll. The man did not seem like a murderer, he wasn't angry and seemed to care about people. The conviction could have been death by electrocution but the jury saw something positive in him that helped lower the penalty to life. It was so kind of the New Jersey court system to keep him alive. Now The Wall was his home. But the charge was murder and Arthur Jones was dealing with it. That was enough said. Nick hadn't really talked to him all that much. In fact few people did because Jones kept to himself. Like a lonely old ghost, he drifted in and out of his cell before and after dinners, before and after exercise and shower time. He never really had a lot to say. But he had a certain air about him. He was always nice to the guards. The prevailing prison attitude and lack of empathy toward him had left Nick wondering about Jones' future. He wondered if some of the other guards would treat Jones the same way. What a wasted life, he thought, stuck within those archaic, granite blocks of The Wall.

Trenton State Prison was home to all kinds of prisoners. Some on the inside appeared to be great guys; on the outside they had deep rooted psychological problems that propelled them to commit murder. Maybe Arthur Jones was in many ways a victim, brought up on the mean streets of Newark without anyone to take an interest in him. His best years were now being spent at The Wall, a virtual dungeon where a man's dignity was ripped from his breast and he was forced to live in a primeval mode of survival. Most people believed prison was by choice. They should have thought twice before they committed the crime. Others thought prison was simply a result of their inability to stay out of trouble or that they just couldn't prevent the dark side of their being from manifesting itself and winning out over their inability to reason. Not having to deal with the struggle between good and evil on the outside, they grew comfortable on the inside. In an odd way they had become victimized by the granite seduction of The Wall.

Trenton State Prison was built in the late 1700s from a colonial blueprint and with manual labor. It sheltered many a criminal, most of who were hardened villains bent on self-destruction and rebellion. Some were cold-hearted psychopaths trapped in a narcissistic world. Many were helpless victims of the Depression, where desperation turned them into robbers and then killers. Others had fallen prey to social injustice and were probably victims of a judicial system laden with blatant racism. The police work too was biased, shoddy at best because of the desperation and pressure to lay the blame. Some may have been political scapegoats who pissed off people with money and found themselves in a struggle with the judicial system. No one was exempt from the hard times of the Depression, but it was especially difficult for those who challenged authority because they ran into the stiff arm of New Jersey law.

The prison was centrally located in working class South Trenton and the prisoners and the locals, many of who were immigrants referred to it as The Wall. Behind it, weathered cement smoke stacks stretched upward toward the sky, a testament to the blessing of jobs that were offered to the multi-cultural mix of Trentonians. Grime from the local factories seemed to cling to the granite wall and also to the many brick houses and buildings. The odiferous mixture of oil, machines, and chemicals seemed to lay motionless and invisible in the air, blending with a toiling humanity that paid it no mind. Kids unfazed by the smells played in the shadows of The Wall, hoping to find one of the little pink prison balls the 'trustees' (prisoners with little prison time left and less serious offenses), would leave behind for them. The guards would allow the 'trustees' to retrieve the balls, giving them a minute's worth of freedom. The only people, who were not oblivious to the smells, were the visitors to South Trenton who ventured in from other parts of the city or from surrounding townships to go clothes shopping along Broad Street. Factory whistles would scream out early in the morning, and not early enough in the afternoon, for all the hard working local people who trudged like drones back and forth from home to work, and work to home day after day. The sweat and grit earned just enough dollars to pay the rent and put some food on the table.

Since the late 1800s, Trenton had evolved into a big industrial city and even after World War II its factories were still very active. Much of the industry could be found in the vicinity of the state run prison. Less than a mile north past hundreds of row homes lining Center Street and cater-cornered to the city's Italian neighborhood Chambersburg, John Roebling's steel cable factory was still diligently twisting out the steel cable for suspension bridges and skyscrapers around the world. The Brooklyn Bridge, Roebling's 'elevated promenade', provided majestic vistas of the steel-boned skyscrapers that became the New York skyline. Not far from the prison in Trenton, a few miles southward along the Delaware, a large delegation of immigrant workers lived in the town that bore Roebling's name. Even some eighty years later, his family still maintained a residence within two miles of the factory and three miles from the prison down on East State Street. Just a few miles southeast from the town of Roebling across the river in Fairless Hills, Pennsylvania {the river formed a natural border with Pennsylvania} workers were blowing out impurities from iron ore to make the steel that was used for many of the technological advancements of not only the 19th century but businesses like automobile manufacturing which dominated the 20th. Connecting both states a half-mile due west of the prison was the famous Trenton Makes the World Takes Bridge. Its six- foot letters would light up the night and reflect off the water down below. The sign like a crusty, veteran sentinel presided over the historic Delaware's white-capped rapids. The local working denizens and even the upper crust professionals from the northern and western sectors of the city were proud of the sign. It seemed to make the city worldly, though few people who were not from the city had ever heard of it or for that matter ever saw it.

Driving closer to the two hundred year old prison, one could have difficulty noticing it and then from out of nowhere it would spring up, a giant medieval castle reigning over the demographic bed of mostly German and Slavic people. Situated behind the main thoroughfares of Broad and Cass Streets and surrounded by the many narrow streets that paralleled each other all the way down to the murky and fast moving Delaware, the prison was an imposing colossal enclosure formed of New England granite and mortar. The pasty mortar uneven and seemingly without pattern, pretended to cushion the huge granite boulders that formed The Wall. Sharpened and barbed wire ran along the top of the walls and all the way down to each corner where it was shadowed by a rippled stone roof. An armed guard sat in the corner tower with perusing eyes cradling a rifle in one hand and a mounted machine gun in the other. Endless lines of deterring wire connected each corner, with more guards and more weapons in each. In the guardhouses were men paid to keep the bad guys behind The Wall, and they were ready to shoot down anyone bold enough to scale the solid granite blocks out to the real world. Unfortunately on rare occasions, there were desperados who made the fateful attempt and felt the wrath of modern weaponry. On the other side down near the concrete ball court, steel fencing separated specified work areas. Some of the most hardened criminals in the state with nothing to gain and nothing to lose, went about their business monitored by the men paid to enforce the penitentiary's security. Everyone interacted with one another. It didn't matter if you were a good guy or a bad guy.

Fear took permanent residence within the minds of the good guys, but rarely did it ever cross through those icy, mental corridors of the convicted. At The Wall they survived because of a lack of it. One day a prison guard came up with a name for this cast of hardened criminals. They were the scum of the earth and for whatever reason the prisoners took to the name.

With his shift supposed to be over at three and running late, Nick hustled to his Oldsmobile, pulled the steel handle on the door and started the ignition. Suddenly, he remembered the envelope and arched his index finger and thumb into his pocket. He looked at the envelope, pulled out the contents and skimmed over the information. After a few seconds, it was easy to extrapolate that much of the contents was about the Lindbergh kidnapping. He wanted to read the entire account but he was hungry and couldn't wait to get home. "I'll finish reading it later on," he thought. He clutched the letter in his hand as he drove around to the exit gate of the parking lot. "I wonder why Jonesy gave this to me?" he thought.

At the stop sign he paused and let the engine idle for a few seconds. He tried to recall some of the facts of the Lindbergh kidnapping case. He would have been just a young boy when the so-called 'Trial of the Century' took place in 1935, so he couldn't really recall too much detail. Gazing out of the passenger side window, he could see the roof of the small death house where the man who kidnapped the Lindbergh baby met his fate in that electric chair they called Smokey. Nick remembered the prison tour on his first day of work. The captain had explained to him how the chair was first used in 1907, and since then a hundred and forty people had taken that lonesome stroll to eternity. The death house was less than fifty years old but it seemed much older. Nick struggled to remember the Lindbergh baby's kidnapper's name... "Richard something." Still holding the note the prisoner gave him; he looked up at the massive concrete fortress before him and toward the death house. "Bruno Richard Hauptmann—that was his name." Suddenly, a cold chill ran down his back. He remembered the lights had flickered on and off in his South Trenton home the night they electrocuted him in that dubious electrical contraption.

"Yeah, Hauptmann," he thought. He stared at the letter. Realizing he didn't want to stay at the prison parking lot any longer, he put the note back in his pocket, pulled the standard shifter down and slowly cruised onto Cass Street. In his mind, he struggled with the image of Bruno Hauptmann getting executed in old Smokey.

Stopping at the traffic light on Broad Street, he again reached back into his pocket and pulled out the note. There were three pages of intricate details; Hauptmann had confided in Jones about the kidnapping. Nick continued to recall the details surrounding the case. He remembered that it occurred in the early thirties and that the Lindbergh estate was not that far from Trenton. "Just up the river to West Trenton and over to Hopewell," he thought. It was a sad thought as he remembered the tragic outcome. A Negro truck driver had found the baby's body on the side of some leaf covered mountain. He remembered that Hauptmann was a German immigrant who had been caught passing ransom money, got convicted after a sensational trial and was sentenced to death. Nick thought again about Hauptmann receiving his punishment right there at The Wall. The thought reminded him of the day last year when as a guard he had to witness an electrocution in that eerie death chamber. The man's body tightened like a cable on a hydraulic lift; the tape covering his eyes was futile as his face turned red and watery. An overwhelming odor of burning flesh was tough for him to stomach. Starting to feel queasy, he shook his head to clear his mind of the chilling memory.

Hearing the car horn behind him, Nick shifted the car back into first and slowly drove down Broad Street. He couldn't help but wonder why Arthur gave him that note. He waited at another traffic light and then made a sharp right hand turn onto Liberty Street. At his home on Smith Street, his new bride Elizabeth anxiously waited for him, nervous about his job but feeling confident because she knew her young husband was street smart and more than competent. Besides, he was from Trenton.

Nick was looking forward to going home and reading the note from Arthur Jones, but he could feel his stomach growling. He would share the contents of the letter with Elizabeth at dinner. He wasn't sure how she would react to the letter. Maybe she would share in his curiosity or maybe she would just blow him off as she sometimes did when he would bring up something about the prison.

Driving up in front of the semi-attached house with the asphalt faux brick facing, he could see she was waiting for him at the screen door. It was a good feeling for him knowing that his wife was anxious to see him. She opened the screen door, obviously waiting for his arrival.

"Your Mom called and said she was making a pork roast for dinner. Do we really have to go over there? You know she hates me, and the only reason she probably called was to collect the rent."

"What? Have you been worrying about this all day?"

"No, but I really don't feel like going over there. I mean I like your Dad and everything, but your Mom is not nice to me."

"I'll call her; we'll eat some of the leftover chicken in the icebox."

"Thank you, darling." She hugged him and felt the envelope in his shirt pocket.

"What's this—a note from your girlfriend?"

"Yeah, right," he said with a smile. "It's a letter that one of the inmates gave me."

"An inmate? What are you--crazy?" shrieked Elizabeth, her voice a mixture of sarcasm and surprise. Nick laughed again as he handed the note to his new bride.

"Read it and tell me what it says because I only went over it quickly." She opened it up and sat on the re-upholstered sofa that was given to them from her parents. She read the first page carefully, and then continued on to the second and third page.

"It sounds very interesting, but why you?"

"Who knows? This guy likes and trusts me. I treated him with respect unlike some of the other people around there."

"What did it really say?" Nick asked Elizabeth as he pulled the uniform shirt over his head, trying to change clothes and listen at the same time.

"Well, it tries to explain a lot of the circumstances surrounding the Lindbergh kidnapping case. It really makes you think about what really happened back then. When was that anyway in the thirties? I wonder if the note is true."

"Who knows? You never know about prisoners, they can be quite creative."

"Yeah and evil too," said Elizabeth.

"But how would anyone in prison gain from making up something like this?"

"Nick, they're prisoners, they have plenty of time to keep themselves busy"

In his thick Trenton accent, Nick responded using a term of endearment for his wife and a hint of his own opinion. "You know, Bett, I really like the guy. I don't think he was a murderer liked they said he was."

"Who? Hauptman?"

"No, no. Arthur Jones, the man who gave me the letter. He said it was the truth and he wrote it down as he remembered it or something like that. I don't know what I will ever do with it but it is fascinating. And I'd be willing to bet that the guy who they fried in that electric chair for the murder of the Lindbergh baby was probably railroaded as well."

"Well I think Hauptman was probably a scapegoat, that's what my Dad always told me, probably took the blame because they had no clue who the real murderer was," responded Elizabeth.

"Or..." Nick hesitated for a second, "they knew who it was and protected his ass. The fact that Arthur gave me that letter may seem interesting and everything, but do you want to know what I really think?"

"What?" she questioned.

"It's time to eat!"

"You're right," she said with a grin. "Let's just eat it cold."

Nick placed the letter back inside the white envelope and casually tossed it into the top drawer of the walnut hutch. He smiled and walked over to the rounded white icebox, removed the tin foil covering the chicken and placed it on the table. They quickly sat down and ate their leftovers.

CHAPTER TWO
A TROUBLED CHILDHOOD

Cottony white swirls crossed through an azure blue sky, partially hiding the burning rays of the sun. The cloud cover prevented the intense heat of the upper plains from totally ruining the late afternoons. Near the town of Little Falls, Minnesota, the sprawling Mississippi River had spread its muddy waters out into murky ponds, creating natural reservoirs. Minnesota was the land of a thousand lakes, but in this area it was the upper Mississippi that provided the animal habitats and the playgrounds for adventure. Although it curved and then narrowed to the north, it still provided plenty of smaller lakes and ponds. Minnesota at the turn of the century was a wholesome piece of America, a virtual paradise for any young boy, and it was in this picturesque environment that the Lindbergh family would establish their roots.

The Lindberghs were not unlike many of the Swedes who made the northern plains their home. The weather and the terrain were similar to their homeland. In 1860, politician Ola Mansson left a wife and children in Sweden and crossed the Atlantic with his mistress and their young son, Charles August. Seeking a new life, they chose a rural setting absent of intrusion and interference. The state of Minnesota would be the perfect place. Amidst charges of blatant adultery, embezzlement, and radical political ideology, he fled Sweden in search of a new life. When his older children in Sweden changed their names to Lindberg, Mansson did the same and even added a new first name August. Later, he added an 'h' to Lindberg anglicizing it. Ola was now Augustus Lindbergh. Bitter toward his homeland, he was now content on raising a new family and living his life as a farmer in the beautiful but rugged north state. Because of the name change, his son Charles was not really a junior; he was Charles Augustus Lindbergh or simply

C.A. as he liked to be called. He grew up in Minnesota with several siblings in a relatively normal setting. As an adult, C. A. went on to a successful career as an attorney and then later he too involved himself in politics. He was distinguished and handsome, and he found himself the interest of many of the single women in Little Falls, Minnesota. Extremely popular; everyone knew C. A. After losing his first wife and having fathered two daughters, he met a woman at the Antlers Hotel on the west side of Little Falls in 1900. Evangeline Lodge Land, a graduate of the University of Michigan like him, was in town looking for a high school teaching position. An attractive woman and the daughter of a dentist; she and Charles quickly became the talk of the town and the next year, they were married in a simple ceremony at her family's home in Detroit, Michigan. They returned to Little Falls and moved into a small cabin that abutted the Mississippi riverbank and was shaded by an enormous, old oak tree. It would serve only temporarily as a humble abode while the couple waited for their dream house to be built overlooking the river. The new house was to be quite large and spacious. According to the plans the new house would have many windows with scenic vistas of the river. From the upstairs windows, one could ogle up and down the mighty Mississippi River.

On February 4, 1902, Evangeline gave birth to a son and they aptly named him Charles Augustus Lindbergh Jr. The baby's birth took place in Detroit, where her respectable family could assist in caring for the baby. After six weeks, the couple returned to Little Falls. Due to the enormous demands of parenthood, they found marriage to be a struggle. Evangeline had a difficult time with motherhood and the parents began to quarrel often, sometimes in the company of their infant son. Despite the tension and conflict, they tried to hold on to the marriage until the new house was finally completed, thinking it might make things better to be in a beautiful new home. The house was well shaded and after the little Lindbergh baby grew up and became a rambunctious three-year old, he was able to spend most of his days romping around the property as his Mom and some of the servants watched over him. The house and its beautiful grounds provided long days filled with great fun until the sixth of August in 1905, when a horrible blaze gutted the new house and destroyed all but a few belongings. The fire helped fan the flames of an already smoldering marriage and this took its toll on young Charles. The little boy stared; sobbing, he watched the house go up in a plume of smoke. His nurse Nettie Carlson, who just happened to be present on that day, quickly snatched him up and carried him to the barn across the road from the house. Against her wishes, the boy turned around from a corner of the barn and was mesmerized by raging flames and billowing columns of black smoke. He wanted to be strong but he couldn't disguise his puzzled and helpless frown, as he watched his parents dream house and his very own world of security crumble within the destructive inferno. The following morning young Lindbergh and his saddened mother could do nothing but stare. Lying in front of them was a twisted clump of glowing metal, jaggedly rising from a blackened foundation of re-fired cinder blocks. The combination of glowing metal and simmering embers from the wood frame fouled the morning air. The two searched for anything of value that might have been spared by the blaze. Fortunately, some of the staff was able to remove some items prior to the total overwhelming rage of the fire, including the upright piano that would one day become a very visible part of the new house.

The second Lindbergh house was built sometime later, but it was not on the same scale as the old one had been. Charles parent's marital problems and the family tensions worsened, manifesting into a routine of adversarial confrontations. Consequently, young Charles would spend much of his time alone, playing near the banks of the Mississippi constantly thinking and questioning why things happened the way they did. In 1906, C.A. won a congressional seat and since it meant he had to live in Washington, DC most of the year, the time he spent with his young son was compromised significantly. For a short time, the family rented an apartment in Minneapolis as C.A.'s political aspirations drove him to seek more exposure, but the youngster had difficulty adjusting to the change. When he threw the landlady's cat out of the second floor window, they thought it might be better to come up with a different plan. They even tried Washington D.C. for a while but that did not work out either. Eventually, they would head back to their home in Little Falls.

Still there were the great times Charles spent on the family property. To the north of the property line, the Pike Creek had become a favorite swimming hole for the young Lindbergh boy and he loved to swim on those hot summer afternoons. He had learned how to swim from his Dad when he was a young boy. It was an unpleasant experience for young Charles when his father had literally forced him to swim. Momentarily the boy struggled to make sense out of the fact that his Dad had left him in the deep water to drown, but after physically fighting the currents and showing some basic knowledge and natural ability, he made it back to the riverbank where his proud Dad was waiting for him. Any doubts he might have developed were quickly erased when his Dad would put an arm around him and give him some encouragement. When his Dad said to him, "I knew you could do it" or "that's my boy," the young Lindbergh boy would light up and smile from ear to ear. Even the overly tough image his Dad often projected wasn't enough to loosen the strong love the boy had for his father. He believed that his father's unconventional methods such as forcing him to swim were normal and would only help him overcome any hardship or challenge that might arise in his life.

Once the young Lindbergh had perfected the sport of swimming, he felt confident in his ability to do almost anything. And once the warm Minnesota summers replaced the cold of winter and the chill of spring, the boy would go to the Pike Creek every chance he could.

When on certain days Charles had tired of treading water, he would experiment with the many offerings that nature had provided for him and learned first- hand about the flora and the fauna of the Minnesota back woods. The young Lindbergh thrived in the outdoors and on those days when the Minnesota winds would abate and the pristine snows of bitter winters would finally melt, he would anxiously head down to the creek or the river not only to swim but to explore. The warmth of summer was short-lived and young Charles had to take advantage of every minute. He enjoyed looking for mud turtles or soft shells, and if he got lucky he might find a wood turtle wandering through the Mississippi brown waters. Crows would caw and red-tail hawks would soar above the tall pine trees. Ground hogs and chipmunks, Pickerel frogs and salamanders, oak trees and mulberries, the blue skies and the endless dreams of an American boy all laid out there for the picking. For a short while these were his playgrounds, a virtual paradise for any young boy. Unfortunately, C. A.'s demanding congressional responsibilities took precedent, forcing him to spend most of his time in Washington D.C. This meant less time at home for the young Lindbergh boy, as he and his Mom took long grueling road trips back and forth to Washington to visit. On other occasions, they would trek over to Detroit to spend time with her family, the Lands. There she could get some parental love and attention for herself, because she didn't get any at home and it would also benefit young Charles as well because he could spend time with his maternal grandparents. He was equally fascinated by the many stuffed animals and preserved specimens that his grandfather had kept around the house.

On a lazy summer afternoon sometime in 1907, Charles had become intrigued by an injured blue jay that had fallen from its nest. He stared at the wounded jay trying to make sense of what had happened. The tightly wound nest was lying next to the bird. It had been jarred from one of the taller scrub pines. A chick was badly injured and had little chance of survival. Twenty feet above his head the bird's parents were in a chaotic frenzy. They swiftly darted downward toward the boy who crouched by the displaced nest. The piercing cries of the bird's parents echoed loudly through the trees and could be heard far off in the distance. Young Charles stared at the bird and with an extended arm held it upward toward the sky. While the bird's featherless body suddenly went limp, he whirled it around and around as if the little bird would find a way to miraculously fly on its own. Again, the adult blue jays screeched, fending off the danger and they quickly darted for the boy's blonde head. Charles pivoted and spun around quickly. He picked up a long stick and threatened to strike out at the jays. The boy shouted to the birds daring them to attack him while still holding their lifeless baby in his other hand. The Lindbergh boy was undaunted and on the offensive. He picked up a small stone, lifted his left leg like a baseball pitcher and gunned it at one of the large jays. The birds retreated back to the pine tree screaming in unison. The birds watched nervously as the young boy lacking in empathy, discarded their baby and ran off, distracted by the voice of his own mother calling him in for dinner.

As Charles got older, those times of enjoying the upper Mississippi became limited because of his parents fighting. And like all children who experienced their parents in conflict, it dominated his thoughts. So it wasn't any surprise that the young Lindbergh sought refuge in the beautiful upper Mississippi watershed. Here he could find solace away from his parent's squabbles. Whenever he got the chance he would play in the Williams Woods to the northwest of the property line. Sometimes the young Lindbergh would get caught up in the intriguing perplexities of nature or in the magnificence and beauty of the Minnesota landscape, and his Mom Evangeline would have to go searching for him, or get some of the other children like Alex Johnson or the Thompson children to help find him.

When Charles turned six, his Grandfather Land gave him his first rifle. A year later, C.A would buy him a Savage 22-caliber repeating rifle and at the age of eight, he gave him his first shotgun. Shortly after that he was firing a 38-caliber Smith and Wesson revolver at homemade targets on the property. For the most part Charles was responsible, but there were times when he and his friend Bill Thompson got carried away. On one occasion they fired their rifles and shotguns at some of the neighbors from across the woods.

Bill the shorter of the two boys, quivered from nervousness as three quick shots rang out in the cool autumn air and echoed through the forest. Someone had fired a rifle and it sounded like it was in close proximity. Bill's eyes grew wide. He trembled terribly while his mouth turned cottony dry.

"Charles, we gotta get out of here. Somebody might be trying to kill us." Charles forced a smirk-like smile.

"If they want to a fight, we'll give it to them." Bill seemed confused but his response was quick.

"The last thing we need to do is fire back. Besides we don't even know if they were firing at us. If we hit one of them whoever they are, we could be hanged."

The young Lindbergh stared at his friend with little emotion, and then his demeanor turned suddenly. "Ah shit, we're not going to hit anybody. We're just trying to have a little fun. Now c'mon Billy Boy, you gotta be with me. You don't want the word to get out that your chicken do you?"

"No you skinny towhead, but I don't want to get my ass shot either." "Look, let's just fire a couple of shots their way and set them straight for firing in our direction."

"Aw Lindbergh, you're so darn hardheaded," replied Bill. The two boys stood up with nothing in their sights but forest. Charles readied his 22-caliber repeating rifle and Bill took Charles' ten-gauge shotgun and aimed.

Lindbergh whispered, "One, two, three". The two let off two volleys of ammo. After a tremendous reverberation they stared at each other.

"Quick," responded Lindbergh. "Let's get the hell out of here." Gulping air, the two boys darted from the forest glade and then sprinted with their rifles by their side held tightly by stiff, outstretched arms. They continued to run hard towards the south end of the estate.

Fortunately, neither was hurt, and they laughed when their run turned to a walk and then to a complete halt. The pair dropped and fell to their elbows and then to their back. They tossed their guns off to the side of the tall rye grass. Both stared upward towards the autumn clouds. Lindbergh let out a laugh. Bill looked at him with bewilderment and then he too broke into laughter.

"You must not tell anyone," said Lindbergh. "No one!"

"You're crazy," barked the other boy, "Crazy as a loon!"

Lindbergh just looked at him and smiled, enjoying the dubious complement. Charles' erratic behaviors made it difficult to keep friends, as he developed a reputation for being unpredictable and stubborn.

There was another time when Charles and his mother had been horseback riding on the edge of their farm. Someone had fired shots in their general vicinity. Once again, the young Lindbergh, who had his rifle with him as he often did, returned fire without flinching. His mother said nothing, and the two headed back to a more secure area on their property.

As the Lindbergh boy grew up, his life would take many twists and turns. The already rocky relationship his parents were clinging to unofficially came to an end, when C.A started a new relationship with someone other than Charles' mother. Although the young Lindbergh was unaware of this affair, he knew that things were not going very well with his parents. Whenever his father ran for Congress it was quite exciting. When he was older he was able to travel around the state with his dad, but the responsibility of being a congressman would place a great amount of unneeded stress on everyone.

In 1916, his dad was soundly defeated when he decided to give up his congressional seat and run for the United States senate. Trying to hang on to a political career, he took aim at the governor's seat and after an ugly campaign where he was attacked for his unpopular stance against the war, he had to back off the political stage a beaten man. Young Charles shifted his attention to great technological advances like guns, cars, and motorcycles. After learning how to drive at the age of ten, he became the family chauffer. By the time he was fourteen, driving was old hat and in 1916 he actually drove his mom and uncle the entire distance from Detroit to Redondo Beach, California. It took him almost six weeks because of poor roads and inclement weather. Once he got to California, Charles and his mother would take up residence there. Charles soon found that California was no different from anywhere else, and once again he had trouble making friends. He rarely attended school and was even arrested for illegally driving a vehicle without a license.

When the experiment of living in California did not work out, the mother and son team returned to Little Falls. Evangeline had her sick mother join them on the farm where the fourteen-year old Charles emerged as the man of the house. He enjoyed the time spent on the farm where he was given most of the responsibility of managing it. This additional responsibility meant more power and that meant he had less people to answer to. He became quite capable, always completing the chores around the farm. By 1917, at the age of fifteen, he was still required to attend school and with all the rules and regulations he had to abide by, he hated every minute of it. He loathed having to take orders from anyone. At high school his attendance and grades were poor at best. Because of the war and America's impending involvement, a Minnesota law allowed him to bypass the responsibility of attending school, as long as he worked full time on the farm. The young Lindbergh jumped at the opportunity. Because he liked being the boss, he thrived at working on the farm. He enjoyed working with his hands and became adept at fixing machines and building things around the farm. For a short time he became a diligent and responsible, teenage farmer. He got up early, was unfazed by the cold ruthless winter and completed all the necessary chores.

At the end of the Great War, Charles' mother enrolled him in engineering classes at the University of Wisconsin. From the outset it was a disaster. Like high school there were just too many rules. Lonely from his father's absence (he continued his relationship with his mistress), and embarrassed that his intrusive mother rented an apartment near the school, he found himself caught in the transition to manhood. Even though his mother wanted to know everything he was doing, she still had difficulty showing him any affection. She was trying to guide her son through life as if she was running a business. Evangeline loved her son but she didn't know how to express her love. As the family dynamics shifted toward the negative, Charles internalized his emotions and became more anti-social. He became more comfortable being around inanimate objects. He relished riding his motorcycles and shooting his guns. He became somewhat of a daredevil and he loved flaunting his riding abilities and showing off his prowess as a shooter. He often taunted those who could not ride or shoot as well as he could. He laughed at those who could not compete with him, as it satisfied his egocentric needs and insecurities. Not attending classes and questioning the rules and regulations at the University of Wisconsin spelled trouble, and he quickly found himself on academic probation. He resented the fact that they could do that to him and quit school. He considered himself above all rules and regulations. He hated authority. It was obvious the time had come for him to fly, literally and figuratively.

Before he could get his wings, he had to drive his motorcycle from Wisconsin to Nebraska. In 1922, he had answered an advertisement from the Nebraska Aircraft Company and was willing to shell out $500.00 to learn how to fly. The owner of the company had one student enrolled and that person was Charles Lindbergh. The owner Ray Page was in the process of selling his company and consequently the aspiring aviator only received about eight hours of instruction. But in the eight weeks he was there, he learned everything about the mechanical side of aviation. He studied the engines, how they worked and how they were to be maintained. He attached propellers, serviced and repaired the planes and kept a close eye on every facet of flying. He watched as the pilots prepared and meticulously went over everything before take-off. Although he wasn't getting the learning experience in the air he was still learning the essential nuts and bolts of aviation.

A short time later he became 'Daredevil Slim', when he started walking on wings during flight. A man named Erold Bahl was so impressed he gave him a job as his assistant and the two barnstormed over towns raising money in the process. He also reinforced his reputation as a daredevil when he learned how to parachute. One time, he cut his chute with a knife as he was descending, and then without anyone's knowledge he pulled the cord of a backup chute and landed safely to the wild applause of the crowd. He enjoyed the attention he was getting and relished the nickname of 'Daredevil Lindbergh'. Before too long Lindbergh would save up enough money and with his dad giving him some financial assistance purchased his first airplane, a Curtis JN-4D a Great War biplane nicknamed the 'Jenny'. With the help and advice from an older pilot, it wouldn't take long for the young aviator to grasp the concepts and methods required to pilot an aircraft. Flying became an obsession as he flew all day and slept with his plane at night. He started making money by charging people five dollars per ride.

During the early summer of 1923, Charles was able to show off his aviation skills to his father. C.A tried to get back into politics by running in a special election after the senior senator from Minnesota, Knute Nelson died. He thought it would be a good idea to use his son's barnstorming antics in his campaign as way of gaining votes. After some successful rides and a couple minor crashes his father had enough. His idea allowed him to spend several weeks with his son but he lost the election coming in a distant third. Despite his father's loss, Charles continued to barnstorm in Minnesota and Iowa.

In January of 1924, Charles, decided to enlist in the army as an aviator. While stationed in San Antonio, Texas and with his intense focus on flying, he continued to acquire more aviation knowledge, specifically aerodynamics, navigation techniques, and meteorology. He was taught the latest in weaponry. Without much enthusiasm, he learned some of the military's ways including discipline and the expectations of officers. After less than a half year of military training, Lindbergh was saddened by the news that his dad was battling a brain tumor. After flying to Little Falls, he was able to spend some time with him before he died, but he did not attend his funeral. Because of the lack of a will, an ugly battle over his dad's estate ensued between his half sister Eva and his mother. All this unexpected stress took its toll on an already lonely young man.

Lindbergh's behaviors would take a strange turn. For the next six months, he struggled to make a lasting relationship. Unable to make friends he seemed like he was in constant conflict with his fellow aviators. His inability to cope with his father's death and his mother's sudden lessening of correspondence made him grow sullen and depressed. He was unable to adapt to the military way of life and had several run-ins with fellow airmen. Angry over his inability to sleep because of a sergeant's snoring, he placed a dead skunk in the man's pillowcase. Even after forcing him to sleep outside for two weeks because of the smell, he took the man's bed apart and reassembled it atop the roof of the barracks. He threw buckets of ice water on anyone who taunted him. He put shaving cream in the mouth of a sleeping cadet, and turned a water hose on another airman who also was sound asleep. Antisocial behaviors took a strange twist when he placed green paint on the erect penis of a drunken cadet. Apparently the young man was bragging about his sexual exploits, and Lindbergh didn't like it. His weirdness prevented him from developing a relationship with the opposite sex, and he looked down upon fellow cadets who were sexually active. He dismissed his awkwardness with women as his own choice. The desire was there, but he was not quite ready, as he was busy fighting the emotional demons that his parents had cast his way. Things became sadistic and almost criminal, when he placed a poisonous viper in the bed of a fellow cadet. Like college, his stint in the military was becoming increasingly difficult for him and on March 25th, 1925, the young aviator was transferred to the army reserve. Immediately, he headed back toward the Midwest where he would resume barnstorming, and pick up some odd jobs with his aviation skills.

Lindbergh's intense pursuit to know everything about aviation, and his love for flying was unmatched. Despite the fact that aviation was in its infancy, where pilots and engineers were still learning and plane crashes seemed to be common occurrences, the young aviator was fearless. His life was now all about flying, and he pursued all avenues to become a better pilot. In 1926, St. Louis, Missouri became his home base where he shared an apartment with an old friend named Bud Gurney. Gurney and Lindbergh were both working as air mail pilots, and became pioneers in the field. Regardless of weather or any other peril that could inhibit his ability to fly, he went on delivering the mail. Despite two near fatal crashes that saw him parachute through darkness, and several near crashes, he continued to fly the mail in army salvage planes that some people were calling "flying coffins".

Still, it didn't take long for Lindbergh's antisocial behaviors to get the better of him. He was passing off laxatives to people he did not like, and also exploded a stink bomb in a man's glove. The worst incident was when Bud Gurney asked him to go out drinking and reveling. The young aviator did not want to go and criticized Gurney for his behaviors. Gurney reciprocated by poking fun at him for being a party-pooper. Gurney went out, had some drinks with some friends, and left Lindbergh alone to stew. When he came back he found a jug of icy water on the counter. Thirsty from the alcohol, and thinking he might benefit from a cold drink, he turned it up and nearly choked. His throat and nasal membranes started to burn. The young man needed immediate medical care. What he didn't know was that his roommate had replaced the water with kerosene. While Gurney was struggling with the poisoning, the young aviator laughed heartedly. Gurney had to be rushed to the hospital. He suffered serious throat and gastrointestinal burning, and nearly died from Lindbergh's bad joke. Fortunately, Gurney did not press charges against him, or Lindbergh could have been facing an attempted murder charge. It soon became clear to some of the pilots that ran in the same circles, that Charles Lindbergh was more than just a strange character. None of the other aviators went out of their way to be friendly with him, and he wasn't fitting in well. He decided to stop delivering mail, and look elsewhere for adventure. The following year in 1927, Charles Lindbergh would transform himself from being the great pilot that no one wanted to be around, to the Great Aviator that the whole world wanted to embrace.

In 1919, Frenchman Raymond Orteig had posted a $25,000 cash prize to anyone or any group who could fly an airplane across the Atlantic Ocean from New York to France without stopping. The flight was supposed to have been completed in five years. With no one having shown much success or interest in the proposal, Lindbergh contemplated making the flight. With Orteig willing to extend the offer, the young aviator found a group of St. Louis businessmen willing to finance the construction of a new plane with a powerful single engine. Lindbergh would oversee the construction; he would make the modifications to make the aircraft lighter, and relocate the fuel tank to the front of the cockpit. Engineers from the Ryan Aircraft Company out of San Diego worked feverishly to complete it in time for a May takeoff. Lindbergh piloted the plane from San Diego to St. Louis. In St. Louis, there was a big promotional dinner with his benefactors. The press snapped photos, and asked questions with the strange aviator. Lindbergh was not quite sure how to take the photographers and newspapermen. Answering questions that he thought were thoughtless and juvenile, such as "What do you think of girls?" gave him a real disdain for the press. He then flew on to Long Island, New York where he would prepare to take the plane that was now hailed as the 'Spirit of St. Louis' across the vast Atlantic expanse.

People were calling the young airman suicidal, but he merely smirked at those so willing to criticize. However, Lindbergh was smart enough to realize that perhaps they were right. Death did not intimidate him. His family was for the most part broken. His dad had passed on, his unaffectionate mom had cut the apron strings, his stepsister Lillian had passed on from tuberculosis, and he doubted he would ever see his other half-sister again. There were no other relationships with anyone, male or female. He had nothing to lose, and was willing to take the risk to make his dream a reality and in the process advance the field of aviation. In addition, he had his eyes on the twenty-five thousand dollar Orteig prize.

On the 20th morning of May in 1927, without much sleep the night before, Charles Lindbergh posed for some more pictures, including one with his mother who decided to see him off. She seemed uncomfortable alongside her daring son, and even refused to give him a goodbye kiss. Someone quickly changed the subject, and asked him if five sandwiches were enough? He smiled. "If I get to Paris, I won't need anymore, if I don't get to Paris, I won't need any more either." With his plane laden down with over 450 gallons of gasoline, forcing the weight to exceed two and one half tons, he declared he was ready. At 7:51 he said, "Let's give it a try". The plane rambled down the rain soaked runway, with lift beneath its wings, and fire in the belly of its engine, the Spirit of St. Louis soared upward. The young aviator his eyes gleaming of determination, was now in pursuit of his destiny. He realized that any time he could find himself in peril, but he was up for the challenge and confident his determination would see him through. On the ground, people wondered whether this tedious trek across the Atlantic would lead him into historical oblivion or into a scientific and potentially economic epiphany.

CHAPTER THREE
A LIFE CHANGED FOREVER:
BECOMING THE GREAT AVIATOR

———————

Crossing the Atlantic alone in the Spirit of St. Louis gave the young aviator much time to reflect. He thought about how far he had come as an aviator. Over 7,000 flights and 1800 hours logged, had granted him the title of expert. To accomplish the feat that lay before him was immense. Others had tried and failed. Some had died trying. Flying over the icy waters of the North Atlantic, required him to shed any fear he may have harbored. He knew the second he departed the Canadian coastline in pursuit of the European continent, that he was the only person capable of such an outrageous act of daring. And only he had the passion to travel that impossible distance, harnessing man's technology along the way. Lindbergh was better than the others because of his absence of fear; he was willing to gamble his life and soar into a foggy sky of uncertainty. The young aviator had to be confident. He continued with his thoughts and jumped ahead two days. What would it be like when he succeeded? His insecurities would shatter like broken glass. No more sarcastic remarks and no more criticism. He would be the greatest aviator ever.

The Spirit of St. Louis with its motor humming kept up the pace. The pairing of man with machine was working flawlessly. Lindbergh had timed it right as he followed the sun. As he curved across the globe, he would only have to endure a few hours of darkness. By the time he made it to the European coast, the sun would already be up. The young aviator persevered. It would take almost thirty-two hours of constantly checking the gages, maintaining a remarkable stamina, keeping his mind clear, and an intense concentration for the task at hand. Fighting two days of sleep deprivation, his mind was fraught with hallucinations, but in the end his determination would win out. In the distance it became clear; the young aviator had finally made it. The beauty of the Irish coast stood out. His mind cleared and he re-focused. Below, he could see the Irish people staring upward, waving at him. All he had to do was let the wind carry him southward, across the English Channel, to the picturesque French landscape en route to Le Bourget Field in Paris. As he approached, he marveled at the throngs of people jumping up and down, their hats waving in the air, and although he couldn't hear them, he knew they were shouting his name. People had been impressed before by his aerial acrobatics and death defying escapades, but now this was different. He had wondered just how much of an impression his accomplishment would have on the world; now he knew what his crossing had done. Not only had he changed aviation, he changed the world.

Before Charles Lindbergh even stepped onto French soil, the crowd had lifted him up so the world could see this daring young airman. In less than two days, he became the world's most famous man. During a time where people tended to break away from society's restraints and live free, Lindbergh soared to the next level. He epitomized the bold American spirit of the 1920s, and ventured where no man had gone before. He had indeed become the Great Aviator.

The French people lavished him with unmatched hospitality. His feat was celebrated with wildness and unbridled enthusiasm. Through the streets of Paris people chanted "Viva Lindbergh! Viva Lindbergh!" Strangers embraced each other, the social elite and the masses, and a huge parade was set to take place along the Champ-Elysees. That night after meeting the French president, he slept in the luxurious home of the United States Ambassador to France. He was awarded the French Legion of Honor. The British gave him the Air Force Cross. His crossing stimulated an outpouring of good will between the Allies. With the newspapers and wires working overtime in the United States, Americans wanted their hero to come home. They too wanted to revel in the excitement of the crossing. President Coolidge immediately sent the cruiser Memphis to pick him up, so that by the time the French were finished with their adulation it would be America's turn. With the unending attention given to him, the Great Aviator could do nothing but smile and enjoy. For the first time people appreciated him. There was no teasing, no sarcasm. Making friends would now be easy; his loneliness gone forever. People would do anything to meet him, to see him in person, to extend a hand and touch his, so they could say they shook hands with the Great Aviator. No longer would he have to force a smile. He could do as he pleased because he was now a true hero. The Great Aviator despite some earlier apprehension with newspapers, enjoyed the newfound attention. He relished and savored the constant admiration.

By the time the Great Aviator returned home, the entire country was in a frenzy. President Coolidge was anxiously awaiting his arrival so he could walk alongside him in the parade that was arranged near the Washington Monument. In New York, they were preparing for a ticker tape parade down Broadway. There he would meet with more dignitaries. In St. Louis, yet another parade was planned. Politicians lined up for photo opportunities. They wanted to be there standing next to him when people screamed his name. "Lindbergh! There he is, Lucky Lindy!" President Coolidge would bestow on him the rank and title of Colonel in the Air Corps Reserve, and award him with the Distinguished Flying Cross and the Medal of Honor. Within days unlimited offers of all kinds would pour in. Companies wanted him to be their spokesman, consultant, even president. Mayors from around the globe offered him the key to their city. Kings and Queens and other dignitaries from around the world inquired about meeting the Great Aviator. A new publication called Time Magazine decided to name him its first "Man of the Year".

To say that the newfound attention had kept Charles Lindbergh very busy was an understatement. He loved flying his airplanes around the continent. On one trip, he flew down to Mexico so the people in Mexico City could shower him with presents and in return get a glimpse of the Great Aviator. A dinner was planned with the wealthy, American ambassador to Mexico, Dwight Morrow and his family. While there he became interested in his daughters. For the first time, he could talk to a girl without worrying about making a fool of himself. Initially interested in the older daughter Elizabeth, he found he was more comfortable and less intimidated by the younger daughter Anne. She seemed shy but very interested. She was educated and bright, but somewhat naïve. After numerous discussions, she agreed to take him up on an offer to go flying. The Great Aviator liked her stock. She was pretty and emotionally strong. She had good form and good health. For the first time he thought that she could be the woman who could bear his children. He wanted someone who could produce strong and healthy offspring, and Anne Morrow fit the bill. Lindbergh believed mating was the most important choice one had to make in life and that strong genes were vital to the continued existence of humankind. He was impressed with the Morrow family's determination and success. Although he rarely engaged Anne in conversations about heredity and genetics, he respected her stock and relished the time they spent together.

The couple spent unlimited hours in the air, where Lindbergh was quite impressed by Anne's ability to learn the concepts of aviation. She was a fast learner and like him, loved the thrill and the exciting rush of adrenaline that flying provided. After a relatively brief courtship that was spent mostly in the air, the two decided to tie the knot. Even with the press snooping around wanting to know when and where, Charles Lindbergh and the Morrows were able to keep the wedding a private and secretive event. On an unlikely day, Monday May 27, 1929 at North Haven, Maine the Morrow's family retreat, the young couple was married. Still, there were some photo hounds and reporters who hid around the grounds trying to get a scoop, or a quick snapshot of the world's most famous couple. They even tried bribing some of the servants for any iota of information. It annoyed the Great Aviator but he knew this was the way it was going to be, possibly for the rest of his life. He would have to figure a way to deal with it. Incognito, the couple left on a long and extended honeymoon, sailing along the New England coast.

It would not take long for the Lindberghs to resume flying. Since Charles was named the Chairman of Transcontinental Air Transport (TAT), he wanted to go out and inspect their new line of aircraft firsthand and Anne became his unofficial assistant. It seemed company executives were more interested in them than business. Everywhere they turned, someone asked for an autograph and Anne wondered why she too was being asked to sign her John Hancock. Aviation was becoming huge, as investors understood the potential market. TAT had solidified the industry, creating several routes across the country and setting up convenient hubs so other aviation companies could link up with them. They were changing the way man traveled and the Great Aviator was instrumental in their growth. Not only was he improving the technology, he was an active participant in the growth of aviation as business. He was also becoming rich. In the eighteen months after the famous flight, he had earned a million dollars for his name and expertise. For Anne, she enjoyed her new lifestyle but she didn't like that her life and even marriage would be shared with so many people. She thought and hoped that at some point she would be able to put her own life out in front, possibly utilize her writing skills and enjoy life as a writer. She could write about her many adventures with the Great Aviator. They knew so many people, befriending rich elitists, movie stars, writers, and artists. The couple had so much going for them it was as if they had become America's answer to a royal family.

In 1930, the Lindberghs continued flying around the world until Anne started suffering bouts of nausea. It didn't take long to realize that she was pregnant. A change was in store for America's most famous couple. Anne wondered how their life would change once a child was born. How would her husband handle the responsibilities of fatherhood? The answers to those questions would require a great deal of pondering. She was only twenty-three and loved the adventurous life that being Mrs. Charles Lindbergh had offered her. There was no way she would give that up. As long as she had someone to help her, she could make the adjustment to motherhood. However, she wasn't sure about her husband. He loved the power that came with being the Great Aviator and he definitely wasn't going to give up his lifestyle. Being a father was a big step for someone who as far as she knew, had never been around a baby before. Affection was a word he was unfamiliar with, and she knew babies craved it. Anne accepted the fact that her husband was not affectionate but how would he be with a baby? Maybe a baby would settle him down and get him to lift up from his heart an emotional reaction he had never experienced before.

On June 22nd 1930, Charles Augustus Lindbergh Jr. was born at the Morrow's estate Next Day Hill. At close to seven and one half pounds, he appeared to be a healthy baby boy. During the first few days the baby slept for long periods of time, but as he got a little older he became more restless, wanting to exercise his lungs more frequently. His father did not know what to think of his young son. After two weeks of steady crying, the Great Aviator quickly scheduled business trips and meetings allowing him to get away from the infant. He left his son in the care of his mother and grandmother. Within weeks, there were servants at Next Day Hill who were given the responsibility of taking care of him. The question of affection was answered within the first month as the Great Aviator avoided the baby's nursery like the plague. As the baby craved food or attention, he was quick to cry. It was like a cue for Lindbergh. The newborn baby was becoming a huge challenge. He continued to spend long days in New York City in his new office at his attorney and friend Henry Breckinridge's law firm. The only thing he could come up with when someone asked him how his baby was doing was to say that, "his son was interesting". When it became obvious the boy would have golden locks and a cleft in his chin like his father, he finally admitted that the boy looked like him. He rarely talked about him, it was as if his son was stealing the spotlight and he resented it. The new mother was also struggling with motherhood missing the freedom of flying and pursuing adventure. Parenthood did not stop the young couple from socializing practically every night while someone else watched over their child.

Anne's questions about parenthood were quickly answered. Neither did very well at assuming the responsibility. The Great Aviator spent little time with his son and everyone at Next Day Hill knew it. At no time did he ever make an effort to bond with the infant. It unnerved him when Charlie cried. "How could my son cry so often?" When the Great Aviator wasn't flying, he was working, and when he wasn't working, he was 'shooting the bull' in the office with Colonel Breckinridge or some of the Colonel's attorney friends like Colonel 'Wild Bill' Donovan or Bobby Thayer. About six months after Charlie's birth, he started spending time with renowned, scientist Alexis Carrel. Carrel, a Nobel Prize recipient, had offered the Great Aviator the opportunity to tour the laboratory at the Rockefeller Institute of Medical Research in New York City. Lindbergh was fascinated with biology and started driving across the river from Englewood, where he enjoyed discussing science with Carrel. Carrel was aware of the fact that the Great Aviator was not educated and that sometimes he acted unrefined, but he could see he had an analytical mind. That impressed the French scientist. Early on in their discussions, Lindbergh had posed the idea of an artificial heart. It was an idea that the two men hoped to explore together. The Great Aviator also started spending more time away from home with Bobby Thayer, a young attorney in respected attorney Bill Donovan's office.

By the end of 1930, the Great Aviator sought more privacy for his family. Charlie was not progressing as well as he had hoped; the child's development was severely delayed. After six months, he wasn't interacting very much and continued to be an unhappy baby. As the press continued to hound them for pictures and information about the baby, the Great Aviator thought it would be a good idea to move to a more isolated location, away from Englewood. He was disappointed that his son seemed abnormal and he did not want anyone to find out about it. Even though the newspapers were constantly demanding pictures, Lindbergh prevented anything about the baby from getting disseminated to the press. A perpetual restlessness, combined with this uneasiness about the baby's health, led him to the scenic hills of central New Jersey. He wanted to move to a secluded, rural area and build a farmhouse where no one would bother him and his family. He would have the privacy that he longed for. Through an aerial search, Lindbergh found the perfect tract of land near Hopewell, N.J. Less than three miles from the quaint little town, the tract was perfectly nestled in the hills about sixty miles south of Englewood. It was the ideal location, not too far from New York City but far enough and secluded enough to keep the news hounds away. Finding it was easy by air, but difficult by land. The location would be conducive for him to come and go, once he cleared a landing strip for his airplane. It would also provide him with great privacy for his family. After completing the land transaction, he worked with the architect from Next Day to draw up the specifications of the farmhouse. Despite Charlie's struggles, it was an exciting time for the couple as they prepared for their new home.

Because Charlie had difficulties with his development, they decided to hire a full time nursemaid who would care for him and give him the attention he needed. In February, they hired Betty Mowat Gow to be the nursemaid. She had limited experience, but after a brief interview the Great Aviator declared her the right person for the job. While the construction was underway, they rented an old farmhouse close to the property near Princeton, and for a while they lived and commuted back and forth. They brought Betty down to the rental house and she fit in nicely.

She was young and pretty and full of energy. She was comfortable with the child, but by the late spring everyone was getting tired of the rental house and they went back to spending weekdays in Englewood. The Great Aviator, restless to fly again, planned a long expedition to the north, where he could survey potential routes for air travel. Anne, anxious as well to take the trip, was confident that Betty could handle the baby, even if he continued to cry often. This was reason enough for the Great Aviator to get back in the air, especially miles away from his son who he resented more and more with each day that passed. At the end of August, they would depart on a four- month long expedition; it would take them across the top of the world and on to the Orient. Betty Gow and the baby had been dispatched to the Morrow's vacation retreat in North Haven, Maine. The day before they left, the Lindberghs flew to North Haven where they stayed overnight. Anne got to see the baby one more time before they were off to the north. It didn't take long before Betty developed a feeling of claustrophobia. It was rare that anyone came up to Maine to visit the baby or Betty. She was ensconced there the entire time playing 'mommy' to the Lindbergh baby. She couldn't help but feel trapped. Fortunately, while there she met a Norwegian sailor named Red Johnson, who worked on wealthy neighbor Thomas Lamont's yacht, the Reynard. The two struck up a friendship and it helped Betty deal with her doldrums. She began to question the baby's slow development and had even discussed it with her new friend Johnson. The couple was surprised by the fact that the boy didn't walk and wasn't talking at all.

The Lindberghs returned from their trip earlier then they had planned. On October 5th Anne received the unwanted news that her father U.S. Senator Dwight Morrow, had died suddenly after only ten months in office. They returned to Englewood two and one half weeks later on October 23rd. A week earlier, while the family was finishing up with funeral arrangements, little Charlie and Betty returned from North Haven. With Anne's emotional state shaky at best, she could not hold back the elation of seeing her young toddler.

In Hopewell, the builders were in the last stages of construction. Plastering and painting was still incomplete, but Anne and her mother decided a good way to get their mind off of Dwight's death was to take a trip to the new farmhouse. One day without the Great Aviator, they took the baby and did the two-hour trip by car down to the estate. The Great Aviator did not go because he was preparing for yet another business trip. For Anne and her mother, the mountain air proved to be therapeutic.

Back at Englewood, Red Johnson was becoming a regular visitor often socializing with not only Betty but other Next Day Hill servants like Violet Sharpe and Marguerite Junge. They were kitchen and dining room workers and likeable employees. Marguerite and Betty had become good friends in a short time. Violet however, was aloof. She thought that one day she would free herself from serving others, and pursue another line of work. She tended to socialize with the men more than the women. Her flirtatious manner had hooked several of the male workers around the estate, including the butler who wanted to establish a serious relationship with the maid. She however enjoyed the company of Red Johnson, even though he was regarded as somewhat of a sportsman. Red enjoyed flirting with all the ladies including Violet, but was most interested in the attractive and petite nursemaid, Betty Gow.

CHAPTER FOUR
BUILDING A LADDER NOVEMBER, 1931

I t was just after noon, when the Great Aviator pulled his brown Fisher coupe up
the drive to his unfinished weekend estate. Maroon and yellow leaves adorned
the hardwood trees that were spaced out along the cinder drive. Tall pines
bowed in the gentle wind, shifting the colors like a moving rainbow. Clouds were
moving in but they couldn't hide the beauty of the country road that led the way
to the large white house. The Lindberghs were now calling the estate Sorrel Hill
and they hoped to transform it into a spacious working farm. It was obscurely
nestled in the Sourland Mountains and it shadowed the rural railroad stop of
Hopewell, New Jersey. With the cloud cover, telling time proved difficult but the
Great Aviator was always aware of the time. He had scheduled the afternoon to
check on the progress of the house and take care of some other business. Inside
the French-style home, voices of workers could be heard bouncing off the walls of
the unfinished house. Masons from Conover's Construction Company were trying
to put the finishing touches to the inside of the house. They had just restarted
after lunch. The slim Lindbergh walked through the foyer and all three workers
turned and nodded to the tall man who they knew only as Lucky Lindy, the nation's
collective idol. As usual, his powerful presence had created a sense of awe and the
trio of dusty masons couldn't help but stare at the iconic Lindbergh. They paused
from slapping the thick brown-coat over the wooden slats, which would allow the
plasterers to apply their smooth white-coat. Conover's masons were hoping to
finish the first coating of the walls in the servant's quarters. It was the last room
left to complete. Lindbergh wanted it to be completed as soon as possible so the
Whateleys, a middle-aged couple already on the payroll in Englewood, could watch

over things for them when they weren't there. They were already staying in one of the other upstairs rooms and Lindbergh wanted them into their own living quarters as soon as possible. But today Lindbergh needed to be alone; he had other tasks to do that he considered more important.

The quiet Lindbergh, a man of few words, felt compelled to say something. "Things are shaping up well. Why don't you gentlemen take the rest of the day off?" He said nothing else. None of the stunned men responded in words to Lindbergh. They just nodded and quickly picked up their trowels and mud-pans. As they did, Lindbergh took a stroll around the house. After walking up the stairwell, he could see that most of the upstairs rooms were completed. The master bedroom was as he and Anne had planned. Off to the side of their room was the baby's room. He entered the nursery where his young toddler would spend a lot of time, and gazed down from the southeast corner window. The distance down to the ground did not seem that far. It surprised him. Walking out of the baby's room, the stairwell was to the left and the front room would be where Betty Gow would stay. It formed a corner of the house. There was a window on the side and another one that faced the front of the estate. Lindbergh peered out of the front window. He could see the three workers putting their belongings into the back of their work truck. Looking away but not totally ignoring them, he tried to get an approximate height from the windowsill to the ground, which was a mixture of soft clay and red shale. A catwalk of wooden slats had wound around the southeast side of the house so the workers wouldn't track clay and mud into the house. Lindbergh walked back to the nursery. He studied the side window and its width. The ground seemed no more than fifteen feet from the window. Facing mostly east, he stared out to an untidy and uncut field of tall autumn grass and brown briars. The green cedars had cast afternoon shadows on the natural landscape. He smiled at the aesthetic beauty of his property. An impressive and picturesque chunk of land that encompassed almost four hundred yards of countryside on one side, it was a great contrast from the North Jersey residence at Next Day Hill and the bustling offices of Manhattan. In fact, it was quite amazing that anyone including the Great Aviator himself could find it; the location tucked in the Sourland mountains and only accessible by dirt road. Bringing back some memories of his childhood he thought of it as his very own farm, one that he would never let go. It would stay in the family. He had earned it with an audacious and daring willingness to take an incredible chance. More people around the world had heard of him than President Coolidge. Before he left office, the American president had awarded him the Distinguished Flying Cross and bestowed upon him the title Colonel. It was a title he would never let go. On more than one occasion he reminded people that Colonel was the name he preferred. He deserved the title because he was the Great Aviator. Lindbergh continued to reflect for a few minutes more, enjoying the attention in his mind, when his head suddenly turned to the sound of a truck's ignition.

The workers had turned their Ford truck completely around and coasted down the cinder driveway away from the white fieldstone house. The Great Aviator was now alone. He quickly descended the stairs and walked over toward the side garage where behind it stood a small barn-like structure used to cover the well. It was in here where numerous building supplies like nails and small sterling pine boards were covered and stored. In one corner there were just tools and buckets of nails. On the outside there were different types of wood including pine, birch, oak and fir and they were covered by a large piece of canvas. There were studs, slats, lathing and even some flooring, most of these in different lengths and widths. Many of the studs and slats were off to the side in one pile. Those of lesser quality were left uncovered by Conover's workers. Other used wood was in an untidy pile on the other side closer to the garage. All this was convenient for the work crews. If they needed something they didn't have inside the house, they just might locate it outside amongst the piles.

The Great Aviator peered into the well shed, and then slowly walked around the woodpiles. He studied the assortment of wood, and after careful thought selected several different sizes including two by fours, two by sixes, and milled five quarter floor planking. Carefully, he lifted each, and with one eye closed and one eye open, he ogled the boards to make sure they were straight. He shook them with an extended arm as if to weigh them. Most of the selected wood was basic yellow pine. Lindbergh was not a master wood worker, but he was not a stranger to carpentry. He had made ladders as a kid on the Minnesota farm, as a vocational student in school, and even last summer before he and Anne left on their three-month adventure to Asia, he had constructed a small light weighted telescoping ladder. It was small enough to keep on board the plane, and to assist Anne as she climbed into their Lockheed float-plane the Sirius, the plane they used for their epic trek to the North Orient.

Lindbergh continued to size up his supply of wood. Those boards that he wanted, he tossed off to the side in a neat separate pile. Because the two by sixes were too heavy, he flipped them back onto the big pile, and decided to use the lighter planking for the ladder frame. Unlike the ladder he had created for his Asian trip, this one would have to be longer but still not too cumbersome and heavy. And it would have to be telescoping. The measurements were important in order to get each part of the extension ladder to sit perfectly in its place. Even though his other ladder was not a carpenter's beauty, it had worked well for him, and he used it before and after his many journeys. This one would be the same in appearance, but it definitely needed to be taller.

The lanky Minnesotan placed his tools that he had taken from his car onto the makeshift worktable. From his pocket, he took a piece of paper. This was the casual blueprint he had already drawn up. The dimensions included the rails and the rungs he had estimated earlier. Like all great engineers, Lindbergh wanted to make sure all the schematics were right, but he didn't have the exact dimensions of the house when he drew up the plan in his New York office that morning. He had hoped that by eyeballing the distance from the window to the ground, he could still create an efficient ladder that would allow him to reach the second floor windows. What needed to be exact, were the measurements that would allow the ladder to telescope, to allow the other rails to expand out into an extension ladder. The Great Aviator hoped that the preparations he had made earlier would be sufficient. The actual crafting of the ladder would be easy, but he would have to tenon the rungs into the rails, mortising them. If his measurements were correct and it was squared out properly, the boards would perfectly nest together. Once he did that, putting it all together would take no time at all. Although it was obvious he was not a carpenter, he considered himself a good engineer, and he wanted the task at hand to be accomplished quickly and properly.

Now it was the industrial engineer that took over. He systematically prepared his workspace. He set up two wooden 'A's that had been left by Conover, and placed two 2 x 6 inch boards into a gap at the top of each to set up a workhorse. Three times he did this, and then rested wider and longer boards on the three horses. In several large tin cans there were hundreds of nails, of all different sizes. He pulled the cans from the buckets that were left in the well shed, and placed them off to his right. A hammer rested on one of the 'A's. Both were now at a close distance where he could easily reach them. Lindbergh then measured and marked, and measured and marked according to the blueprint. He was methodical and intense. He was adept at using both hands well. Meticulously, he used a carpenter pencil to draw the squares that would be used to line up the rungs. He used a handsaw to get the right length and width. He was unsure of the width of a standard ladder, but whatever that might have been; he wanted to make sure it would not be too narrow for him to descend quickly if carrying at least thirty pounds. And the Great Aviator did not want his long legs to be impeded by ladder rungs that were not spread far enough apart.

Carefully, but with force, he slid the planer up, and then down the rails. He used his chisel when he had to. Again he used the handsaw. He used a sickle knife to gouge out the squares he had cut with the saw. Lindbergh knew it wasn't going to resemble a professionally made mill bought ladder, but it would work, and hopefully work well. Each rung would have to be the exact width so they could fit tightly, and allow the ladder to extend into its proper position. To Lindbergh what was most important was that the ladder had to work, the telescoping pieces had to slide. It would show his engineering prowess. The look was secondary. With force and precision, he routed holes with a hand drill. He twisted and twisted until he had made a perfect circle on the inside ladder boards, and then he widened them into squares with the knife and chisel. He slid the rung into place making sure that it worked. Several times he did this for two sections of the ladder. When he had the measurements just right, he attached the flat rungs, and then decided that it was taking too much time. The damp cool weather chilled his hands; it hampered his coordination. Lindbergh frowned, as he noticed that not all the rungs were flush with the rails. And because he was running out of time, he had to nail the rungs on the last section. In his haste, his cold hands had failed him, and he nailed crookedly. It was not what the Great Aviator had wanted. But Lindbergh was determined to finish his project, even if his ladder wasn't up to his usual standards. Rushing to complete his project, he had to abandon his normal obsession with perfection, but he was determined to make the ladder slide with ease. If the rungs were not perfect; he could deal with that. What he could not deal with was a telescoping ladder that didn't slide properly. He considered himself a great engineer; it had to work the right way.

With the autumn afternoon transitioning to evening, Lindbergh's only quest for perfection centered on the telescoping of the ladder. With full concentration he became relentless with his planer and wood chisel, shaving the rails, and making sure the pieces of the ladder would fit well enough to slide up and down. Realizing that he was close to finishing, Lindbergh's pace slowed. He paused for a few moments, took a deep breath, and then shaved one of the rails one more time. He then wedged the tenons into the rungs making sure they were snug. Everything would fit now, he was sure of it. He stared down the side rails and checked the pine rungs. From a casual observation it was not fit for sale in a mill or lumber yard. But it wasn't just any homemade ladder. Not every amateur could devise a telescoping three-piece ladder out of scraps of wood and basic tools. Lindbergh knew what he wanted, and it would serve his needs. In the mind of the Great Aviator, it was a relief that his project was complete.

Now that he was finished, he couldn't prevent his mind from going over the reasons why he wanted to construct a ladder in the first place. In his mind it gave him a sense of assurance, as if he was trying to justify it to someone else. Like the reason that propelled him to make a ladder before, this one too was for his own convenience. But even though he would never admit it, this time there were devious and immoral implications. The Great Aviator had made up his mind to stage the kidnapping of his own son. He would place the ladder beneath the boy's room, climb up and into the nursery, take the boy out through the window, and turn him over to someone else down below who would take the child away. This would be the perfect kidnapping. An unknown intruder enters the nursery window, takes off down the road with child in hand, out to a getaway car, and never to be found. A phony ransom note, a frustrating investigation, strong alibis for everyone, and the cops left in a quandary. And no one would dare question him. For the Great Aviator, the bottom line was that he would not have to deal with a tarnished image or the responsibility of taking care of a sickly child. He did not want to bring harm to his only child, but he felt he couldn't give the boy the attention he demanded. The child barely knew him and would scream or cry when his father got too close. The fact was the boy was not healthy. His battle with rickets had slowed his motor skills. His hearing was not what it should have been due to the long plane rides he had to endure as a seven-month old fetus. His mother Anne was forced to fly alongside her husband as he continued to pursue records. Although Charles would not admit it, his main concern was satisfying his own ego, not the care of his pregnant wife. But the Great Aviator was concerned about his reputation, and it troubled him deep down that his only son had all these deficiencies. After all, he and Anne were the perfect couple. They had to have the perfect child.

The Great Aviator wanted to live in a perfect world. He had long conversations with his friend Alexis Carrel on the theories regarding genetics, and the importance of eugenics. The idea of eugenics, to create a master race by eliminating the weak members of society only fed Lindbergh's troubling dark side. He often allowed Carrel to stroke this dark side by telling him how Swedes were a better brand of people. He showed him a poster of a strong Nordic farmer standing in a field that said, "Only healthy seeds must be sown". It was a propaganda poster for Charles Davenport's eugenics movement. Since his paternal lineage was totally Swedish, Lindbergh easily bought into it. Carrel was highly respected. In 1912, he was the first person to win a Nobel Prize in medicine. But the scientist had no qualms avowing his extreme ideologies. Since they spent so much time together in New York City working on the perfusion pump, he and Lindbergh could bounce their demented life philosophies off each other. He told Lindbergh on more than one occasion that it was effective to kill off the worst of any great race and keep only the best people, as if he were breeding dogs.

The Great Aviator repeatedly went over the kidnapping in his mind. It made him feel better when he justified it. Although death was not part of the plan, there was absolutely no way he could be the father of a genetically deficient child. He wanted a fit family. People judged others by their offspring; he had to have a healthy, strong, robust baby, and Charlie wasn't fitting that bill. A child reflected his parent's chromosomal fabric but Charlie didn't mirror his parent's genes. Lindbergh's plan was to give the boy to a couple overseas in Germany who would raise him. He would pay them well to keep the secret, and he hoped they would take good care of the child. Having an offspring with special needs required immense responsibility, and the Great Aviator did not have the time or the patience. He refused to accept an unhappy child; one who cried every time he came near. Charlie was abnormal, and having a retarded child would tarnish his hero image, and in some way imply that he was inferior as well. He had enough insecurities and he did not want them to get the best of him. Now that he was the Great Aviator, he had a reputation to uphold. America's blood needed to be pure; its children strong and he would do his best to keep it that way. The offspring had to possess great qualities. Like the specifications of an efficient airplane, they would have good form, they would run flawlessly and there was no room for error. Now that they suspected Anne was pregnant again, he knew they could produce more children. Having two young children, one genetically deficient, would be more than the Great Aviator could tolerate. Not only would it put a real damper on his reputation, it would hamper his ability to do what he wanted, including flying around the world and meeting with the hordes of followers. He wouldn't want all his followers ridiculing him for having a slow child. How could he have a retarded child? It didn't make sense. Lindbergh was the Great Aviator. In a paradoxical but more sinister way, he had to satisfy the insatiable narcissist skulking around his troubled mind.

Lindbergh made sure the rungs felt secure as he shifted the telescoping ladder smoothly on its side. His eyes shifted across the ladder carefully, and then he smiled at his creation. With care and pride he pulled it off the wooden workhorses and stood it up. The Great Aviator placed his large black shoe on the bottom rung and lifted the nesting rail upward. It slid perfectly. He then balanced the ladder and pushed up the other telescoping piece. It too worked. He smiled as he wiped some of the sawdust off the rails with the rag. He let the rails drop back into place. Again, he slid it up and then down. Now, Lindbergh lifted the entire ladder up above his head. It was extremely light in weight.

"About thirty-five pounds, no more than forty." Under his breath, he questioned himself, "Would it be sturdy enough to hold me?"

Since Lindbergh was alone at his getaway farm, he was able to pull the ladder away from the well shack, and stand it up without anyone seeing what he was doing. Its modest weight allowed him to easily lift it on to his shoulder, and he walked it over to the house. With two bent elbows, he carefully leaned it against the side of the house, making sure not to put a mark on the beautiful white fieldstone. Looking at the house and then the ladder, he wondered for the first time if the ladder was of the right size. The length didn't seem right.

"Would it fit up to the second floor windows? Were his dimensions the right size?" The Great Aviator wondered whether he had placed too much emphasis on the telescoping aspect and not enough on length and sturdiness.

Had he miscalculated? In his mind, he knew that he had miscalculated before, but he hoped he didn't repeat the behavior again.

The Great Aviator then walked the ladder around to the southeast side of the house, and without its full extension, placed it under the nursery window. Again, he was careful not to leave a mark on the house. It was way too short. He then extended it all the way out. This time it was too long. If he placed it directly beneath the window, the bottom rung would be too far away from the house because of the distance between rungs. He wouldn't need all three pieces. Lindbergh then doubted himself.

"Why did I waste my time making this a three piece ladder?" He paused for a second, staring upward to the second story window. He pulled one of the sections out and casually tossed it to the side. Even with a two-piece extension ladder, it didn't seem right.

"Dammit! I will have to climb the ladder on an angle." He realized in his attempt to accommodate his long legs, he made the rungs too far apart, and the ladder did not measure up evenly with the sill to allow him to climb into the window. He then positioned it to the right of the window. From this position, he would have to almost swing from the ladder into the window. He knew he could do that, but he wondered if he would be able to get back on the ladder with the child.

Again, the Great Aviator paused. His arrogance allowed him to blow off his questions from earlier. Not totally realizing the difficulty such a maneuver would entail, he mistakenly thought that his ladder would still work perfectly. Lindbergh then stepped onto the bottom rung to ascend the ladder. Carefully, he lifted his long leg upward to the second rung. Suddenly, he heard a crunching sound, and the top side rail splintered, forcing a rung to pull away slightly.

"Ah, shit!" With no one around the Great Aviator didn't hide his disappointment. "Son of a bitch!" he shouted. The All-American kid from Minnesota was spewing some colorful language, and then spoke to himself in a mumble, "All the goddamn time I spent trying to create the perfect extension ladder was just wasted, not to mention the effort."

"Shit." He cursed again. He was angry at himself. "All that time, I should have realized this could happen. I totally messed this up. Now what?" The Great Aviator paused to gather his thoughts. He spoke to himself. "Oh well, I guess I could hammer some more nails into it."

He was quick to realize that even if he nailed the side rail, it was unlikely that the ladder would hold more than a hundred pounds. His thoughts shifted. They dashed across his troubled mind.

"Forget using the ladder to get the child. I could just lean it against the house to make it look like someone used a ladder to enter the nursery. I'll figure out a different plan to remove the boy from the house." Instead of just scrapping an immoral plan completely, the Great Aviator had ventured down an even more dangerous path of deception. The ladder would be a ruse and the police investigators would be his dupe.

After a few minutes, he let the ladder back down to its normal size without telescoping it. He lifted it onto his shoulder, and toted it back to the well shed.

"I can't leave it here either," he thought. He covered it with some burlap, and carried it out into the field over a distance of more than a hundred yards to the south, and close to the road. He noticed a growth of thick briars below some wild dogwoods. He figured he could hide the ladder beneath them. Because the ladder was so light, he didn't think too much about carrying it such a far distance from the house. It had to be far enough where no one would find it, but in an area where he could come back to get it later on. He could even pick it up and place it in his car, and drive it around and up the drive to the house. Still disappointed, Lindbergh flipped the ladder off his shoulder and without the care he had earlier, tossed it down to an entanglement of briars. With a straight back, and arms extended, he pulled it under the thickets and then let his shoe violently shove it underneath so no one could see it. He placed the burlap over it. He was angry with himself. He shook his head and turned back toward the house. With an easy gallop, the Great Aviator headed through the woods back up to the house. He wanted to get a drink before he headed north to Englewood. In the kitchen, he splashed some water onto his face and wiped his brow with a hand towel. He gulped down some cold, well water, and then locked up the house. The Great Aviator got into his car to make the return trip back up to North Jersey. He would tell Anne that he had been to the house, and that it was coming along nicely, but he would not tell her that he spent the entire afternoon there building a ladder.

CHAPTER FIVE
MEETING THE OLD PEDAGOGUE

The Great Aviator was desperate to get out of the office, even if the time he spent as a consultant was limited to a few days here and there. But he had been spending a great deal of time with Alexis Carrel at the Rockefeller Institute working on their heart perfusion pump, which had the potential of replacing a human heart, by pumping blood outside the body. The summer months were taken up with his grueling tour of the Orient. With the winter closing in, and when the opportunity arose to get out of the office, he took advantage. Encouraging him to take an occasional respite from his new office regiment was his friend Bobby Thayer. He and Thayer had become more than just co-workers. At times they would share some personal issues, which always seemed to end up with the Great Aviator dominating the conversations. Lindbergh confided in him about his frustration from a lack of privacy. It seemed every news outlet wanted to know about his personal life. He loved the attention, but he was frustrated because he had not figured out a way to control the newspapers, and the one thing he hated most was not being in control. Hounded by newspapermen, and being in the public eye often drove him to disguise himself, and he and Thayer would sneak down to the heavily wooded areas near the swamps around Throg's Neck. With the cold weather moving in, the sporty confines of City Island were less accessible and Throg's Neck became an alternate hangout spot for them. By going to the coastal areas Lindbergh could relax, and even though there were people who would occasionally spot him, they were mostly German and Austrian immigrants who spoke German and kept to themselves. Being around the water, even if they were the murky, polluted waters of New York Harbor and not the beautiful waters of the upper Mississippi, brought back childhood memories of times that were much easier for Lindbergh. He always relished hunting with his Dad or walking with his Mom, and hanging out with friends, even though he had few back then. Getting out of the office and spending time with Bobby Thayer was relaxing and therapeutic. Thayer was easy to talk to, especially on a man-to-man basis. Both men were about thirty years old, and they could talk about the things they had in common.

The Great Aviator was really fascinated with Thayer's underworld connections. Thayer, a graduate of Harvard University, was fortunate enough to get a job in the law firm of Colonel Bill Donovan a big Republican powerbroker. Donovan was a good friend of another colonel, Henry Breckinridge, who was Assistant Attorney General under Woodrow Wilson. Breckinridge worked with Anne's father Dwight, and became a close advisor to the Great Aviator. Thayer, because of those connections, befriended Lindbergh. In his quest to be a criminal attorney, Thayer found himself indoctrinated into the world of organized crime. He got to meet many of the well-known mobsters that were constantly jockeying for racketeering position. Through a local thug named Mickey Rosner, he even met Jack 'Legs' Diamond a cohort of Al Capone. Rosner was always trying to hustle a buck, and was well known among the city's criminal ilk. He did a lot of the legwork for the notorious hustler and famed owner of the Cotton Club, Englishman Owney Madden. Rosner was very accessible and Thayer liked hearing the latest about the city's underworld. That was if Rosner was telling the truth. Before he married his heiress wife, Thayer often frequented many of the city speakeasies, where he was known to go dancing with the ladies or brushing elbows with audacious people like Mickey Rosner. Despite the fact that the country was economically depressed, there was still much money to be made down on the west side Chelsea docks or in the smoky, backroom labyrinths of downtown Manhattan. It seemed there was always money to be made, and most of it was not legitimate. Thayer, through Donovan's law firm, had become quite acquainted with many of the hustlers as they deceptively eased their way in and out of the judicial system. Growing up in the backwoods of Minnesota never provided Lindbergh with information on the seedy underbelly of society, so he was infatuated with Thayer's stories. Despite being a polished attorney, he like everyone else in America was equally in awe of the Great Aviator. Thayer, the shooting star from Harvard, suspected Lindbergh wasn't the most educated and sophisticated man but he was quite intelligent and like himself was a gambler who lived life on the edge. This character trait is what Bobby Thayer liked most about him. Lindbergh's daring escapades during the Roaring Twenties had captured the imagination of everyone. And the Great Aviator seemed equally enamored with Thayer's underworld connections and his reputation as a sportsman with the ladies. The pair had a reciprocating relationship and they became good friends. Even though Thayer was married and was a promising attorney, he still managed to spend some time with aspiring mobsters and easy women. Going down to Throg's Neck or any of the beaches nearby like City Island proved to be entertaining for both men. It was on one of these trips to Throg's Neck that the 'Old Man' made his appearance.

The old man was John Francis Condon, well known as simply 'Doc' Condon. He was a large, unusually athletic looking man of about seventy years old. He was loud and boisterous but smart and cunning. He appeared to be quite obnoxious, but his age and eccentricity were also an easy and convenient excuse. On the first day they met, he asked Lindbergh a huge assortment of questions, but it only prompted the Great Aviator to laugh at the odd, elderly gentleman. But Lindbergh was quite impressed with his knowledge and oddball personality. Thayer kept his distance from the old man, and socialized with some of the other folks down along the beach, often inquiring about the latest, ingenious, method of making a buck. Lindbergh however, seemed intrigued by Condon's strange, overly obnoxious personality. The old man fascinated the Great Aviator. But that was not unusual. Old Doc Condon seemed to have that initial effect on most of the people he came in contact with.

"So tell me about what it was like to be alone over the Atlantic? How did you feel when all those people came out to greet you in France? How about seeing all those fans, who showered you with ticker tape? What was Coolidge like? Was he really as weird as they said?"

Initially, Thayer was protective. He intervened during the interrogation, and imperatively told the old man to go easy with all the questions, but Lindbergh found the old man's tenacity and curiosity amusing. Condon told Lindbergh that he was a retired schoolteacher and principal, and that he lived in the Bronx. He also related that he occasionally did some part time teaching at the College of New Rochelle, and even lectured some at Fordham University. His profession interested Lindbergh, and the Great Aviator returned a line of questioning to the old man about education. Condon would answer by going off on tangents about the youth of the 1920s being reckless and without morals. Somehow, he would transition the conversation to a rant on how the Italian immigrants were ruining everything.

Over a period of several weeks in the late fall, it seemed Condon was always hanging around Throg's Neck, and he told Lindbergh he had a real estate office over on City Island. Lindbergh after feeling comfortable with the old man, would sometime disguise himself and venture down to the beaches to 'punch the bag' with him. The old educator was quite perceptive, and was good about maintaining privacy for the Great Aviator. But even though he was in awe of Lindbergh like everyone else, he did not want to jeopardize his private afternoon bull sessions with him so he kept their relationship a secret. Lindbergh would make him promise not to tell anyone that he would be there, and Condon agreed. Lindbergh was impressed by the old man's vigor, and his ability to turn the charm on and off. He was in great physical shape, and could adapt to any conversation. At times, he was an eloquent, sophisticated educator, and then in a flash he was one of the cheap foul-mouthed conmen that so often frequented the beaches near the waterways. And this fractured behavior the Great Aviator found fascinating.

CHAPTER SIX
EARLY JANUARY 1932 A CHICKENWIRE PEN

January in northern New Jersey was not the same as Northern Minnesota. Snow wasn't normally piled three feet high and the frigid arctic weather didn't consistently stay around for months without some thawing. Yet it was not totally unheard of to have temperatures dip below zero or see an occasional snowstorm dump more than a foot of snow on New York City's western neighbor. Of course when the arctic fronts would hang around too long, so would the snow, sometimes all the way into March. It didn't always remind the Great Aviator of his picturesque home state of Minnesota but he seemed at home during the cold winter months of northern New Jersey.

Next Day Hill was in a semi-urban, but secluded setting in Englewood just across the Hudson River from the big city. Blanketing the estate grounds was a coating of snow hardened from a steady northern wind that blew across the top of it. The Great Aviator had just finished nailing chicken wire onto a primitive frame of pine two by fours. The cage was about four feet by six feet, and it was perfect for Lindbergh's plan. His plan was not to put the family dog into the pen, as several of the staff might have thought when they saw him building it. Instead, he was going to put his baby in the newly crafted device. The Great Aviator had hastily built the pen so that his eighteen-month old son could get used to the cold temperatures. Betty Gow and his wife Anne weren't paying much attention to the Great Aviator, as it wasn't uncommon to see him working on something around the house on the rare days he was at home. Getting Betty to dress the baby up in his snowsuit, so that his Dad could take him outside, was no problem at all. Betty surprised and elated at the father's sudden interest, did not hesitate to get the boy ready for the frigid North Jersey weather. Thinking that Colonel Lindbergh was going to take him for a nice little walk around the grounds, Betty felt compelled to inform Anne what was going on. Elated, she too was quite surprised by the father's new and sudden interest. She was excited. Charles was finally adopting the role of a father.

"Come on It, we're going outside. Let's see what you're made of." Mother and nursemaid smiled with appreciation of Charles' newfound parenting skills, but they were not overly excited about the odd term of endearment. Away they went, as the Great Aviator scooped up his only son and headed outside.

"Now It, you will remember this one day, and you will appreciate me doing this for you. Without anyone at Next Day Hill aware of an ulterior motive, the Great Aviator had no trouble removing the child from the baby's mom and nursemaid.

Young Charles was a little more than 18 months, when his father acclimated him to the cold, winter weather. The Great Aviator had two good reasons for this. One, he thought exposing him to the winter weather would serve to toughen the toddler up and give him some discipline. The second reason was to get him used to the cold, because he knew as part of his bigger and more complicated plan he would be exposed to some cold temperatures for an extended period of time.

To the dismay of the child's nursemaid and mother, Lindbergh unexpectedly placed the child in the pen.

"What in the world is he doing to that baby?" asked Betty disgustedly, as Lindbergh pulled the chicken wire over top of the child. "Why, I don't know," said Anne puzzled, but as usual too naïve and too afraid to ask. Instead of speaking up, and with a bizarre look of adulation, she just smiled weakly toward her husband. Seeing the women getting nervous, Lindbergh nonchalantly waved them off in an attempt to stop them from worrying.

"Don't worry," he shouted, "he will be just fine. I'm not going to hurt the boy; it's good for him. It will toughen him up. It will teach him to be strong." As the Great Aviator walked away from the crude pen the baby started to cry loudly. Again Lindbergh waved the women off. Showing her angst over this new development, Betty again looked at Anne waiting for her to make a move. When she didn't do anything, Betty's Scottish brogue came on strong. She couldn't hold it back any longer.

"Mrs. Lindbergh, you can't allow him to treat the child that way. He's going to get sick, not to mention, its scaring the lad to death. He's just a baby—he can't handle this kind of rough treatment."

"I don't know what I can do, Betty. You know how strong minded the Colonel is."

"Yes, but someone must do something." Anne pulled the window up. "Charles I think that is enough, the boy is crying."

Lindbergh again waved her off but this time he was stern. "Don't worry about him, he will be fine."

The Great Aviator strutted up the steps and joined the women. All three silently watched the little boy crying for someone to help him. The child struggled with the loneliness and the frigid temperature. The crazy event that was going on outside the house at Next Day Hill started to generate interest within the house as well. Many of the staff, including servants Emily, Violet, and the butler Septimus, looked out to see the crying child, and then became equally baffled as to why the parents were letting this go on. The painful ordeal went on for two hours, until the Great Aviator finally went out and pulled the top off the pen. He lifted the child out and carried him toward the house.

"C'mon, boy, I bet you feel tougher now, don't you? It, this will teach you some discipline. Believe me; you'll appreciate me doing this for you. Lindbergh handed the child off to Betty, while Anne headed toward her bedroom to write in her diary. The Great Aviator said nothing to Betty, and went in to the kitchen looking for something to eat. "I sure am hungry; working out in that cold really builds up your appetite." Looking over to Violet the serving maid, he commanded her. "Get us something Violet; the boy might be hungry too. Better ask Betty what It eats." Lindbergh grabbed his handkerchief, blew his nose, and stretched his arms out above his head. He plopped down in the dining room chair and waited for Violet to serve him.

CHAPTER SEVEN
MIDDLE OF JANUARY 1932

The Great Aviator liked Betty Gow's new friend Red Johnson. He was a rogue sailor who had the gumption to travel to the states and procure a deckhand job on Thomas Lamont's yacht. Lamont was a good friend of Dwight Morrow. With the yacht docked in North Haven, where Betty had been living during that summer and fall as the Lindbergh baby's nursemaid, the two struck up a relationship. With the Lindberghs busy flying around the world and the Morrows constantly busy, Betty spent many nights alone with the Lindbergh child. On one of the rare nights when Mrs. Morrow volunteered to watch the baby, Betty was able to take advantage of the opportunity and went dancing with the Norwegian sailor. It was a relationship that grew out of convenience. Both were lonely, craved a relationship and just happened to be in North Haven at the same time.

When the Lindbergh's trip was abruptly cut short because of Dwight Morrow's death, they were forced to return home on October 23rd. It was at the end of October when the Great Aviator met Red Johnson for the first time at Next Day Hill. On Sunday November 22nd Betty and Red drove down to Hopewell to visit the new home and take in the beautiful countryside. Lindbergh gave Red a special tour of the estate, and it made the Norwegian feel quite important spending time at the farm with the world famous airman. Red seemed at ease with him and Lindbergh respected that. He had little tolerance for people with no self-control, and absolutely loathed anyone who tried to brown-nose him. But Red carried himself well. The Great Aviator contributed this to his Scandinavian pedigree.

Again on New Year's Day 1932, the two men were able to spend some time together. After the chicken wire episode, Betty had to tell Red that the Great

Aviator was not such a great man, that he had flaws like everyone else. On more than one occasion she had seen the dark side of his personality. She had been critical of him before, even confiding in Red her disgust over the Lindberghs spending so much time away from their child back in the fall. It was easy for everyone to make excuses, but it still troubled her. Just because Lindbergh was researching and flying planes, didn't absolve him from his responsibility as a father. She couldn't help but feel that she had been dumped on with the immense responsibility of being the Lindbergh baby's nursemaid for almost four months. Most of that time was spent alone with the Lindbergh child. She knew that their trip would have been longer had Dwight Morrow not died. She remembered watching him force his young son into the chicken wire cage and then preventing anyone from going to him. She hated the thought of the baby out there in the cold, crying for someone to come get him. Lindbergh was sadistic and everyone at Next Day Hill knew it. Most of the staff was keenly aware of the child's health impairments, and wondered how he could treat the baby that way. Since Betty was the principle caregiver, she keenly saw how tense Charlie got whenever his father got too close to him, and witnessed on several occasions the child screaming for someone to come to his aid. And then he wouldn't allow anyone to consul the child when he cried continuously. In her mind, a caring person would not behave in such a manner. When the Great Aviator asked her if he could meet with her and Red one afternoon in January, she could not help but wonder what he was up to. During a weekday when Betty was not scheduled to work, he set up a meeting with her and Red. When the couple sat in his car and shared a box lunch near the beach at Throg's Neck, she couldn't believe what the Great Aviator was suggesting.

"Look I know this sounds callous, but if you look at it from a different perspective you will realize it is the best thing to do. Betty, I know how much Charlie means to you so I feel confident, you will agree with me. I know someone who is willing to take Charlie and give him the attention and medical service that he needs. However, there is one problem. If the press found out that we did this, they would crucify me. I have not told Anne of my plans and I cannot let her in on this."

"Colonel Lindbergh, why are you telling us this information?" asked Betty.

"Because, I want you and Red to help me." He mentioned Doc Condon, and Red immediately knew whom he was talking about. He had seen the old man around City Island and like most people who had met him they couldn't forget his odd personality.

"Doc Condon, a friend of mine, has volunteered to assist me in this endeavor. He knows three men and a woman who are willing to take the child to Germany, and set him up in a nice home over there. The problem is that we must do this without anyone's knowledge even Anne's. That is where you two come in. I will pay you to help me pull this off." Betty and Red were bewildered at the proposal.

Betty wondered at the real motive behind the Great Aviator's plan. She knew he was not a good father. Had he given the boy some attention and showed some patience, Charlie might not have been so cranky around him. She was aware that both parents lacked parental instincts. Anne struggled with her father's death, and was preoccupied trying to deal with that. When she showed signs of overcoming her father's death, she had to deal with the morning sickness from her second child. Throughout the whole month of December, the expectant mother was bedridden with nausea and fatigue. It meant Charlie spent more time with Betty, and it bothered her. It did not help that Charlie's needs were increasing because of his rickets. It was as if the Lindberghs were afraid of confronting the challenge of taking care of a needy child. The more she thought about it, Lindbergh's plan was making more sense. The child would be better off in a loving environment, even if that environment was in Germany.

"Colonel Lindbergh are you sure that this would be the best thing for Charlie?"

"Betty, I am sure he will be well taken care of. I have thought about this for some time."

"What about Anne?"

"Yes, what about your wife, Colonel?" Red Johnson echoed Betty's question.

"I know it will be hard on her, but Betty you and I both know that he is closer to you than he is to her. And you know the boy hates me. If he is given to a couple that is willing to dote on him and tolerate the crying, he will be much better off. Anne is new at motherhood and does not seem to have the maternal instincts like you do. An adoptive mother and father would be just what he needs. I cannot because of my commitment to aviation give him the needed attention, and I certainly can't afford to have the press boys criticize me because I can't give him that extra time. Nor can I allow them to criticize me for having a retarded child."

"He is not retarded, Colonel, he is just a little slow in developing."

"Whatever it is Betty, he will be better served in Germany with two loving parents. Betty was skeptical, but when the Great Aviator said he would be better with loving parents, she knew he was right. The Lindberghs were not good parents and everybody at Next Day Hill knew that.

Again, she thought about the day just two weeks earlier, when he put Charlie in the wire cage.

"I am willing to pay you both to help me. Betty all you will have to do is put him in the proper place when the kidnapping takes place."

"Kidnapping?" asked Red.

"It's the only way we can pull this off. Doctor Condon has assured me his men will take the baby to a temporary shelter until the coast is clear and then take him over to Germany. A German couple will take care of him and then accompany him on the trip across the ocean. I will assure you he will be in good hands. Red I want you to drive Violet Sharpe down to Hopewell so she can take the baby to the German couple. It will be easier to pull this off down in Hopewell than up here at Next Day Hill. I will give you more directions once Doctor Condon and I figure out every detail. I can assure you this will be well planned, and everybody will be protected. I will need you to remain silent and not tell anyone of the plan. There are certain things that need to be in place to make it work. Betty, you will need to be the inside person to make sure the timing will be just right. And Red I want you to be a driver. I hope you are willing to help me. As I said it will be the best thing for the baby." Betty and Red did not know what to say. But they knew that this was the Great Aviator speaking to them. If anyone could pull this off, it was him. And he did know enough people who could help him pull it off. Betty knew she had an attachment to the baby, but she was also aware how sadistic Lindbergh was with him. Anne was an absent parent, always too sick or busy to take care of the boy; now she was bedridden because of the morning sickness. She spent little time with the baby, and was out flying for four months when she and Charlie were cooped up in North Haven. Anne just wasn't ready for motherhood. She wondered how the parents could be so unattached to a child his age. Charles had nothing to do with the boy. Whether it was because of the baby's slowed development or his own selfish interests she knew that he was right, he would be better off. The baby would be happier and healthier in a place where someone could give him the proper attention. She agreed with the Great Aviator that Charlie needed parents who were willing to stay at home, and give the boy the love and medical treatment he might need. By the end of the hour-long lunch, without much consideration, they had agreed to assist the Great Aviator in the kidnapping of his own son and in sending him off to a new home in Germany.

CHAPTER EIGHT
INTROSPECTION AND PLANNING

The Great Aviator was alone in the parlor of his private wing at Next Day Hill. A blast of salty air had misted its way in from the lower Hudson, and hung like a shroud over the grounds. It had mixed with an arctic north wind that was rushing frigid air from the top of the world, creating minute crystals of precipitation. The winds were jagged and unrelenting, and combined with the moisture from earlier in the day had once again locked Next Day Hill into a wintry landscape. Instead of pristine snow, an almost translucent blanket of silvery sleet had glazed over everything on the grounds. Lindbergh was alone, his wife and child were asleep, as was his mother in-law and most of the staff. It was almost midnight, and a nearly full January moon was intrusive as it invaded the tall windows and illuminated the room. Foreboding shadows slowly crept up along the glossy wooden floor like an uninvited stranger from a Dickens novel. As the precipitation started to give way to clearing, reluctant gray clouds struggled to block the phalanx of milky stars as if they were caught in a heavenly power struggle. The gray clouds in desperation fled an impending gloom, and the lunar orb acting like a well-mannered host, danced in and out like a lonely ghost. The beautiful Morrow estate, a mixture of architectural and natural majesty seemed impotent against the cold, overwhelming forces of nature.

The Great Aviator couldn't elude the uneasiness of his own dilemma. He wanted to make sure his plan would be an efficient one. It would have to work and there could be nothing to make it fail. Part of that plan would be Lindbergh's complete dominance and control of the investigation that would follow. He was banking on his own reputation, and a public and a police force that was, even five years after the flight, still in complete awe of him.

Deep within his complicated psyche, Lindbergh knew he was afraid of failure. The failures he experienced as a child, and the lack of parental support to aid him through those challenges haunted him still. His insecurities were not always obvious, except when he relied on practical jokes to divert the attention away from him. But deep down, he knew he really was the Lucky Lindy that everyone called him. Afraid of the truth, he never dreamed that the country would embrace him like they did. Sure his famous plane ride was a tremendous accomplishment, but his transatlantic flight was really an almost suicidal escape from his own tormented life, a life that in many ways haunted him every time he replayed it in his mind. His father's own inability to show him the love he longed for, and the pressure of a stoic but overbearing mother, were now playing out again. The abandonment by his staid father was still a tough pill for him to swallow, almost twenty years later. All he ever really wanted was to penetrate his father's iron casing, and get him to acknowledge some respect for him. He longed for his father's love and attention that was so comforting to him as a young boy, but he resented him for his abrupt departure during his pre-teen years. In his mind, he also resented his Mom's inability to deal with his dad's departure and her own refusal to give her son the love he so needed and craved. She had a weak personality unlike his Dad. He loved his mother, but he did not like her. She could be cold and distant toward her only child, and rarely showed him any affection. He loved his father too, but there was a great deal of anger there for the abandonment, that just didn't want to go away. The man certainly never respected Charles' mother and never really took his own son seriously. The elder Lindbergh once admitted that he was frustrated by his own son's inability to smile and have fun. But Charles was sure had his Dad been alive for the famous flight, he would have earned his respect. C.A. was never able to communicate his love for the boy, especially after he and Charles' mother grew apart. Maybe it had something to do with C.A.'s resentment toward Charles' mother, and his disgust for her that prevented him from getting closer. He wasn't sure. But trying to reconnect and restore their relationship became frustrating for both father and son.

Even as early as Charles' fifth birthday, C.A. was becoming less and less visible and his estranged wife's cold but smothering treatment of the boy only compounded the situation. But earning his Dad's love was another story, and the problems that the Great Aviator had seeking social acceptance because of these issues were enormous. Every time he attempted to make friends he did something stupid. His college classmates hated his arrogance and know it all attitude. All the practical jokes he used to do on his 'temporary' friends in the service were just futile attempts at striking up a stable relationship with a man or woman. Lindbergh just didn't know how to do it. All the tall tales he told, and all the embellishments were just desperate ways to get accepted. And always he failed. In his mind, he always thought he would never be able to live up to his father's expectations, and certainly not be able to accomplish what he did. But now the tide had turned dramatically, and the world had reached out and embraced him. The young man had now become a messianic icon; a legend who embodied the spirit of adventure that would symbolize the 1920s. He was Charles Lindbergh the Great Aviator.

Lindbergh's life had now entered a new stage, and for him to maintain his image he had to come up with the plan even though it may have been sinister to the outside world. In his mind however, the plan was his only option, his only choice. There were still kinks in the plan, but he was sure they would be resolved. And he still had some doubts about whether it was the best thing for everyone concerned. Could Anne, the absent but proud mother (despite the child's inadequacies) handle such a stressful situation? Lindbergh knew she must never find out about his plan, it simply could not happen. If she did, he would be destroyed, and the Great Aviator would revert back to being a loser, the loner that no one could stand being around. Only this time there were heinous criminal implications.

As the Great Aviator gazed into the darkness of Next Day Hill from his tall leather chair, his mind continued to race. "Charles Lindbergh is an arrogant man, despite his insecurities." He smirked as he thought it. The Great Aviator began railing himself within his own mind. As usual, he was quick to make excuses. The fact that he was able to recognize his insecurities only heightened them, but was strong proof of his intelligence. He couldn't hide the meandering thoughts of doubt, but he knew he had to carry the plan out despite the enormous implications.

"Maybe I seem arrogant to others, but I did do something that no one else did or had the courage to follow through with."

He couldn't help but feel proud. The Great Aviator thought back to the crowd sprinting toward him when he landed outside of Paris, and the blizzard of ticker tape, tons of it, falling down on him at his homecoming parade on lower Broadway. Millions of people turned out to get a glimpse of the Great Aviator. He remembered the looks on their faces, the adulation and the awe, and the never-ending attention. Despite the shortcomings in his own mind that re-surfaced periodically, and the elapsed time since his flight, he was still arguably the most famous person in the world. But he knew his fame could not get in the way; he had to be careful and persistent with his kidnap plan. He justified it in his own egocentric mind. Little Charlie hadn't really progressed like he had hoped. Physically he was weak, and a Lindbergh couldn't be weak. And the little boy never showed any love for his father. Because of the miniscule amount of time the Great Aviator spent with him, the boy never called him Dad nor did he ever attempt to get close to his father. At times the boy would run fearfully toward Betty if he saw his father coming toward him. The only real time the boy would acknowledge his father was when he would call him 'Hi' and no one really knew what the child meant when he said it. His father never called his son by his real name. Sometimes he would call him Buster but most of the time he referred to his son as 'It', which most people thought was just an unlikely term of endearment.

"My own father didn't respect me and now my very own son doesn't either," he thought. Not realizing the child's age or ignoring the fact that he was rarely around the child, he projected his very own frustrations on him. It was quite obvious to everyone at Next Day Hill that the child just never felt comfortable in his father's arms. He never smiled around him and the only person the boy really responded to was Betty. Occasionally, he seemed comfortable with Anne and her mother, but since the death of Anne's Dad's in late 1931, the two women had not been the same. Beside he had no intentions of hurting the boy; he was merely sending him to Germany, where he would be given the attention and care he needed. Maybe he would even grow up to be a normal adult. Right now the last thing the Great Aviator needed was a deficient child or a child who did not even like his own parents, especially his father, the most famous person in the world. There wasn't much room for compromise on these two issues and Lindbergh had learned to defend himself quite well within the steel studded, concrete walls of his own mind.

The fact that he and Anne were constantly soaring above the clouds, thousands of feet in the atmosphere when she was almost eight months pregnant, and the uncompromising steady hum of propellers did not faze them. Certainly it could not have been too nurturing to an unborn child. The unborn child's health was secondary to Lindbergh's fame and fun. Even after the birth of the child, the parents were still too busy flying around the globe, often for long periods of time. It was Betty who tended to him, and it was Betty he grew closest to, and this placed a tremendous amount of responsibility on her. The pressure of all this was scaring her and she had grown tired of the responsibility. She was becoming the child's mother and the day would come when she would have to separate from him. She too had a life to live; she was in her twenties with little prospect of marriage. Charlie's parents at no time understood the ramifications of being absent in their son's life. Their trip to the Orient began in the summer of 1931 and Lindbergh and his wife did not return home until October. For over two months they played, while young Charles clung to Betty Gow. She was indeed the replacement mother and father for the Lindbergh baby. At no time did the thought ever occur to the Lindberghs, that maybe the child would feel the estrangement of his parents and suffer anxiety from the separation. For the Great Aviator, he was caught up with his own fame and although his wife may have thought about it, she did she never challenged her domineering and egotistical husband. She was only 23 years old, she had been sheltered and like everyone else seemed to be taken in by the Great Aviator. She placed him on a pedestal that he relished and he adeptly used this to his advantage.

Bold gusts of wind unforgiving and relentless, drove down on the northern New Jersey house, forcefully lifting the painted wooden shutters from against the house and slamming them back down again. Air made its way in below the windows and beneath the mortared sills and it whistled lightly through the parlor. There were no goose bumps rising up on the neck of the Great Aviator. He was beyond all that. After all, he had learned not to be afraid of being by himself. Aside from the times he spent alone as a young man, he had flown in blizzards by himself, one time having to parachute to safety. He had performed various feats of daring, including wing-walking all by himself most likely because he enjoyed the attention he received when people thought he was a bit crazy. And he had an acute habit of brushing things aside, rarely showing any emotion. Flying over the Arctic during his trips to the Orient saw him make emergency landings, mainly because of miscalculations. Some of these landings were absolutely terrifying to his wife. One of the most perilous landings happened over China. He accomplished this dubious feat by bringing his plane down between two monstrous mountains in a narrow valley that could have easily swallowed him and his plane. Again this was done because of his own ineptitude. Of course his greatest solo accomplishment was his trek across the Atlantic. For almost thirty-four hours, he battled hallucinations and loneliness in his single engine monoplane the Spirit of St. Louis to legitimately become the Great Aviator. And there was absolutely no denying this incredible accomplishment. He was after all the first man to ever cross the ocean in an airplane.

The eerie noises from a drafty house on a January night had no impact on him. Lindbergh again tried to concentrate on the task at hand. He carefully crafted his plan. He had thought things out over and over again. All the people he needed were in place and all of them would be instrumental in making the plan work. They would do as he said or they would have to answer to him. There would be no mistakes, and make no mistake about it the Great Aviator would call every shot. He would stonewall any unneeded interference by the police. The last thing he needed were hot shot cops poking around and telling him what to do. Charles Lindbergh knew what to do and he was going to do it his way. He was going to call every last shot.

Again, the wind played with the shutters. On the baby's nursery window the wind rattled and it disturbed young Charles' sleep. He turned his head, let out a slight whimper and went back to sleep. Only the Great Aviator heard the toddler and he listened intently for a few seconds and as the child did not emerge from his slumber, Lindbergh continued analyzing the plan in his mind. He knew that he could deceive the work staff but he did have reservations about the police. There were no local police in Amherst where his estate was located but there were cops in the town of Hopewell a few miles away that would be the first ones called in to investigate. Lindbergh had more concerns about the New Jersey State Police but he was sure his fame would neutralize them, even though they had already developed quite a reputation. He had heard how intimidating they were and they were certainly imposing in those bright blue uniforms and black leather knee boots. Could he get over on them as easily as everyone else? In his mind he knew could. "Uniforms and hearsay mean nothing. They're just as inept and incapable as everyone else. I will have them eating out of my hand." The Great Aviator loved the power; it fed his ambitions.

During the late 1920s, Charles Lindbergh had everybody eating out of his hand, and he grew adept at it. For whatever reason, people seemed to discount his strange, erratic and sometimes reckless behaviors. Once Charles saw that people didn't understand him or felt fearful of him, the narcissist in him went to work. And now in the 1930s the narcissist was at work again, only this time in a more sinister manner. In his mind, he could always find a way to justify his behaviors. But he knew he was reckless and this thrill of adventure made the adrenaline rush through his icy cold veins. It did not matter that many of his behaviors were abnormal, but he had a deviant streak that was often immoral and threatening to others.

Creating a flawless and perfect kidnap scenario was not only challenging to the Great Aviator but it helped feed his craving for attention and power. If at certain times a sense of guilt may have randomly crossed his mind, he rationalized things by thinking that his great scheme wasn't really a kidnapping but something that was in the best interest of the child. And it would benefit him in the long run. To the general public the welfare of the Great Aviator was important, but not nearly as important as it was to him. The moral implications of his carefully crafted plan like every other aspect of it were quickly put to rest because in his mind he wasn't doing anything wrong. What was perhaps the most frightening aspect of all of this, was the Great Aviator's perverted beliefs in natural selection and eugenics which somehow became a justification for sending his only son to someplace where disabled kids could not be seen or heard. And that was in the best interest of mankind. Lindbergh did have a strong argument that sending his son to be raised by caring parents was a good thing. But his abusive behaviors were inexcusable and obscene. Besides putting him into a chicken wire pen on a snowy day two weeks earlier, there were other questionable behaviors that the

Great Aviator had exhibited toward his only son. He enjoyed throwing pillows at the child knocking him over repeatedly. The child would struggle to get up and Lindbergh would laugh as he told people it was good for him, the very same thing his own Dad would tell people when he deliberately frustrated the boy by holding him underneath pillows when he was a toddler. It was obvious to the staff, the Morrows and Anne that Lindbergh enjoyed antagonizing the child. Thinking it was funny, he liked to flick the child's ear with his thumb and index finger repeatedly. After awhile, little Charlie didn't think it was very funny at all.

There was an incident at Next Day Hill the day after Christmas, when Lindbergh was so abusive to the boy that during a baby bath, he dunked his son's head under the bathwater to build character, or so he said. Young Charles was only a year old and in the eyes of the Great Aviator a child's need for soft contact was not manly. He wanted to teach the child to grow up like a man. There were people in the Lindbergh household who sat idle while these behaviors went on. Like everyone else, they were fiercely intimidated by the Great Aviator. The immoral implication of these behaviors was never brought up, and Lindbergh scoffed at anyone who bravely mentioned that his teaching methods might be a little too harsh. Anne, the silent bystander, was equally as negligent, because she was the child's mother and let this abuse continue. Being young wasn't a good excuse. There was no way to justify any of these demented behaviors. The main responsibility for the Great Aviator and his wife was without a doubt their son. But it was quite apparent to anyone ever connected to Lindbergh that he often shed his parental responsibility faster than a lightning bolt. And it was unfortunate for the child that his Mom did the same thing. Five years after the historic flight, she was still caught up in the Charles Lindbergh mystique. Running into her room to write in her journal every time something didn't seem right, was an easy way out. It was a behavior many people thought to be strange and irresponsible.

It was a fact that Charles had been fighting demons in his own mind for years; few people if anyone were aware of it. As a child, he struggled to face up to the reality that his Dad wasn't coming back to live with him and his Mom. In addition, his two stepsisters had formed an alliance against his mother and on more than one occasion things ended up ugly. Shouting and physical altercations would take place between the girls and their step-mom. The girls looked at Charles' mother Evangeline as a crazy woman. She resented them because she felt C.A. dumped them on her when he left. There were physical fights between his parents as well. Even his dad had become violent with his mom striking her more than once, and although his parents tried to shelter him from the tense confrontations, he knew about most of them, including the time his mom threatened to shoot his dad with a pistol she had stuck into his temple. C.A. told her to "Go ahead and pull the trigger." She threw the gun down and ran outside, into the woods. Young Charles hated this, and it pained him to think about the old memories. He tried to extricate them from his mind but they were always there hiding in his memory bank. From out of nowhere they would appear, raising their ugly heads; haunting and taunting him. And then all too often, they manifested themselves in ugly, erratic behaviors that were cast onto others. A genetic predisposition of unpredictability inherited from both sides, and combined with these abusive environmental effects, coerced his subconscious mind to confront things with narcissistic solutions. People who tried to get close to him would find his abrupt and abrasive behaviors intolerable. Consequently, he projected the blame for everything bad away from himself and onto others. No one could get too close to the Great Aviator.

The issue of morality might have been something that Lindbergh brought up occasionally in the company of others but his philosophy on most issues were more in line with a robber baron like Andrew Carnegie or his friend Herbert Spencer and his theory of Social Darwinism. And two years before his history making flight, the scientific Lindbergh discounted the moral issue of teaching about Charles Darwin's theories in school, poking fun at the aged William Jennings Bryan for his moral stand in the Scopes monkey trial. Why, he even laughed when the old man passed away a few days later. "A beaten extremist; a religious zealot," he mused. It had been said by some at the time and even later on, that Charles Lindbergh's moral conscience was at the least suspect, and he enjoyed ruffling people's feathers a little too much.

Lindbergh studied his plans. Pulling the blue Sheaffer fountain pen from between two thick oversized children's pencils and his ceramic ink well, he carefully orchestrated his plan. After checking the almanac from one of his flight books, he was able to schedule the kidnapping on the night with the least amount of moon light. On the first of March after the leap year, the moon would be a waning crescent and not visible until the following morning. The evening sky would be charcoal black; no one would be able to make out the get-away car. Essentially, his cohorts would be able to slip out of Hopewell as quickly as they slipped in. The Great Aviator continued with his deceptive hoax. He was systematic and deliberate. He was organized and thorough. He listed details down to the minute. Abbreviations and initials were easy for him to decipher, but to others it meant nothing. He was careful not to keep anything incriminating around the house for fear that Anne or any of serving staff or even the nursemaid might find it. This would also include the staff at the farm in Hopewell as well. Lindbergh kept all written plans in his leather briefcase in his study, and he kept them with him wherever he went. Of course no one would dare come up to him and ask him what he was doing, including Anne who may have quietly questioned his validity on some issues, but always gave him plenty of room and respected her husband on his accomplishment and his knowledge of science and engineering. When he was working in the study, she never interrupted him; she always figured that what he was doing was work related. And if it wasn't, it was not any of her business anyway for he was indeed the Great Aviator.

Lindbergh knew that he might have to include at least two of the staff in his plans, and he was sure they would comply even if he had to force them. Forcing them would be easy, if they couldn't be tricked into the roles they would play. Violet Sharpe would be an easy target. She acted younger than her late- twenties, she was not really attached to anyone romantically which could be an avenue to exploit, and she just seemed terribly naïve when it came to relationships. Because of several difficult relationships that she had been involved in, she was emotionally vulnerable. Getting Betty Gow would not be that difficult either, as long as the Great Aviator got her to understand that everything was really in young Charles' interest. Lindbergh was unaware of the fact that Betty already had great reservations about the care the boy was receiving from his often-absent parents. Of course if any of the servants did become a problem, or in any way made waves not only would they be deported quickly, they would have to face the wrath of an angry Colonel Lindbergh. The Great Aviator knew enough people through Bobby Thayer to have them vanish literally without a trace. It was no secret that the employees at Next Day Hill were intimidated by Lindbergh's immense power. They felt that sense of power immediately whenever he entered a room, or when he would often speak down at them in his imposing manner. They were quite aware of his thirst for power. There were some people around both estates that may have questioned his validity as an international hero, or even saw through his image as an intellectual, but they never underestimated his power for fear he would find out. The fact was Charles Lindbergh was very perceptive and aware, that people were in awe of him. He could sense danger or weakness in others and it was easy for him to exploit people, even his own family.

The early morning wore on. The Great Aviator had worked hard putting together his plan to send his only child off to Germany to live with someone he really didn't even know. His relatively new friend that he met near Throg's Neck Doc Condon would become a principle player in the kidnap plans. The old man had assured him that he would make sure the child would be in good hands and be given the proper care. Condon had been a schoolteacher and a principal and despite being a bit eccentric and strange, was organized and competent enough to serve as an overseer to the operation. Condon was very believable when he assured the Great Aviator that he would make sure that everything would work perfectly without error. Of course, Lindbergh conveyed to Condon that he would be the one with the ultimate power and control and that Condon had to go along or he could be the big expendable. But Lindbergh knew that Condon had the right contacts, people like Isadore Fisch and his business partners Charlie Schleser and Richard Hauptmann, who were more than willing to do anything for the right fee. Lindbergh was forceful in his demand that nothing go wrong and he was going to do his best to convolute and complicate matters so that those trying to investigate would be confused and frustrated. If there were any mistakes made, those responsible would pay dearly, some with their own lives. But Lindbergh did relate to Condon that he would make sure everyone would be protected should the police get too suspicious. Doc Condon liked that assurance from Charles Lindbergh. It made him feel important working secretly with the Great Aviator and getting the thousands of dollars was quite alluring. Those who would be working for him would obviously need money during these difficult and hard times and were willing to do anything to get their hands on it.

Lindbergh had agreed to pay Condon a hefty fee of $20,000 to pull the scheme off. Condon had met a lot of interesting characters as an educator, and he somehow managed to keep in contact with some of the more undesirables. During his retirement, he was a visible character around the Bronx and he could often be seen hanging out down near Throg's Neck or City Island. Sometimes he would go to Hunter's Beach but more often than not it was too crowded with couples. When the weather turned cold there wasn't much to do near City Island or Hunter's and there were less people around. Condon would get a lift from one of his buddies and take the short ride over to the swampy hangout of Throg's Neck. Most of the people he came into contact there were immigrants from Germany. Others were displaced Germans from places like Austria and Yugoslavia. They all spoke German and for the most part ran in the same social circles. Many were unemployed men looking for a way to make a buck. Without anyone knowing of where they were going, Lindbergh and Thayer started going down to Throg's Neck because they enjoyed their talks. On occasion there were German women who would sometimes flirt with the two Americans. Lindbergh would don his fedora, pull up his coat collar and get away for a while. Condon knew many of the men down there. Land deals and illegal stock transactions were convenient ways for Condon to pick some extra cash. The ilk that Condon had been associating with had formed small but successful operations that included phony real estate deals, fake business operations where they could sell stocks to gullible immigrants and occasionally a little money could be made selling fur pelts. The principle players involved in these activities were German immigrants who were willing to make some extra money doing whatever it took. There were no hard criminals within the group. Most were illegal immigrants looking to make a buck or just people who sometimes found that desperation would encourage easy criminal solutions to fit their needs. Most of the people that Condon knew from Throg's Neck, City Island, or Hunters Beach had made their way over to America and found themselves (like a lot of other people) wondering where their next meal would come from. Somehow they quickly learned how to make enough money to get by. There were many hard working people trying to earn a decent living but still the majority of the people socializing with Condon were trying to work their way up the criminal ladder. The elderly pedagogue was always around the area. People were aware that he ran a real estate business on City Island with his friend ex-heavyweight boxer Al Reich. The business had an office that Condon could use for his various schemes.

The Great Aviator was fully aware of the tremendous risks he was taking. He was intelligent enough to know that the unsavory, criminal element he would be dealing with couldn't always be trusted but he seemed infatuated with gangsters and was willing to take that chance. He also had a plan that would protect him should something go awry, one that was based on convolution and projection of blame. Even though he did not want to, the Great Aviator could find someone within his scheme to be the scapegoat if it came down to that. He loved taking chances and he loved stepping over the line into a world of danger. His flight over the Atlantic was a dangerous gamble that many people believed would end in disaster. But that was Charles Lindbergh, living on the edge, always willing to challenge that line. It thrilled him. It made adrenaline rush through his icy veins, and it fed his huge ego. To him, his scheme to send his young child overseas for someone else to rear would be no different, and despite the criminal and moral implications of such, he somehow in a perverse way thought the challenge to be adventurous and thrilling.

Lindbergh arose from his upholstered oak armchair and pushed it up against the matching desk. He walked over to the window and stared out into the darkness, across the snow covered stately grounds of Next Day Hill. Gazing out, he struggled to focus and make things out in the darkness. The grounds of the estate were gripped with an icy and wintry look. The wind rocked some of autumns remaining leaves as they poked through the icy cover and Lindbergh couldn't help but wonder how his life had gotten to this point. He pondered where his life was heading. What would his life be like without young Charles? Would the Great Aviator be given the total respect from a new child like he believed he truly deserved? Anne was already pregnant expecting their second child. Would he or she also become a burden to the Great Aviator? Would the new child meet the rigid standards that the Great Aviator had proclaimed he deserved? With little Charlie gone he wouldn't have to worry about what people might think about his unaffectionate son humiliating him in public, or in front of his inner circle of friends and advisors. And if he set up his plan perfectly, there wouldn't be anyone who would dare question the integrity or reputation of the Great Aviator.

The early morning had finished wrestling for control from the dark night, and a new day seemed to be hiding around the corner. As time seemed to be moving faster than usual, the Great Aviator couldn't stop analyzing himself and his devious plans to ship the young boy to Germany. He couldn't help but think that he was caught in the middle of some power play with the unknown or some source more powerful than he, who was arguably the most powerful man in America, if not the civilized world.

Lindbergh walked away from the icy window. The wind was finally beginning to abate and the howling suddenly turned to whispers, the soft whispers mimicking a child's voice. The voice called out to him. Lindbergh quickly turned toward the sound and then hesitated. He was tired, and he knew his senses were playing tricks on him. He remembered the hallucinations he experienced during the last leg of his transatlantic flight and concluded that the time had come for him to retire for the night. Once again the whispers broke through the silence. Lindbergh then realized it was his young son Charlie innocently mumbling in his sleep. Since the boy had trouble hearing he didn't always hear himself making noise, especially in his sleep. The Great Aviator ascended the stairs and stared toward the nursery. He paused for a second, yawned and walked into his bedroom where he took off his gray wool slacks and white shirt and quickly fell asleep.

CHAPTER NINE
THE DREAM

L ike newly broken glass, Lindbergh's sleep was sharp and jagged. His sub-conscious mind was uneasy. His tall, lanky body shifted from position to position in an attempt to get comfortable. Not relenting, his dreams were fast and continuous. They were disturbing and bothersome. And there was the same pattern in each of them. In these dreams he was continuously crouching to receive a running, crying child. The boy was a toddler of the same age as young Charles. In every instance the child ran to him but because of some hidden restraint the child never made it. He would get close and then things would get slower and slower and then stop. After a second or two, they would resume back to the child running to him. He would crouch to receive him, but again it was the same frustrating situation with Lindbergh desperately trying to catch the child. As the child got close, Lindbergh could only get a glimpse of the boy's face and then it would turn dark like a black slate. As the dreams were repeated, Lindbergh's uneasiness grew worse. Like a continuous, repeating nickelodeon they replayed. He turned again and again, frustrated by the inability to sleep and the inability to make sense of the dreams. He struggled to make out the face. The child's cries were loud and piercing. The boy appeared to be lost and was inconsolable. With his outstretched arms the boy was desperate looking for someone to hold him, someone to save him, someone to rescue him. And Lindbergh wanted to but he couldn't. He was the Great Aviator, why didn't the boy come to him? The Great Aviator stretched and reached but he just couldn't make contact. He was so close but yet so far away. His body rolled over and then back again, struggling with his unconscious mind.

The dreams came faster and faster, and by this time they were annoying Lindbergh tremendously. His body twisted and turned. In one dream he could hear the child, but he couldn't see him at all. A dense, impenetrable and icy mist, like the January weather, shrouded his mind. It merged with the annoying sound of an engine humming, creating a muffled scream for help. His subconscious mind recalled the memory of the last leg of his historic flight when he battled hallucinations. The sound of the motor and the chilly fog frustrated him, as his thoughts jumbled, meandered in and out. Some thoughts broke through the mist; others were denied. His subconscious struggled with an opaque barrier that blocked his sanity, trapping him in an abyss where rational thoughts seemed lost forever. Minutes seemed like hours, and then for some reason the last dream slowed. It glided into a halt, and then like an old fashioned picture frame it was paralyzed in time. Now, both the boy's face and body appeared as the Great Aviator began to visualize. The little child moved closer and then darted toward him. Intently, he focused on an innocent distraught face. A disturbing image took on more shape. It was a face flushed with silky tears, crystallized on fair white skin and shadowed by flaxen hair. His cheeks were shiny. The child was now crying loudly staring out through piercing blue eyes. The Great Aviator's body was tense and taut and he stared inward focusing on the face. The icy fog was now lifting and the muffled sounds were slowly fading away. Lindbergh's burden was gone and he peered inward. The boy's face was in front of him and he could see it clearly now for the first time. The image was so close; it pained him, yet he continued to bore in on it. He wanted desperately to help the boy, but there was some powerful force that prevented him. Suddenly, Lindbergh took a step back in his dream. His shoulders dropped; his neck stiffened in a defensive posture. Now it was obvious to him who the child was. It was he, Charles Lindbergh the Great Aviator.

Lindbergh rose up quickly from his bed and he stared out into a black room; his wife was sleeping soundly. His hands trembled and perspiration soaked his body. He thought of the dream. He couldn't help but think of his father, the father he desperately wanted to please but couldn't. The little boy was seeking help, seeking satisfaction; he just wanted his Dad to rescue him from his pain. He wanted it so bad. He remembered the times after he left, when he wanted his dad to pick him up and hold him tight. Just hold him, and squeeze him, and show his love for him, but his Dad just couldn't do it. He was six years old and his Dad was nowhere to be found. Maybe he was too busy; his job too demanding. Maybe he was just incapable of love. And now it was twenty-five years later. Was this a cycle that was repeating again? Lindbergh fell back in the bed, his wife Anne stirred. She sat up and asked him what was wrong. The Great Aviator sighed deeply. So many things had crisscrossed his mind at once, the past, the present, and the future. His nightclothes were damp and his body cold. A chill rushed up his back. He used the back of his hand to wipe the sweat from his brow and answered his wife, "Nothing, Anne, nothing."

CHAPTER TEN
RECRUITING THE GERMANS

I t was late November of 1931 when two of Doc Condon's acquaintances were first introduced to Charles Lindbergh by happenstance. Charlie Schleser and Isadore Fisch had stopped down by the water as they often did looking to sell something or even try to involve some of the people in their phony business deals. They too had struck up a relationship with the old man a month or so earlier, and on one day they happened to meet up with Condon when the Great Aviator was there. They were not aware of Condon's friendship with America's hero, nor Lindbergh's private little getaways from his consulting job in Manhattan. On this day, the two Germans along with Condon were discussing ways to sell some fur pelts and hustle some stocks in one of several businesses they had started. The trio had conspired on different schemes while down near Throg's Neck. Schleser, Fisch, and Condon had helped each other on more than one money-making scheme. Condon knew plenty of people because of the real estate business that he operated on City Island and over the years as a New York City public schoolteacher he came in contact with many folks who were struggling to make ends meet. Like most people trying to survive during the leans years of the early thirties, they were willing to do anything to make a few extra dollars. Lindbergh seemed to relish the time talking to Condon and over a period of several weeks got to know a few of Condon's buddies. One man who started stopping by with Fisch was Richard Hauptmann who by trade was a carpenter. Hauptmann had a nice, convenient car, and Fisch allowed him to get involved with some of the moneymaking schemes. Schleser was somewhat leery of Hauptman and didn't want some Johnny come lately to move in on the territory but Fisch liked Hauptmann and assured Charlie Schleser that Hauptmann was a good fellow. Schleser still kept his distance from the quiet Hauptmann. The dynamics of this strange cast of characters initially meant nothing to Lindbergh who simply enjoyed an occasional respite from work. After a while he enjoyed the time interacting with the old schoolteacher Condon. Whether it was a fascination with him, an interest in lawless behavior, or some deeper psychological motivation he was harboring, Lindbergh continued to take his incognito jaunts down to the swamps near Throg's Neck. In December, Thayer was tied up with his legal profession, as the courts rushed to end things before the new-year and was unable to accompany the Great Aviator down to the swamps. As Christmas approached, the Great Aviator was in a hurry to implement his scheme of sending his son overseas and he knew who the best person was to help him pull it off. He was the man who knew everyone and everything, the garrulous intellectual, Doctor Condon.

During the cold months of December and January, Lindbergh and Condon's relationship became more complicated. After numerous dissertations and orations, they found they had a lot in common. Even though the two men were willing to befriend some of the German immigrants, much of their discussions centered on their shared nativist views and disdain for unappreciative foreigners, who were bringing the country down and competing for limited jobs, legal and illegal. Condon was always railing the Italians and Lindbergh was always railing those people he referred to as inferior.

Lindbergh also continued to work with Nobel Prize winning physician Alexis Carrel. Together they were still trying to perfect the blood profusion device, which could pump blood outside a person's body. As their relationship grew, they shared more spiritual and philosophical conversation. Carrel continued advocating for eugenics and Lindbergh was fast becoming his best student. By the end of the year, the two had mutually agreed that there were humans who were born intellectually and physically inferior and they contributed to the decay of mankind. They both agreed that systematic euthanasia could be a cure-all to eradicate this rot that had befallen the human race. The eugenics movement was becoming more and more popular in the early 1930s with more members of the scientific intelligentsia attaching their names to it. Old Doc Condon who viewed himself as a pillar of the community, agreed with Lindbergh and Carrel's demented philosophy, but it seemed he had a bias not only based on intellectual and physical deficiencies but also a bias based on ethnicity.

During one those random conversations with Condon, Lindbergh brought up the unpleasant admission that his own son had not met his standards because of his physical problems. He also confided in the old educator that his son had not progressed mentally as he had hoped and that the boy hated him. He told Condon the boy cried all the time, especially when he came near and how he had the child had become a burden to his parents. Lindbergh brought up the unthinkable, and to his surprise Doc Condon assured him he could help.

"Doc, I have to tell you I have thought about sending the boy away to Europe, a place where a family could raise him and give him what he needed. My wife is frustrated because the boy only relates to his nursemaid. Because of rickets he has trouble walking and he doesn't talk much."

Condon was eager to please and asked no questions. He mentioned nothing of the child's age or condition. The old man just wanted to do whatever he could to help and to penetrate the inner circle of the Great Aviator. He could then tell people what a good friend he was of Charles Lindbergh. Excited to assist in any way possible; Condon felt the need to deliver an oration.

"Colonel, I think I could help you out with your dilemma but first let's start from the beginning. Your child has an infliction of which there is no cure. Although rickets can be treated, it often leaves behind a debilitating and scarred body. Your young son is plagued by this cruel hand of nature that will render him a cripple for the rest of his life. But your time is so precious to you. Sir you are indeed someone who has significantly contributed to modern science and it is of great importance that you continue to do so. Colonel you have risked your life to further the world of aviation technology. And now you must continue to pursue your interests and innovations. What we must do Colonel is find someone who can assist you in this endeavor and most importantly provide a safe refuge for your sick child."

Lindbergh interrupted the old man's speech, "What I am thinking of doing Doctor Condon, is sending my son overseas, where someone can take care of him without newspaper guys asking questions all the time. I just can't do it alone. And I must insure that this undertaking is done in secret. If people found out that I did this I would be ridiculed. That is why I have devised a plan."

Before Lindbergh explained his plan, Condon interrupted. "Precisely, Colonel Lindbergh, and I believe I know some people who can help you. But I'm afraid such an undertaking would be costly. It might mean you would have to pay someone thousands of dollars."

"Look Doc, I'm willing to pay whatever it takes. I have the money, what I don't have is the privacy to pull this off. I have thought of staging a kidnapping but I simply can't do this alone."

"Yes sir, I understand your dilemma or should I say your paradox. Colonel, there are many people around here who would be willing to help you get your son to a place where he could get the proper care."

"It's not that he can't get the proper care here, it's just that I can't have a son who is a burden to everyone." Lindbergh's eugenic leaning was starting to surface and his dissatisfaction with his first offspring was apparent. Had he not been talking about his own son he might have been more drastic with his plans. But the Great Aviator was willing to shed his paternal responsibility to little Charlie if he could. As he had said over and over in his mind, he was only doing what was best for Charlie and everyone else. With a new baby on the way Lindbergh would still have paternal responsibilities, but hopefully Anne would give him a strong intelligent child who would grow up to be a productive person and not become a burden to him or anyone else.

"Well, Colonel, give me a day or so to think about how I can help you. Can you meet me again in a few days? I will come up with a plan to help you."

"Doctor, I do have some ideas about staging a kidnapping. What I would like for you to do is figure out who could help us without telling anyone of our plans. We need a few people we can trust. It is imperative Doctor Condon that we don't tell anyone of this conversation. Once we come up with the right plan, we can discuss this with the right people, if you know what I mean.

"Yes Colonel, I know exactly what you mean. As I said give me a few days and we can meet at my real estate office on City Island. Better yet, I have a vacant house down on Jerome where we could meet. Even though I'm sure you will be disguised, there will be less chance of anyone recognizing you there because there are less people around, unlike my office. Colonel, I believe between the two of us we can put together a viable plan. You have my word sir, that I will not discuss this with anyone. You are a great American, I understand this paradox and together we shall solve it."

For another few minutes, Lindbergh and Condon 'punched the bag' about nothing important and then went their separate ways.

Three days after talking things over with the Great Aviator, Doc Condon already had a plan in place to help him with his dilemma. He knew exactly where he could find the right people to assist him in making the plan work. Looking for them was easy; they liked to hang out at the same spot near the old dock on Throg's Neck. After meeting with Lindbergh, he hitched a ride down to the dirt road that led to the swamps. He was sure he would find the Germans down there. Since it was cold now and the winter had set in, the sporting season was over at Hunter's and City Islands. Throg's Neck was closer and it served their needs well. During the afternoons it was not uncommon to find the Germans killing time. They were always discussing ways of making money. Isadore Fisch and a couple of his friends like Charlie Schleser, and Joe DeGrasi were constantly on the lookout for naïve prey. Newcomer Richard Hauptmann wasn't really part of the group but had become pretty tight with Fisch. Fisch was impressed with Hauptmann's knowledge of the stock market and his willingness to be a participant in the latest money making scheme. On this day, DeGrasi was nowhere to be found, but the other three men were busy discussing ways of parlaying fur money into the stock market. Schleser who was a skilled, real estate huckster was anxious to hear how they could use the stock market to get rich quick.

Two of Condon's men were there. Fisch and Schleser were right for the job. Condon did not know Richard Hauptmann that well since he was a newcomer, but he surmised he was like the others; willing to make a buck. He was going to float the kidnap plan and see what type of reaction he would get.

"Gentlemen I hope this day finds you in good spirits despite this economic mess we have found ourselves in. I am not quite sure of these proposals Mr. Hoover has put in place. It seems this new fellow Roosevelt has a great deal of proposals to alleviate the lack of jobs. Of course, we don't have to rely on some shallow politician to make some jack; there is plenty of the green stuff around if you look hard enough." Condon could not help being dramatic, it was his way, but he was really setting things up to see if his German friends were willing to help him in his plan.

"Hey, how are you Doctor Condon?" asked Charlie Schleser, who knew the old man from the real estate business.

"Vats knew?" "How are you, Doktor?" Isadore Fisch and Richard Hauptmann were polite as they both acknowledged the histrionic Condon. The three Germans seemed elated to see the old man.

"Well, fellas, I do have a proposal for you. I am quite sure that you are aware of the money that is being made these days in the snatch racket. I can provide you with an interesting opportunity to make a great deal of money."

"Uh, uh, no sir Doctor Condon," replied Schleser. "I do not vant any part of kidnapping any little crumb stealers. The three Germans laughed.

"Yeah. Count me out, too, Doctor. I don't vant no part of the snatch racket," echoed Hauptmann. Isadore Fisch was not intimidated by Condon's mentioning of starting a kidnap ring. The snatch racket, as it was commonly referred to, was becoming a lucrative business.

"Tell me, what exactly is the good Doctor up to?" Isadore Fisch wanted to know more. If it involved money, it didn't matter how it was to be made; he was interested.

"Well, if you gentlemen would be so kind to permit me to make a brief presentation, you might find that you will be very interested in this. A very good friend of mine has a young son that is daft, or shall we say he is slow. He is a very busy man and does not have the time to provide the child with everything he needs. I have told him that I knew several men who would be willing to help if the price is right."

"Why doesn't he just send him off to one of those nursing hospitals where they pay people to look after them all the time?" Charlie Schleser had a good question for the retired educator.

Condon explained, "Well, Charlie, it's not that easy. You see this father is extremely well known. He will need some good fellas to help him pull this off. That is where you fellas come in. We would like to stage a kidnapping with some people on the inside to make it work."

Fisch did not trust anyone probably because he was always trying to get over on everybody. He wanted to know more, but he was quick to throw up a red flag and wasn't quite ready to attach his name to the scheme. "It sounds like a recipe for disaster, if you ask me, Doctor Condon."

Condon was not amused by Fisch's comment. "Before you gentlemen turn down my offer, let me finish my proposal. This father would be willing to pay you gentlemen more than ten thousand dollars each to carry this thing out for him. Now beside the great money you could make, here is the best news. This man can guarantee you won't get in trouble."

"Who the hell is this guy, Doctor Condon? Has Bismarck risen from the dead or something?" Hauptmann smirked after he posed the question. He was looking for the same reaction from his buddies and they obliged him with their own shit-eating grins.

"You fellas know who I am talking about. As a matter of fact you have met him down here before."

"I bet it's Lindenburg," said Hauptmann.

"It's not Lindenburgh, it's Lindbergh" replied Schleser. "Is that who you are talking about Doc? Charles Lindbergh? The Lone Eagle, Lucky Lindy?"

"Exactly, Charlie. He came to me because he knew I would be the right man to help him pull this off. I have spent my entire life assisting people in many different ways. He was aware of this and that is why he selected me. Now that is where you guys come in."

"So Lindbergh wants to send his own son off somewhere? Where does he want to send him?" asked Fisch.

"Well that is why I will need some good people to assist me. The Colonel would like to give him to a family in Germany. Do you know of any family who would be willing adopt a young child? Maybe one of you has some friends or relatives who would be willing to take on this responsibility. We would have to keep the boy's identity secret."

"Well, what is wrong with the boy?" The gray haired Schleser seemed concerned.

"According to Colonel Lindbergh, the boy has not yet walked because of rickets and it appears as though he has hearing problems. The Colonel also tells me he wails incessantly."

"Doctor Condon, I know enough people in Germany who would be willing to adopt a child. How much money did you say Lindbergh would pay?" Schleser seemed willing to involve himself as long as the money was right.

"He told me he would pay fifty thousand dollars to the right bunch of fellas. Let me tell you gentlemen how it would work. We would need to do this down at his farm in Hopewell. This will keep the press out for a while. The Colonel would have the nursemaid signal someone to come into the house when no one was around and then take the child to the car. They would drop him off at a safe house until the coast was clear and a few days later, take him up to New York where they would board a steamer and sail for Europe."

"I'll drive my car, Doctor. How much is that worth?" Hauptmann now seemed interested as well. The lure of ten thousand dollars appeared to be the prevailing factor.

"Look, gentlemen. Here is what I think would work. The nursemaid will hand off the baby to someone he knows so he won't start crying. It might be the Colonel himself or it might be another person, we're not quite sure yet. Let's say Richard does drive the car and Fisch is his navigator, that other person will be needed to hold the baby and care for him. I think we will need a navigator because the house in Hopewell is very secluded. It is in the Sourland Mountains and extremely difficult to find. The next step would be to take the baby to the safe house. I believe the Colonel already knows of a cabin that is totally hidden. Apparently, he spotted it from the air. We will need a woman to help take care of the child until we can get him out of the country. Someone could leave for Germany right away to make sure there is a home ready for the baby when he arrives. We will probably cut the boy's hair to disguise him; maybe dress him as a girl. I know this sounds jumbled and there are a lot of people involved, but I will have all the kinks ironed out before we carry this endeavor through."

"Doctor Condon, I believe my wife would be a good person to take care of the boy. Are you sure the safe house is well hidden? Where is it?" Schleser was offering the services of his wife, and like Hauptmann seemed already committed. Isadore Fisch however was still cautious. He wanted to know more, and did not give the old man time to answer Charlie Schleser's question.

"Okay, Doctor Condon. I have a question for you. What guarantee do we have that Mr. Lindbergh will protect us?

"My good boy, he is the Great Aviator. People will do whatever he says including the police. He will oversee the investigation and call the shots. The two of us will have this thing worked out I can promise you that." Condon was sure of himself but he never really answered Fisch's question.

"How about you boys think about it for a few days? I will contact the Colonel and we will go over some of the logistical components to the plan. Let's say I stop back here in two days around the same time and see what we have. There is one thing that I want to say and that is most important. There is an issue here of secrecy. You must not tell anyone of our conversation, not even DeGrasi or your wives. NO ONE! You boys got that? The Colonel is a very powerful man and we will need to uphold a code of silence."

"But Doc, don't you want me to talk it over with my wife? Schleser asked.

"I suppose but remember—we do not need any loose lips. We will need absolute secrecy."

Because the old man had gotten dropped off, he now needed a ride back up to Jerome Ave. He asked Hauptmann if he could drop him off. All four men got into Hauptmann's dodge. They drove along the dirt road eventually past St. Raymond's cemetery, and out to the friendly confines of the Bronx.

Two days later, Doc Condon called the Great Aviator at his office and then met him at the unoccupied house on Jerome that he had purchased through his real estate business. They discussed their plans for a while and with the Great Aviator incognito, the two men headed over to Throg's Neck where the Germans were waiting for them. Condon and Lindbergh had been fine-tuning the plan and now they wanted to see if the Germans were willing. The Great Aviator told them of his dilemma and his willingness to pay fifty thousand dollars. He promised to protect them from the police but he was adamant about the need to make sure everything was done as planned, so there would be no need to have to protect them. The Germans had made up their mind to help and were ready to do whatever the Great Aviator asked. They went over the plan and had agreed to meet again with the last meeting to take place on the morning of the kidnapping. The Great Aviator informed them he needed twenty-four hours of flexibility to announce when the exact day of the kidnapping would take place. Condon and Lindbergh would continue to perfect the plan adding a few new details. They met again with the Germans, updated them, and told them they would meet one more time and that would be on the morning of the kidnapping.

CHAPTER ELEVEN
THE MORNING OF THE KIDNAPPING
MARCH 1ST, 1932

D oc Condon's real estate business on City Island wasn't overly profitable during the lean times of the 1930s but on rare occasions someone would get him to sell a house. His house on Jerome was left vacant at least temporarily until it had served its purpose. The old man thought of himself as quite a salesman with his eloquent speech and convincing delivery and wanted to sell it. However, he was willing to wait until his new friend Charles Lindbergh finished his business. The old codger was confident after weeks of incubation; the house was the perfect hideout to hatch the kidnap plan. It was here at the Jerome house without anyone's knowledge but the conspirators, that the detailed plan to move Charles Lindbergh's only son to Germany had been thoroughly formulated.

The principle players were all there. They surrounded the Great Aviator as he sat on an old dining room chair. His suit was expensive, but as usually it hung limply on his lean and straight frame. He had already shed himself of a disguise that consisted of an old topcoat, rounded sunglasses and a Russian peasant hat. With his collar pulled up to meet the sides of the hat, no one would ever know that he was Charles Lindbergh, the Great Aviator.

Lindbergh's demeanor was stern but he smiled as Doc Condon told the punch line of a favorite Italian joke. It was something about 'wops' keeping their underwear on all winter and not ever changing, his dislike for Italians overtly apparent. Condon was his usual self, loud and obnoxious making sure everyone was focused on him. The swarthy Fisch said nothing. He was short and skinny with big ears and black hair, and he watched everyone almost with a sense of distrust as if trying to figure everybody out. Hauptmann was also quiet but he laughed at the demeaning ethnic joke about Italians. A crooked smile below piercing blue eyes hid an air of uneasiness. But he had strong Nordic features including a pronounced chin. He was thin and muscular and despite the uneasiness, he looked strong. He looked toward Condon and Lindbergh as if he wanted their acceptance. The well-dressed Norwegian Red Johnson was to Lindbergh's right, and he sat there as if he was the Great Aviator's right hand man. He looked extremely short next to the tall and slim Lindbergh but unlike the two Germans he seemed comfortable in the presence of the Great Aviator. He kept a casual smile as he sat there listening to Doc Condon. Lindbergh leaned over toward Johnson with interest and asked him if he had a place he could hide his money after he was paid. Johnson was surprised and told him he didn't. Lindbergh told him he should parlay his money into the stock market because stocks had become cheap after the crash in 1929. Ignorant about the market, he asked Lindbergh what was a good stock to buy. "Anything in aviation," said the Great Aviator. The two Germans, who had done some dabbling in the market, glanced away from Condon and listened intently to Lindbergh's advice. They pushed their bottom lips out and nodded toward each other. Hauptmann felt smart because he had already invested in several aviation stocks. Since Lindbergh and Johnson had socialized on more than one occasion because of Betty Gow, the fair-haired Norwegian sailor definitely felt at ease next to the Great Aviator. Knowing he was going to make some money for a change, he asked Lindbergh if he could write down some names of stocks. Lindbergh acknowledged his question with a nod and then stood up ready to start the meeting.

The group of five knew what their roles were. Even the egotistical Doc Condon was willing to relinquish control to the Great Aviator. He understood the magnitude of Lindbergh's plan and what he had at stake, so there was no doubt about who would run the meeting. And like the other meetings it was Lindbergh who ran the show. This was the last meeting, a thorough going over of the plan that was to take place that evening.

Missing from the meeting were the nursemaid Betty Gow, the servant Violet Sharpe and the German couple, the Schlesers, who had the important responsibility of taking care of the baby and sneaking him out of the country to Germany. Betty Gow, an integral player, was well aware of her responsibility and had been in constant contact with the Great Aviator on the phone and also through Red. There were other conversations with him as well at Next Day Hill. Violet Sharpe had no idea that she too would be an important cog in this wheel of deception. Her ignorance of the kidnap plan was exactly what the Great Aviator wanted, and he hoped that she would remain that way. The Schlesers had also been in constant contact with Condon, had been given some money, and were ready to go. Condon and the others looked directly toward Lindbergh as the Great Aviator spoke.

"I want you fellows to know that the Doctor will have your money. He'll give you each a few hundred, and when we execute this plan without a hitch and everybody does as they are told, then you will get the remainder, which will be the ransom money. I called Anne last night to tell her we will remain in Hopewell for at least one more day. And Betty has just received the call from Anne. Red talked to Marguerite Junge at Next Day Hill and she confirmed that Anne had called from the farm to Englewood. Henry Ellerson, the chauffer at Next Day is going to drive her down to Hopewell in about an hour. Red is going to meet Marguerite and her husband tonight at their apartment, as soon as he can to establish his alibi. By the way, Anne still knows nothing. Last night when I called her, to tell her to call for Betty this morning and that we would be extending our stay-over at the farm one more day, she agreed and never suspected anything. You fellas probably wouldn't know this, but my wife is very naïve and now that she is pregnant again, she hasn't felt very well. She spent the whole month of December in bed. Because of her health, she hasn't been interested in too much. Besides, she tends to go along with everything I say any way. Lindbergh wondered to himself if he was giving out too much information, but he wanted to reassure everyone that Anne would not complicate the operation.

Red Johnson smiled as if he knew what the Great Aviator was talking about. He had been down to Hopewell with Betty and had also met Lindbergh's wife up in their summer home in Maine and also at Next Day Hill. He was aware of Anne's pregnancy. She had been sick and heard through Betty that Anne as usual seemed to go along with everything her husband said. The Great Aviator continued.

"I want to review everything one more time, but before I do I want you fellows to know there can be no mistakes and no loose lips. Anybody who messes up will pay; you fellows know what is at risk here."

Doctor Condon interjected. "Colonel Lindbergh I can assure you that my men here will uphold their end of the bargain."

A pensive and anxious Colonel Lindbergh smiled at the comments and cut the old man off. "There is no bargain here, Doc. This a straight deal and there can be no mistakes. I want everyone in this room to know I mean business here." Lindbergh was quick to reiterate, "There can be no mistakes. We all have something at stake here and remember you are all getting paid. If one person screws up, we all go down."

"Yes sir, Colonel," responded Condon. The three immigrants all nodded in agreement with the Doctor assuring the Great Aviator that they would indeed take care of business.

Lindbergh spoke again, "Okay let's go over everything one more time. Betty will be there early this afternoon. She will make sure everything in the child's room is the way it should be, which will mean she is going to remove all fingerprints with a warm soapy cloth. I also did some fingerprint removal myself the other morning. This will serve to frustrate the cops. When Betty is finished putting the boy down for the evening she will signal me by turning the light on and off. At that time I will make my move."

"Before I get ahead of myself, let me back up a bit. Richard, you and Mr. Fisch will pick up Violet in Englewood. You need to pick her up at the bottom of the drive at exactly five thirty. Don't delay. You guys cannot engage her in conversation. Fish, your job is to help Richard navigate his way to Hopewell. Even though you went there yesterday on a practice run, you know those roads aren't the best and the farm can be almost impossible to find. So help him out." Fisch and Hauptmann nodded.

"You also need to keep the conversation going so Violet doesn't get too nosey. She must accept the idea that she is helping the child out. You fellas might not know but Violet can be a bearcat. Red, you need to help out on this issue as well. Not to embarrass you, but I think she's in love with you. You're gonna need to perform your Norwegian magic.

"The Norwegian's got himself a real smarty," quipped Fisch.

Red Johnson smirked, his face matching his hair color. The other men all laughed because they had heard about Violet's habit of falling in love. And although no one wanted to exploit Violet Sharpe, they knew from previous conversations with Lindbergh that even though she could be fiery when she had to, she too was naïve and quite vulnerable. They also knew from discussions with Lindbergh that she was the only person besides Anne, her mother, and Betty Gow, who could keep the baby quiet.

"I know she seems close to Charlie so he will not get upset when she carries him to the car. I will bring the child out through the front door and hand him to her. Originally, I was going to have Violet go get the baby but that would be too risky. Her main job is to hold the boy while Richard and Fish navigate their way back to Princeton."

"Let's get back to the house. Betty will make sure that everything is set up properly. I have gone over this with her several times and she knows what to do."

It was obvious to everyone that Betty Gow had to be the inside person to oversee everything. The Scottish nursemaid supported the Great Aviator's plan to give the child a decent life in Germany with a couple who could provide the boy with the love and attention he so deserved.

The Great Aviator liked the fact that he had everyone's attention. His audience was well aware of the fact that he had thought about this for a long time. Even though Lindbergh seemed tense and repeated himself often, they knew that his plan was systematic and well organized. Like attentive school children, the men stared at their taskmaster, as he continued to layout his carefully crafted kidnap scheme.

"After the baby goes to sleep which should be a little after seven o'clock we will make our move. The staff and Anne know not to go into the nursery between seven and ten. I made that a rule back in November. Ahh….but tonight Betty wants to make sure the boy is well prepared for a chilly night in that cabin. I think she is going to add some extra clothes, so I just told her to make sure the lights are out as soon as possible, no later than 7:00. When she finishes tending to the baby and she is ready, sometime between 7:45 and 8:00; she will turn her bedroom light on and off three times. Betty will then go downstairs and keep Anne at bay at her desk, where she goes every night to write. She will block the doorway so Anne won't be able to see me. I will enter the front door; Elsie and Oliver will be on the west side of the house in their quarters eating, which is usually what they do every evening as well. Oliver takes the dog with him back near the pantry. I can guarantee no one downstairs will hear me. I will then go up the front staircase. Anne and Betty will continue their conversation. The baby should be asleep. I will go to the nursery, grab the baby and quickly descend the stairs. Exiting through the foyer, I will hand off the baby to Violet will be waiting at the front door. She will then carry the baby to the car. If anything goes awry, I will eventually come outside and call everything off. Obviously, I am hoping that won't happen. However if it does, we will try again tomorrow as long as the kidnap idea has not been exposed. If someone does find out about it, I will say I was just playing a joke. Everyone at the farm will believe me because I've done that kind of thing before. This was in case I needed a cover. Also if they notice Violet, than I'm going to say that we need to take the boy to the doctor for a check-up. If we absolutely have to, we'll take him to the Princeton Hospital and try not to bring too much attention to us there. This will also keep Violet from asking any more questions. Red, you can still take her home. If we don't show up in thirty minutes you can pick her up at the hospital, it's not that far from the theatre. I think it's about a mile outside of the town proper. Once again, if for some reason things are not working the way they are supposed to but our plan is still intact, than we will meet here tomorrow at the same exact time." Again Lindbergh repeated himself.

"Let's just say the same exact plan will still be in place." Lindbergh hoped that he had made things clear for everyone. He realized, as he had to catch his breath for a moment that he had been rambling somewhat. He hesitated. When no one asked any questions he went on.

"Alright where was I? Ah, like I said I am confident it will happen tonight. When I get to Hopewell around dusk, after Anne takes her walk and they settle in for the evening, I will put the ladder in the proper position against the house just after sundown. This will be a useful ploy. I want it to confuse the police. As soon as we get Violet and Charlie into Mr. Hauptmann's car….hmm." With so much on his mind, Lindbergh again rambled. He paused and took a deep breath. He tried to keep his mind on track, but not able to do so, he went on reiterating things once again.

"Richard, you need to get to Princeton as fast as you can. Once again, Fish will have a map if you need it and will help you." Hauptmann interjected.

"I do not need the map, Colonel Lindbergh. I know ver I am going. Remember, I vent there yesterday."

"Excellent, Richard, but I just want to make sure; there can be no mistakes." Lindbergh paused for a second, and got back on track. "Once you get to Princeton, to the Garden Theatre on Nassau Street, the Schlesers will be there. At this time, they are making sure the old fishing shack near Stoney Brook is ready for the baby. You fellas dropped them off yesterday. Red will pick Charlie up at around seven and they will be at the theatre when Richard, Fish, and Violet go by. I spoke with Charlie Schleser early yesterday morning before they left, he assured me his wife was ready and they would take good care of the boy. As soon as things die down a little, and they can disguise the baby, they will head up to New York and board a steamer. As you know, they have a friend who owns an old house in the German countryside near Dresden. They will take care of him there, until they can find him a permanent home. Hopefully there won't be anyone snooping around over there either."

Lindbergh had captivated his audience of conspirators. Silent under his hypnosis, they were not only mesmerized by his ability to lead, but were equally amazed at his organization and precision. Even the pompous educator Doc Condon, who was known to pontificate on more than one occasion, was impressed by the Great Aviator's ability to manipulate his audience and maintain a keen eye for detail. Of the four men, it was Condon who understood with some sense of clarity what was at stake for Lindbergh and why he was so determined to pull the abduction off perfectly.

"Remember, time is crucial. If everyone is back in their homes by ten or eleven, you will all have an alibi. At one minute before ten, I will give the signal to Betty to go into the nursery. We're hoping to announce to everyone that the baby is missing at 10:00. That would mean that if you were a kidnapper you would have to be able to pull it off and be back in New York City in less than a half hour or so. That would be virtually impossible. Of course you can all stay out of trouble by not saying a word to anyone about where you were or what you did. If we follow directions there will be no problems. Everyone will get the rest of the money, Charlie will be in a home where he will be taken care of and in a few more months Anne will have a new baby with no problems. I will make sure the balance of the money will be unmarked. Remember loose lips sinks ships, and this ship is not going down. Anyone who crosses me will go down. I have nothing else. Doc, what do you have?"

Condon nodded and asked the group if there were any questions. When there was no response from the group, he took advantage of the little time that the Great Aviator allotted him by showing off his own oratory skills.

"Remember gentlemen, Colonel Lindbergh is a great American. This is important for our country as well as for him. This boy has some physical handicaps that will require much time and attention. He will have a long and difficult road ahead of him. Fortunately, there will be wonderful people who will be there to help him. Little Charlie will be in a home that can give him the special attention he needs. The Colonel has much research ahead of him in aviation as well as other scientific endeavors. He cannot be impeded in his tremendous pursuit of knowledge. Our operation may not seem so noble at this time but in the larger scheme of things it will be most beneficial to every American, not just the child."

Lindbergh did not like the admission that his child had physical or mental impairments even if most of the people there knew the boy was battling rickets and deafness. He felt a twinge of guilt when the old man mentioned the wonderful people who would take care of him. In truth, the Great Aviator had no idea who would be taking care of the boy in Germany. He stared at the obnoxious Condon, wondering where the retired educator was heading with his outlandish comments. It was quite obvious that Condon was an opportunist trying to portray himself as kind and altruistic. He loved any opportunity he could get to pontificate, except he didn't realize he was intrusive when he described the child's problems. No one shook a head in the affirmative, choosing instead to just listen to the old man drone on. While Lindbergh was patiently waiting for him to stop talking, the Doctor seemed surprised that none of the immigrants wanted to add to his commentary.

The only response was an irrelevant question from the irreverent Isadore Fisch. He looked toward the mustached old man with some confusion, and then nodded toward Hauptmann who was riding on the same brain wave. The slender hustler whose black greasy hair was neatly combed straight back, did not hesitate. "When do we get the second part of the dough—you know, the jack?"

Lindbergh seemed relieved that the subject had been changed and was quick to respond to the swarthy German.

"I already told you, you'll get paid the rest when the job is done. We pull this off without a hitch; you will get the balance in a few days when Doc Condon gets the ransom money to you. I can't take any more money out of the bank right now because they might get suspicious. Although I seriously doubt that they would question me, I want to make sure that I'm not the one the police investigate."

The Great Aviator hesitated. "Or anyone else for that matter." Lindbergh didn't want it to sound as if the police were more inclined to investigate someone else. When there were no other comments, he went on. "Doc Condon is going to place a call to the house at around 8:30. That will give Red the alibi he needs. Because he has been to the house before and people have seen him with Betty, he needs to have a strong alibi. He is also going to make an appearance at the Junge's apartment as soon as he can get back. No one else should need an alibi especially if we all play our cards right. The ransom money as I said will not be marked. You fellows follow the plan and everybody will be happy. Remember, when this thing settles down and you've got your money and you're fat and happy, you still can't say anything. If you do, you cut your own throat."

Condon was quick to reply, even though the wind had been taken from his sails when no one responded to his long-winded oration. Because of his ethnocentric views, he had always harbored doubts about anyone who was not American, but the present group of immigrants had provided him with some opportunities to make some extra cash. He was sure that as long as everyone received their money, the operation would be a success. He also knew that with Lindbergh's support and influence, no one would dare cross him, including the Germans.

"None of these fellows is crazy enough to sing or rat on each other, Colonel, and I can assure you again that we will do our part. And there won't be any coppers snooping around either Colonel Lindbergh," said Condon. Wanting to keep the Great Aviator feeling confident that the plan would work, he continued to placate Lindbergh.

"They will not have any reason whatsoever to implicate anyone of us. As long as we don't do anything stupid, like sing like canaries to anyone, we won't have anything to worry about. That means you too, Richard. Don't say a word to your wife. And Red, you and Betty cannot discuss anything about this undertaking—anywhere, ever." Red nodded, while Hauptmann smirked, and then waved his hand in front of his own sculptured face.

Fisch looked toward Johnson and tried to be funny. "You can only discuss it in your bed." Red Johnson's face matched his hair. Richard Hauptmann smiled. Fisch wasn't finished. "I wouldn't laugh either, Richard. You better be careful around Louise."

Hauptmann glared at Fisch and then laughed. "Louise is interested in me, not me interested in her. I bet you'd like to get Gerta in a closed room, Izzy," said Hauptmann. They were both referring to women they knew and were interested in.

Doc Condon quickly restored order. "Richard, seriously—you cannot say anything to your wife."

"I say nutting to her and she knows nutting, what I do."

Lindbergh said nothing in response to Hauptmann but he was quick to defend Red Johnson. "I can assure you too, Doc, Red won't say anything to Betty or Violet. Fish, who's your latest squeeze? You have any Jewish girlfriends we need to know about?" Lindbergh smiled but he was only half-kidding when he asked him. He tried to hide his obvious dislike of Jews.

Fisch didn't know how to take Lindbergh's questions, but he was quick to answer the Great Aviator with a comeback question of his own. "No, you got anyone for me, Colonel? Maybe a Jew?" The conspirators laughed at Fisch's response and it eased the tension of the meeting.

"Okay, any more questions?" asked Condon, as he saw an opportunity to take over the meeting. If not than we can go get something to eat somewhere and prepare for the evening."

The meeting broke up earlier than everyone expected. Lindbergh gave Red Johnson a dollar and told him to fetch him and Condon some pastrami on rye sandwiches. With speed the Norwegian did as the Great Aviator had told him and rushed down the street on foot to a local Jewish delicatessen. Meanwhile, the two Germans pulled up their collars, descended the stoop and got in Hauptmann's blue dodge. They hurried off down the narrow street.

CHAPTER TWELVE
WRITING THE RANSOM NOTES

Red Johnson dropped off two sandwiches for the two men. Lindbergh, pretending to be a nice guy, told him to keep the change. Red told the Great Aviator that he needed to call his brother in Connecticut to tell him he was going to stay with him that evening. He also told his two new bosses Condon and Lindbergh that he was going to do some work on his automobile and stop at a friend's house later on before he left for Princeton.

"Well, you make sure you establish your alibi before and after," Lindbergh told the wiry Norwegian. Before you leave for Princeton make contact with some people, anybody, and as soon as you get back to Englewood and drop Violet off, you need to make sure someone sees you up there too. This means you're going to have to hurry back from Princeton after you pick up your girl, Violet."

Red smiled at the 'your girl' remark and told the Great Aviator in his Scandinavian accent "not to fret, I'll take care of everything. And by the way she's not my girl." He paused for a second and told the men as they laughed, "he sure hoped his brother had that place for him to stay tonight." As if in some big hurry he got into his car and sped off down Jerome Ave and then slowly disappeared into Manhattan.

The Great Aviator and Doc Condon finished eating their sandwiches and sat down at a small round table to discuss the ransom note. Lindbergh had already made up his mind about the amount of money that the note would demand. Fifty thousand dollars was the original amount proposed, with Doc Condon being the overseer who would pay off everyone for their efforts. Lindbergh told Condon to make sure he gave everyone their fair share for he did not want any of the conspirators to feel like they had been cheated in any way. Lindbergh and Condon had assured everyone that more cash in the form of unmarked ransom money would be paid out once the child had been taken from the house. Lindbergh reiterated to Condon in no uncertain terms that anyone who had loose lips would be expendable and his friend Bobby Thayer knew enough people to help him make that happen. Although Thayer had no knowledge of the plan, Lindbergh was adamant about the need for secrecy and liked using Thayer's connections to the underworld as a way of enforcing his rules. The gang was well aware of Thayer's connections.

Condon reassured the Great Aviator that he would distribute the money without incident. He was to receive the $50,000 in addition to the original payout of $20,000 that Lindbergh had given him as a down payment for his efforts in organizing the strange network of conspirators. That would mean he would pay any miscellaneous fees incurred so far for minor items, the expenses the Schlesers would need in their stow-away locale outside of Princeton, steam ship tickets for Fisch, the baby and the Schlesers. The expenses of setting the boy up in his new home in Germany and the cost of return tickets back to the United States for the Schlesers and Fisch would also be taken care of by Condon.

The plan then called for there to be several ransom notes with the fifty thousand dollars to be paid with unmarked bills. The group would then be able to collect the balance of the money from Condon when he would meet with the so-called kidnappers somewhere to distribute the ransom money. Everyone would then be happy with the payoff. Lindbergh was sure that with his influence he could pay with unmarked ransom money. He felt that once the payment was made things would die down as they waited for the return of the child. The child's return of course would never come. He would be safe on a steamer from New York, well on his way to Germany with the Schlesers. His curls would be cut, he would have little earrings in his ears, and he would be wearing a plain little dress that would not bring a lot of attention. Since the child spoke very little and seemed only attached to Betty, no one would ever suspect 'she' was the Lindbergh baby.

The two discussed the phony ransom notes before they decided to sit down and write the first one. The Great Aviator wanted the ransom notes to sound as if a German immigrant had written them. This would make it easier to point a finger at someone in case things did not work out. They both knew that Hauptmann or Fisch would be easy targets because of their German heritage. Charlie Schleser, also a German, was a convicted felon but his wife had seemed to tame his wild ways by leaving him at one point, and he now seemed willing to cooperate and help the Great Aviator. His job, along with his wife's assistance, was to keep the baby until they could get him out of the country. But he too was a German immigrant, even if he seemed more reserved than the younger Fisch and Hauptmann. Portraying Hauptmann or Fisch as scapegoats would be easier should things go wrong. Schleser wasn't overly friendly toward Hauptmann and kept his distance. He even seemed perturbed at him because he was horning in on his and Fisch's business enterprises. Condon had assured the Great Aviator that Schleser would be a team player. It was still easy however, for the patriotic Condon to put the blame on Germany for the Great War, and he wasn't quite ready to let them off the hook. The Norwegian Johnson was well liked by Lindbergh, and the Great Aviator was willing to protect him if he had to. Lindbergh liked Red because of his relationship with Betty Gow and their shared Scandinavian heritage. These two reasons alone, made it easier for the Great Aviator to like him. Condon strongly supported the Great Aviator's plans to make the kidnappers foreign. In fact, he could combine characteristics of all three if he had to come up with a fake suspect. They were both aware that Fisch's Jewish ethnicity and all three men's Germanic background, could work to their benefit if they got into a jam and needed a fall guy. Much of the public's attitude toward Germans had become more negative after the Great War, especially after the Versailles meetings twelve years earlier, had shed more light on their aggression in the conflict. A defeated country, Germany's response to the peace treaty was to fire off more rhetoric, with some of it becoming increasingly more anti-American. Americans like Doc Condon became increasingly more anti-German and anti-immigrant. Condon had a real disdain for Italians but there were no Italians in the kidnap crew to exploit. Making the kidnapper a German would only be logical. But Lindbergh also thought Fisch would be an easy scapegoat because he was a Jew, and he disliked Jews. The problem with that angle was Fisch's confusing personality. Like everyone, Lindbergh had difficulty reading Fisch He seemed somewhat unpredictable but the Great Aviator felt strongly that as long as there was money involved, Fisch would do as he was told. The word was that Fisch would do anything to make a buck. Both men were also in agreement that the ransom note needed to be overwhelmingly confusing to everyone. They also would try to make it sound like it was a gang, like the mafia, that was behind the crime. With two different theories going in two opposite directions, any resulting investigation that included any handwriting experts would be hampered significantly. It would also confuse any overzealous investigators who wanted to make a name for himself. The last thing the Great Aviator needed was some renegade cop who was bent on being a hero.

It was Condon's idea to use a code or signature to make it look like a professional job, and Lindbergh agreed. At Fordham University, he had actually conducted research on symbology and theosophy, and had used this information in some of his classes. After some careful thought, Condon devised a special code but added a spur of the moment twist. He lifted the round Mersman table they had been using and placed it upside down. He unscrewed a foot-long wooden brace that held it together. He told Lindbergh they would use the brace to make three matching holes in the ransom note. In addition, Condon wanted to use different colors for what he would call the 'singnature'. All this would help to confuse the police. The Great Aviator had no problem agreeing with Condon because it appeared he had done his homework on writing ransom notes. They both thought diversions and convolutions should be part of the scheme. And even though Condon was a know-it-all and could be overbearing at times, Lindbergh was tolerant of him. Whatever perception of Condon Lindbergh might have given off, the Doctor was still well aware of the fact that he was subordinate to the Great Aviator. He never questioned Lindbergh, and at no time was there ever a doubt about whose plan it was and who was in charge of calling the shots.

Lindbergh wanted to write the note by himself, but he could tell right away that the old educator was chomping at the bit, anxiously wanting to assist. He watched over everything the Great Aviator did.

From a duffle bag Condon took out two pairs of gloves and a paper Woolworth's bag. He handed Lindbergh one pair of gloves and stretched his large hands into the other pair. From inside the paper bag, he lifted a package of cheap linen stationary that he purchased from the five and ten cent store downtown. He placed it on the tabletop. Lindbergh removed the paper from the packet. Angling his gloved left hand and cradling a fountain pen, he wrote the word "Have". He then switched hands and wrote 50,000 $ with a gloved right hand. Condon watched intently. Continuing on the first line Lindbergh switched again to his left hand and wrote 25000 and the word 'in'.

Condon looked up and cackled. "We will be here all day, Colonel Lindbergh."

Lindbergh forced a smile then he moved down to the next line. With great focus, he switched again to his right hand and wrote 20 $ bills, 15000 $, and then 'in' with his left. Continuing the deception, he switched again and wrote 10 $ bills with his right and then 'and' with his left. On the next line Lindbergh used both hands, again alternating on the one line. He concentrated on the perverted deception while enjoying his criminal role. The next line he wrote entirely with his natural right hand. His Rs and Fs reflected his usual handwriting as well as the word the, but he didn't seem to mind because he knew no one would dare insinuate that he wrote a ransom note. He continued. With Condon's encouragement he misspelled several words deliberately. He wrote 'mony' for money, 'anyding' for anything and 'gut' for good. He accentuated the 'y' on money and the 'g' on anyding with a flare. The intention was obvious. He wanted to create the perception that the note was written by a German person who had great difficulty with the language. He also interjected the word 'for' as some immigrants who struggled with the language often did.

"Because we will need to write one more ransom note, I'll write this on the bottom." said the Great Aviator excitedly. At the very bottom of the note he wrote the words "Indication for all letters are signature and three holes." Again he switched from left to right and back in the process.

The old man looked at the note, thought for a second and pointed at the top of the paper. "You forgot to write 'dear sir', Colonel! You were too busy switching hands," he said laughing. With little emotion Lindbergh wrote a large and fancy 'D', and then smaller than he normally would, wrote 'ear' in his normal handwriting to make the word Dear. He then scribbled a large exotic 'S' and wrote a small 'ir' to make the word Sir. "What do you think Doc, is that better? Is that sufficient?"

"One second, Colonel." Condon grabbed the pen from Lindbergh's hand and placed an exclamation point after sir. "Now, that ought to do it Colonel." Condon smiled at the Great Aviator expecting approval for their joint effort, but as was often the case with the socially deficient Lindbergh, he got no response.

The note read:

Dear Sir!

Have 50,000$ redy 25000$ in 20$ bills 15000$ in 10$ bills and 10000$ in 5$ bills. After 2-4 days we will inform you were to deliver the mony. We warn you for making anyding public or for notify the polise the child is in gut care Indication for all letters are singnature And 3 holes

Condon nodded as if to show his approval. "Now let me do the signature," he said excitedly. It was now Lindbergh's turn to be observer as he gave Condon the okay. Carefully, the old man took the two inkbottles. Using a pen and the cork from the blue inkbottle he drew an arc around the bottom onto the letter. He then took the top cork from the red inkbottle and using the red pen drew another arc onto the ransom note making two different color arcs. When ink started getting everywhere, he was unable to get a full circle from either bottle and decided to leave it that way. He waited for the ink to dry and picked up the wooden table brace from the floor. Lindbergh seemed puzzled as he watched the old man place the template near the bottom of the note. Reaching into his trouser pocket, Condon pulled out an ice pick. Making sure the holes lined up perfectly, he pushed the pick through the template and then on through the ransom note.

He did this three times and the Great Aviator smiled and shook his head as if he was the one who was now confused. Because one of the fountain pens was also leaking it had made a mess in the bottom right corner of the ransom note. The finished product wasn't what Doc Condon had hoped for.

"It's not pretty, Colonel, but I think we have done a great job at disguising things."

Lindbergh held it up to the sunlight that was penetrating through the top of the curtains. "Doc, it sure is strange and ugly but it should work perfectly."

"Let's just say it is unique, Colonel."

"I'm afraid though, if things get too complicated you will have to write the rest of these notes all by yourself, and I am confident you will take care of that. You know, Doctor Condon, with all the extras, the note is even more than unique." Looking down at the note, Lindbergh gave a sly little laugh that had an accompanying tone of deception. "Just keep the immigrant theme going," he muttered under his breath.

Condon heard him and saw this as an opportunity to rant. "I will tell you Colonel Lindbergh, I do trust our group, but I can't say that about all of these immigrants—especially those damn Italians. They come over to our country and take advantage of what we have here and they really don't appreciate anything. I know they are trying to take over everything even here in the Bronx, the most beautiful borough in the world. Look at how they have moved in to take over the docks."

Lindbergh nodded but was in no mood to discuss immigration and quickly went back to the business at hand. He wanted to make sure that Condon would be able to duplicate the same unusual pattern. "You're going to hold onto that template right?"

"Of course, Colonel Lindbergh. I will have to write more ransom notes. As a matter of fact, let me use the template right now to punch more holes in the rest of my paper. This will mean they will all line up exactly." Condon lined up the template with the stationary, and using his ice pick punched through the paper.

"Making another one will not be a problem Colonel. And let me say sir, you shall have nothing to worry about. In fact, punching a whole stack of paper, so they will all be uniform will prevent anyone from trying to duplicate them."

"Since there may be police snooping around the farmhouse, the note writing is all yours Doc. It seems you have quite an efficient system going and the last thing I want to do is interfere. I will have enough to do stonewalling the investigation."

"As a matter of fact, Colonel Lindbergh, why don't we make the second note right now while we have the two inkbottles and the rest of these materials? We can get it done together and beside we certainly don't want to leave any of this stuff sitting around." Condon took some of the same paper and started right into the second note. This time with the Great Aviator looking over Condon's shoulder, the two men again combined their writing skills.

"Wait a second, Colonel. Let me write something here." Condon took the fountain pen and without any flare he wrote *Dear Sir*. His 'D' and 'S' didn't have the same fancy loop as Lindbergh's note. The two men studied the note for a second. Condon continued, as he desired the Great Aviator's approval. He started with his left hand. He did this for the first four lines with Lindbergh telling him what to write and using the first note as his guide. He even added some of his own ideas to the ransom note with Lindbergh's approval and he continued the deception of making it look like a Germanic person had written it. Using his left hand was not as easy as Condon had thought. Lacking the dexterity and endurance of the younger Lindbergh, the old man struggled with the second and third lines. Several words were barely legible. When things were taking longer than he thought, and with the Great Aviator laughing at him, Condon switched back and used his right hand. Condon tired but still tried to disguise his handwriting. "My W is very similar to yours. Do you agree Colonel Lindbergh?" "Yes, I would Doctor Condon. They have a bent line before they drop down." Again they laughed, and then went on. Sharing their thoughts on what to write including warning the police to stay out, the two men were able to finish the second ransom note in about fifteen minutes. Condon used his newly found trademark signature by making the circles with the corks from the inkbottles. This time keeping the pen on an angle, he was able to make more complete circles. He used the template to see if both notes matched up. He took the first note and lined up the holes and the margin with the second one. The ice pick slid through the holes flawlessly. Both notes were now complete. The old man was proud of his accomplishment. He held them up to the light. He could see through the holes in both. "Perfecto!" he shouted.

"Like I said I will use the template and ice pick again if I have to punch more notes." "For God's sake Doc, how many will we need?"

"I'm not sure Colonel how many we will need, we will have to play it by ear, but they will all match up together perfectly. We don't want anyone trying to duplicate these and make things confusing." Lindbergh nodded in agreement. He was impressed with Condon's deviant ingenuity and smiled.

The second note read:

Dear Sir,

We have warned you note to make anyding public also notify the police

now you have to take consequences that means we will have to hold the baby until everything is quiet. We can note make any appointments

just now.We know very well what it means to us. It is rely necessary

to make a world affair out off this, or to get your baby back as soon

as possible to settle those affair in a quick way will be better for both.

Don't by afraid about the baby keeping care of us day and night. We

also will feed him According to the diet

We are interested to send him back in gut health. And ransom was

made aus for 50000$ but now we have to take another person to it and

probably have to keep the baby for a longer time as we expected. So

the amound will be 70000 2000 in 50$ bills 25000$ in 20$ bill 15000$

in 10$ bills and 1000 in 5$ bills Don't mark any bills or take them from

one serial nomer. We will form you latter were to deliver the mony.

But we will note do so until the police is out of the cace and the appers

are quite. The kidnapping we prepared in years so we are prepared

for everyding.

In order to keep control of the investigation that would soon follow the kidnapping, the Great Aviator had to have the ransom notes reinforce the potential of danger to the baby should he not cooperate with the kidnappers. Lindbergh was sure that he could lead the police into thinking that the kidnapping was the work of gangsters. He knew as well that the police would go along with everything he said simply because of his influence. And there was no way they could take the risk of having something happen to the child of the world's most famous man. This made him look like a worried father protecting his son but yet it would allow him to continue his deceitful plan. Lindbergh also felt like he needed time to assess everything at some point after the kidnapping, so his next steps had to be well thought out. He and Doc Condon also knew there was no way the public could be kept in the dark and they would need to use this to their advantage as well. And even though the Great Aviator had said on more than one occasion he did not want the newspaper people messing things up by being too nosy, he was willing to make an exception this one time. He was sure on the night of the kidnapping the press would descend down onto Hopewell like a swarm of locust. And that would be fine with him. He would have them trample every bit of evidence and place their fingerprints all over the ladder just to keep everything as confusing as possible. Hopefully, Charlie Schleser and the rest of the group would get the boy out of the country as quickly as possible. After a few weeks everything would calm down. Lindbergh and Condon decided to add $20,000.00 to the ransom just in case the police made them mark the bills. They thought that if they had to make the payoff quick they could keep the extra $20,000.00 clean. He did not want his co-conspirators not getting paid or getting caught spending marked ransom bills. He knew it would become real difficult for him to withdraw money from the bank without someone finding out once the kidnapping had taken place. Condon was aware of this as well and as he usually did, went along with everything the Great Aviator said.

"Don't worry, I will take care of writing the rest of the notes, Colonel. As for the handwriting, I don't think it will really matter at all. I can make them all look similar. Remember, we have the same W s. " The two men smiled simultaneously. "And I think I can write the same dialogue by myself if I have to. I will keep the same German look to it, but Colonel, those notes really are one of a kind. However, sir, writing with my left hand might be tough. You have to admit, Colonel they are quite grotesque."

Lindbergh nodded toward the old man and again gave him his approval. Condon had taken on an unusual role of playing student to the younger Lindbergh, and in a strange way enjoyed playing subordinate to the Great Aviator. Since the day Calvin Coolidge gave him the title of Colonel, Lindbergh savored being in charge; delegating and barking orders to as many people who would play his subordinate. As if he was taking to the air on another dangerous flight, he wanted to once again make sure everything was set up efficiently.

"Make sure you don't use the disguised handwriting when you write your letter to the Bronx newspaper because the cops will catch on to you right away. You know what you're going to say right, Doc?"

"I can assure you Colonel Lindbergh my letter will not give anything away. They know me well over there and will actually assist me in this enterprise without even knowing it." Lindbergh nodded. He continued his obsession with organization before Condon finished talking.

"Several times during the early investigation we may need to talk," he said, going over what appeared to be obvious to both men because they had discussed this before.

"Once you get the so-called response from the so-called kidnappers, you will come down to the farm and make your claim that you have been in contact with the kidnappers. All you will need to do is call and then describe the signature. Anyone involved with the ransom note will know what you're talking about. Keep calling if you don't get through right away.

Suddenly Condon shouted. "I will tell them that the letter is Siciliano! It has the sign of the mafia! It is a trigamba! A three- legged monster that will create peril for those who don't cooperate!"

For the first time, Lindbergh laughed hard and then sensing that the time was getting closer, became even more restless. "Doc, I hope we have all our bases covered. I mean this has got to work."

Trying to make him feel more at ease, Condon smiled at the Great Aviator confidently. "We are ready to go Colonel."

Lindbergh nodded and handed the old man the second ransom note. He put the first one inside his shirt pocket. The lengthy meeting had finally adjourned.

CHAPTER THIRTEEN
VIOLET SHARPE AND THE GERMANS

———————————————————

L eaving at five-thirty had proved difficult for Violet. She had to rush out of Next Day Hill without telling anyone of her plans. When the call had come in from the man she believed to be her lover and confidante, she did not hesitate. Henry Red Johnson had called that afternoon with instructions for Violet to hurry down to Hopewell just as the Great Aviator's plan had called for. Red like Lindbergh was reassuring, believable, and convincing, and Violet would do as he had asked. There was no doubting that. Red was also adamant about her not telling anyone where she was going including the staff and Mrs. Morrow. He informed her that she was needed in Hopewell by 7:30 and there would be someone there to pick her up at the bottom of the driveway at precisely 5:30. The Norwegian immigrant had been quite secretive since they started dating a few weeks earlier. He had asked her out one Saturday evening at the Morrow estate when Betty Gow was in New York. Red had told her that he and Betty were just friends. Since that time he had kept their relationship secret because many people had seen him out with Betty. He did not want anyone to accuse him of being a sportsman and he certainly didn't want anyone to question him about Violet. But Betty was keenly aware of the new relationship with Violet Sharpe. There was nothing to it; it was part of the Great Aviator's plan. Violet too had become quite discreet about their relationship for fear someone at Next Day Hill would find out. Both sides were being secretive for different reasons.

At 5 o'clock, Violet's shift was over but because of her fondness for Red and her allegiance to Mrs. Morrow, she was willing to work overtime. She was however confused about Red's role in all this. Why hadn't Mrs. Morrow asked her to go to Hopewell instead of Red? Had she known that Red, the Great Aviator, and

Betty were all well aware of her schedule and they were using her in their plans, she would have been more than just confused.

Smoky gray clouds were doing their best to keep any sunlight from penetrating the North Jersey sky. Still there were glimmers of gold poking through the cloud cover, now that the snow and icy rain had moved out. The time was almost five-thirty and there was still light left. Since it was March the first, it was obvious the days were getting longer and spring was just around the corner. But as the moisture had moved out, the cold north gales were moving in; March's lion was still roaring. Violet had dressed warmly, and she walked down the long shaded driveway to the entry road where a blue dodge was waiting for her just as Red had said. There were two men sitting in the front seat, facing away from the 56 acre estate. Both turned, nodded and said hello as Violet climbed into the car. Both had German accents just as Red had said they would, the sandy haired driver with the strongest. Violet had become accustomed to the Nordic accent since dating Red Johnson. Even though Red was from Norway and the two strangers were German, to the Irish Violet Sharpe their accents all sounded similar. Working in Northern New Jersey and being so close to New York City with all the different languages and ethnicities, Violet was getting used to being part of the melting pot. Most of Mrs. Morrow's staff had immigrated from the northern part of Europe.

Riding down to central Jersey, Violet struggled in her mind to make sense out of Charles Lindbergh's decision for her to pick up the baby. She remained puzzled why the man she fell in love with ...Red Johnson, was the one making the call to her. Red relayed to Violet on that afternoon that Lindbergh had told him that he wanted her and two of his friends to pick up young Charles from the farmhouse in Hopewell around 7:30. They were then instructed to travel about eight miles southeast and drop the boy off at the office of Doctor Charles Mayer, whose wife was a nurse. Red told her the couple lived near the Princeton Hospital not far from the university in Princeton. He also told her that Dr. Mayer was going to examine the boy because the boy had been coughing a lot lately and Lindbergh wanted to make sure the child wasn't getting pneumonia. Red had also told Violet that according to Lindbergh, Mayer was an expert physician who was well respected in the area, and that he did not want them traveling too far with the baby because of his cold and with the weather being so raw. He said that Mayer was the best medical person available who could help, and that he didn't want any gathering crowds at the local hospital in Princeton to invade his privacy or suspect that there was something wrong with the baby. He said he was really worried about the boy's cough, and he wanted to get it checked out immediately.

Another big question that Violet kept asking herself was how well did Lindbergh know Red Johnson? Because it seemed so odd that he would instruct him to tell her of his plans, Violet continued to ask herself more questions. Had he seen Red with her on some occasion? Could it have been that Lindbergh couldn't get in touch with her so he had to contact her through Red? Why didn't he just tell Mrs. Morrow of his intentions?

Violet tried to make sense out of things, but the whole scenario was perplexing. She knew however, that she had to do whatever the Great Aviator told her because she was on the payroll and anything that was connected to the Morrows or the Lindberghs was her responsibility. But persistent questions remained. "Why couldn't Betty Gow take the child to the doctor? After all, Betty was the child's nursemaid and had spent at least one or two weekends down in Hopewell. Wasn't it her responsibility to tend to the needs of little Charlie at Hopewell? Violet's responsibilities were as a serving maid in Next Day Hill in Englewood not at the Hopewell estate although she did enjoy holding the child and playing with him from time to time. What did Lindbergh know about her relationship with Red Johnson anyway? Did the Great Aviator know that she had been smitten with the Norwegian from the first time she met him and now he was constantly on her mind? Did he know how hard she had fallen for him?" Violet had wanted to contact Charles Lindbergh in New York at his office but knew she would be unable to get through. She figured he was out of his office as usual. Red told her that Betty needed the evening of March 1st off because she had some personal business, and that Mrs. Lindbergh also had some business to tend to as well. Violet thought that was odd since Betty had headed down to Hopewell that afternoon. Red told her Lindbergh was going to be delayed in New York City because of speaking engagements and would be unable to make it home in time. He was adamant about keeping the appointment with the Mayers. Violet didn't believe for one minute, that even if Charles Lindbergh had been home he would have dropped the child off anywhere. He had never done anything like that before. It simply wasn't his business and not in his nature. Violet was apprehensive. To complicate matters, she had to drive all the way down to Hopewell with two Germans she had never met before, although there was an air of familiarity about both of them.

The driver of the dodge was serious and business-like. He had chiseled features with sandy hair. He carried himself well but seemed arrogant, as he saw nothing wrong with letting his steel blue eyes run up and down her body. The other man looked familiar but was aloof. He was thin and gaunt and stared out of the passenger window. His hair was greasy and his dark eyes beady, both the color of charcoal. His rounded ears stuck-out, making his nose appear larger than it was. Violet surmised that he was probably not as old as he looked. Both men were well dressed. The sandy haired driver identified himself as Richard and his wily friend as Izzy. Richard smirked as the darker complexioned man had responded by saying he preferred to be called Fish not Izzy. Neither was very proficient at English and their accents differed slightly. Both accents were Germanic but Fish had an accent with a swaying inflection that almost sounded Yiddish intermixed with German. His English was much better than his counterpart's. Despite the differences, they communicated well with each other and only occasionally intermixed English. Both men seemed to isolate Violet from their conversation, and Violet was unsure if it was deliberate.

She continued to analyze the strange events as they were unfolding. It seemed quite odd to her that another strange part of the plan was a request by the Great Aviator to take his child from Hopewell to Princeton to the doctor's office. Why would they wait until now to do this? The unlikely trio was to drop the child off at the house of this doctor she had never heard of. Violet struggled to figure things out. She wanted to communicate with the two men in an attempt to figure everything out, but neither was forthcoming with information about the itinerary. After a while she realized it was a wasted effort because their language barrier only made things more difficult. A bumpy ride, the steady hum of the car's motor, Violet's unrefined English accent, and the strong accents of the two Germans made for a troubling concoction that not only made the journey down to the picturesque Sourland Mountains of central New Jersey awkward but terribly frustrating.

Still Violet was able to extract some information. She learned that Richard was Richard Hauptmann, a German immigrant and carpenter. He had immigrated to America after the Great War, fleeing from a humiliated country to cash in on the prosperity of 1920s' America. Later through the combination of broken English and German, she was able to extrapolate that Hauptmann was a carpenter by trade but had figured out over the last year or so how to make money doing other things. She suspected that both men were not much older than thirty, and they liked to engage in illegal activities. They laughed together when Fish brought up some type of a pie business, a business that included a mutual friend named Charlie. In his native tongue Richard declared he did not like Charlie because he could not be trusted. Fish mentioned another company and said he liked Charlie, and Hauptmann just needed to get to know him. The conversation turned back to German and something about Hauptmann's wife Anna. At first Violet could not understand, and then Fish not realizing he was acting as an interpreter, switched the conversation back to English. Richard said he and Anna had cooled off and he was interested in a mutual female friend named Gerta. Fish shouted "Ahh Gerta, Achtung!" Both men laughed. Hauptmann responded with a comment of his own.

"Her husband, Karl Hinkel, he step in horseshit. He is a lucky man to get her. He come over from Germany and all of a sudden they get married. Fish, ve were in das wrong place at the wrong time. Ve both vould love to have some of Gerta." Gerta was a running joke, and they quickly switched the conversation back to German before they stopped laughing. Violet suspected Gerta was someone other than a mutual friend, maybe a mutual love interest. Her ability to interpret everything they were saying proved difficult because Fish and Hauptmann continued to switch back and forth from German to English. While the pair was discussing some of their mutual Germanic friends from Throg's Neck and Hunters Island, she discerned that each had run-ins with the law, were involved in moneymaking schemes and engaged in risky stock transactions. At one point they even discussed the old country where Hauptmann gave Fish some minor details on his life grow-ing up in Kamenz, Germany, but that was about all she could figure out from the conversation. She would never learn that Hauptmann had armed robbery and burglary convictions in Kamenz. Although he talked a great deal about his past, his convictions were something he never talked about.

Fish did not appear to be as forthcoming with information like Hauptmann. Hauptmann appeared to almost boast when he talked, while Fish was an attentive but somewhat muted listener. Sporting a constant grin, there was something about him she didn't trust. Violet would eventually surmise that Fish as he preferred to be called was Isadore Fisch, a part time furrier who always hustled to make a living and was planning to move back to his native Germany where he still had family that he was close to. Like Hauptmann, he never mentioned any run-ins with the law in Germany. He also never mentioned he had few ties in America and that he bought and sold anything even if it was hot, including any type of furs. She didn't know that Fisch had a reputation as a conman and a huckster, and would sell anything so long as someone was willing to give him a fair price. This included hawking phony stocks. And he never mentioned that he was always the first one to initiate or negotiate a bargain both as a buyer and a seller, or that he always carried cash in his pocket (even now during the economic struggles of the early 1930s). Both men were coy enough not to mention Charles Lindbergh or the old man, Doc Condon. There were a lot of things that Violet would never know about this strange duo but she had her doubts and continued to watch the men intensely. Even the two Germans wondered why she just seemed to stare at them with fixed eyes during their conversation.

Violet felt angry that she was left out in the cold on what was going on with the Lindbergh child. It seemed no one was very forthcoming with information, and she assumed Red was doing just what the Great Aviator had asked him to do. The assignment that was given to her was complicated and convoluted. She hated it and sensed something wasn't right.

CHAPTER FOURTEEN
LINDBERGH IN HOPEWELL

I t was just before six, and it seemed too easy for the Great Aviator to get through Hopewell without anyone recognizing him. He drove his sedan eastward to a road running parallel with the property line of his Sourland estate. In a remote patch of tangled briars fifty yards from the dirt road, Lindbergh found his homemade ladder. Covered with burlap and shrouded by scrub trees and wild dogwoods, the ladder blended in so nicely that unless you were looking for it, you would never know it was there. Lindbergh remembered the exact spot where he had left it back in November. Because of the lacing of thorny vines and stubborn weeds, he had to use some force to remove the ladder. Once it was free, he lifted it onto his shoulder and as the winds increased, he hauled it with difficulty to his car. With the car's back window rolled down, he slid the ladder across the top of the front seat with the two top rungs protruding out the passenger side window. Lindbergh took a seat behind the wheel and then drove straight down the road to a bend. He steered the wheel to the left and then bounced along the dirt road following the property line. After several hundred yards, he suddenly pulled the car across the road to the left side. Up near a set of mailboxes from across the farm driveway was another vehicle. A young, dark haired man was out of his car and reading his mail in front of a set of mailboxes. Since Lindbergh was to the far left side of the road, it would be difficult for the young man to see him. Taking his time, the young man read through the mail and then he caught sight of Lindbergh's car. Fifty yards away, he glanced toward the car window. The Great Aviator slowly pulled his chin down to his chest, but the young man kept staring into the car as if he was trying to find out who the driver was. Lindbergh remained calm; he flipped his fedora down carefully so the young man couldn't recognize him. Both men hesitated for another minute and then the younger man got back into his car and pulled it off to the side. Lindbergh waited. When he saw the car pull back onto the road and head in the opposite direction, he pulled his sedan back onto the road in the proper lane. When the car turned right, Lindbergh eased past and then sped up. He continued on down to the gravel driveway of his estate. By now it was after six o'clock, and the early March sun was waning. Not quite a mile up the winding drive, Lindbergh shut off the engine. Still out of sight from the house, the Great Aviator would have to wait again, this time for darkness to replace the light. Later, he would wait for Betty's signal.

It was 6:45. With the darkness prevailing, Lindbergh got out of the car. He pulled the ladder through the passenger side window and lifted it onto his shoulder. The wind and the cold were feeding off each other, making it increasingly uncomfortable. The Great Aviator struggled with the daunting weather. He rubbed his hands vigorously, cupped his hands and blew into them. He grabbed a large piece of burlap that he had originally wrapped around the ladder and with one foot on one side, he ripped it in half. As he sat on the edge of his car, he pulled the burlap up around his shoe and then his ankle. He tied it in a knot. He did the same to the other leg. He was determined to hide his large footprints.

Inside, Betty was to do her best at keeping Anne, Elsie, and Ollie from the east side of the house. Seeing no one around and being as quiet as he could, the lanky Lindbergh carried the ladder over to the east side of the house and strategically placed it near the nursery window. He put his burlap-covered foot on the bottom rung and pushed down making a weak impression. He stepped back and placed the ladder to the right of the window, but as he did the relentless gales nearly picked the ladder up. Because it barely weighed forty pounds, he struggled to keep it against the house. Unable to do so, the Great Aviator tried lifting it onto his shoulder, but the wind was even too strong for him to carry it. Frustrated, he tucked it beneath his shoulder and wrestled it to a distance of about fifty yards from the house. He knew he could still show the ladder to the police later on.

Lindbergh walked back down the driveway, away from the house. Sitting on his bumper, he pulled the burlap covers from his shoes, shook the clay out, and stuffed them beneath the front seat of his sedan. Again he sat in his car, waiting for 7:30, when Fisch, Hauptmann, and Violet Sharpe would arrive.

CHAPTER FIFTEEN
INSIDE THE HOUSE ON SORREL HILL

———————————————■———————————————

etty Gow was alone when she carried Charlie upstairs to his room at 5:45. She had placed a cloth bib over his clothes and proceeded to feed the boy a large bowl of cereal. She wanted to make sure his stomach was full, for he would have a long night ahead of him. By six o'clock the toddler had finished his dinner. With so many mixed feelings swirling through her mind it was amazing that she was still able to read a short story to the boy without getting upset. For twenty minutes she did just that. Like the Great Aviator, she could justify things by saying that the boy was going to be better off with two parents who could give him the love and attention he needed. She knew the boy was getting too attached and she wouldn't stay in the United States forever. There would come a time when she would have to separate. Deep down she held out the hope that one day she would be able to see the child again at his new home in Germany. At around 6:15, Anne joined Betty in the nursery and the two women prepped the child for bed. Anne tried hard to be the maternal overseer but as it always had been it was Betty who was leading the way. Dressing the child warmly for bed because of his cold would be important for any mother, but in this case dressing went beyond just nightclothes. It was Betty who took on the responsibility; she knew what the child was in for. It was important for the boy to have enough warm clothing to protect him from the frigid nighttime temperatures. She really did not know Charlie Schleser and his wife, but the Great Aviator had assured her that the couple would take good care of the child. But the wind was blowing hard and cold, and as far as she knew the old fishing cabin was not connected to electricity. She also knew that it might be more than a few days before the couple would be able to get the young toddler out of the country and on his way to Germany. With all these factors it was imperative that he be dressed warmly.

After the two women cleaned the child up, they lathered him with Vicks VapoRub. This would allow him to breathe a little easier with his nasal passages blocked because of his cold. Betty went back to the front room and using her sewing abilities, put together a short-sleeved shirt from some leftover flannel material. Anne looked after the baby as Betty easily completed the shirt. Re-entering the nursery, she pulled the child up and then placed the shirt over his head. She covered him again with another woolen shirt. On his bottom were two diapers and plastic underpants. As if this wasn't enough, she then placed a gray Doctor Denton sleeping suit over him. As Anne usually did, she watched as Betty placed him into the four- post crib and covered him with yet another blanket. She went to affix the boy's thumbs to two metal thumb-guards that the Colonel had deemed mandatory to prevent the boy from sucking his thumbs while he slept. As Anne turned to toward the window Betty decided against putting the thumb-guards on thinking that it might slow down the Great Aviator when he went to take the child. Not thinking anymore about it, she placed the two thumb-guards in her pocket.

The two women then checked the shutters and as they had noticed before, one of the shutters would not close properly. With maternal instincts, Betty scanned the room to make sure everything seemed comfortable for the toddler and at the same time made sure everything was in place for his father as well. Everything appeared to be the usual when little Charlie went to sleep for the night. Betty then left the nursery and walked up the hall to her room in the front of the house while Anne stayed with Charlie for a few minutes more and then went downstairs. When she did, Betty re-entered the child's room. With a damp piece of some remaining flannel she went over everything she could in the room to erase all fingerprints. Anne by this time was sitting downstairs in the living room writing at her desk. This was something she did often while waiting for her husband to come home. After finishing the wipe down, Betty closed the nursery door and entered the bathroom. She washed some of Charlie's clothes and placed them in a wicker basket together with the flannel rag. She descended the second floor stairs and also the cellar stairs so she could hang up the wet clothes. On the cellar floor near some moving boxes, she noticed a pair of the Colonel's shoes that were covered with dry clay and mud. An unplanned idea came to her to make muddy footprints in the baby's nursery. She splashed water on the dirty shoes to make them muddy and then placed them in the basket. Cautiously, she opened the cellar door and seeing no one around, covered the shoes with some clothes and headed back up the stairs. She removed the muddy shoes. Quickly, she went back into the nursery and made footprints around the room. There wasn't enough mud or clay to make well-defined footprints, so she merely dabbed the shoes around the room just enough to make clay smudges. Under the window she dabbed the suitcase. In and around the crib she did the same. Betty seemed disappointed that she couldn't make the footprints defined enough to simulate an intruder walking through the room. The clay smudges would have to suffice.

It was now 7:30 and the baby had fallen asleep. Betty Gow eased out of the room and headed back down to the cellar with the basket of clothes and muddy shoes in tow. She rinsed the Colonel's shoes, dried them with a towel, and neatly tucked them under the same moving boxes. Again she headed back up the cellar steps and seeing Anne busy at her desk, she went upstairs to signal the Great Aviator that the time had come.

CHAPTER SIXTEEN
RED JOHNSON PICKS UP
THE SCHLESERS IN PRINCETON

Red Johnson had made sure to stop at a friend's house in Englewood at about 5:00pm. William Boland was an acquaintance from Englewood and Red made sure he stopped long enough to establish his early alibi. He stayed just a few minutes, because he had to get to Princeton by seven. An alibi albeit a weak one, was important for him because he was the so-called boyfriend of the baby's nursemaid. Beside Betty, Red knew many of the staff at Next Day Hill, including his new and convenient girlfriend Violet Sharpe. The Great Aviator promised Red he would do his best to keep the police from asking him too many questions. Lindbergh in fact had promised Betty the same thing, and he was going to try his best to keep the cops away from Violet for fear of her spilling the beans. Red was certain he would get a call from the police asking him what he knew about the Lindbergh baby's kidnapping, and whether he knew that the Lindbergh's were staying over at the farm on Sorrel Hill. He was only one of a handful of people who was privy to that information and he would need to be able to recall his whereabouts on the evening of March the first. For the Great Aviator it was a matter of importance that Red get to Princeton as soon as he could, drive a few more miles to pick up Charlie Schleser near Stoney Brook and then be back at the theatre by at least 7:30 where he would wait for the baby to arrive sometime around eight o'clock.

Red's role in the kidnapping may have seemed minor to most of the people involved. But Lindbergh felt he was the right man to pick up Charlie Schleser and to take Violet back home. On the return trip to Englewood, Red could explain to Violet the importance of the operation. Getting her back up to Englewood quickly would also keep any inquisitive cops from asking questions. Everyone would assume the baby had been kidnapped at around ten o'clock. Red would also work well with Charlie Schleser. When he and Schleser got to the theatre in Princeton they would have to wait for Violet, Hauptmann and Fisch with the baby. The Germans would then drop Violet off with Red and then take Schleser and the baby back to the cabin. Red and Violet then would rush back to North Jersey. Their alibi would then be set.

It was a plus that few people were aware of the secret relationship Red had with Violet Sharpe. Those who knew about them were Betty who thought that it was just a matter of convenience for the kidnapping plot, the Great Aviator who knew about a couple late night rendezvous he had with the Irish servant, and those in Condon's kidnap ring who may have known about her relationship with Red, but knew little about Violet. Red hoped that none of that information would come out in any investigation. Not because of Betty, but because he really did not want to get Violet in any trouble. He wasn't in love with Violet but he was fond of her in a plutonic way and he definitely didn't want to hurt her. He was aware that she might be used as a pawn, but it was in an effort to help little Charlie find a place where he could be given the attention he needed. Because Violet had a fondness for the little child, he was sure that she would understand that. She had complained to him once before about how irresponsible the parents were with the child, especially the Great Aviator. Red was confident that Violet would support the plan, after he told her everything was done in the baby's best interest. And since she really liked Red, it would be easy for her to cooperate with him.

Red knew exactly where the cabin was located, but wanted to make sure he was there to pick up Charlie Schleser before it got too dark. The cabin was so well hidden down in the brush and thickets along the brook, and he worried he might have trouble finding it after nightfall. He along with Hauptmann and Fisch had made it a day on Monday driving around the Princeton countryside making sure they knew all the roads in and around Princeton and Hopewell.

At 6:45 Red Johnson had made it to the cabin. He picked up Charlie and his wife. Charlie told Red the Great Aviator said it would be okay if Charlie's wife went along with the two men to Princeton. This was not included in the original plan but Red did not think it would matter and said nothing. By seven o'clock, he parked his car under the barren sycamores near the theatre and the three of them walked down Nassau Street toward the Baltimore Lunch, an all night diner. Red did not go in because he did not want anyone to take a mental picture of him just in case he did become a suspect in the case. The Schlesers were quite at ease with their roles going inside to get a cup of coffee. Red told them once he saw Hauptmann's Dodge he would walk back to get them. He did his best to obscure his pale face beneath his white felt hat. The estimated time for the trio of Hauptmann, Fisch, and Sharpe to pass through Princeton was approximately 7:15. Hauptmann wasted no time as he sped down to Princeton. From there, he had fifteen minutes to get to Hopewell. Hauptmann told Lindbergh he could do it. The Great Aviator expected them to be there in the driveway at precisely 7:30. He did not want them to arrive early. He feared that the inquisitive Violet Sharpe would exploit the opportunity to ask a lot of unnecessary questions.

Still waiting for Hauptmann's Dodge, Red held on to his hat as he walked back down Nassau Street. For a while he stopped near the side of the theatre but facing Nassau Street. He checked his watch and saw that it was nearing 7:15. There were few cars driving down the main corridor of Princeton. If the trio had not been spotted by 7:30, Johnson was to put a call into the Lindbergh household to Betty to inform them they had not arrived. The darkness of the sycamores and the dreary weather made the side of the theatre a conveniently shady place to hide and conduct business. Like a hawk, Red kept watching for Hauptmann's blue Dodge and then he saw it heading south on Nassau Street. Traveling at a speed of about twenty miles per hour, the big car came lumbering by. He huddled within the darkness, not wanting Violet to see him. He could see the two Germans in the front seat but he could not see her. He assumed she was in the backseat. The damp air and stiff winds chilled his bones, and he hurried out of the dark shadows back up to Nassau Street to the front of the theatre. It was 7:20. He turned and kept walking southward until he could see the Schlesers standing in front of the Baltimore Luncheonette.

"I just saw them go by."

"We did too. That should put them right on time," said the bespectacled Charlie Schleser.

"C'mon," said Johnson. "Let's get out of the cold. We can wait in the car until they get back here with the baby. It will be at least another thirty minutes until they come back. Richard knows exactly where I parked my car, right underneath those tall shade trees. Are you folks ready to spend a week with a screaming baby?"

Schleser's wife answered in broken English. "Ve are ready for the baby as best ve can be. Ve have plenty of food and clothes but it is so dark and cold out there. Ve have to keep a kerosene light on so ve can see vat ve're doing, it does noting to stop cold. I did not vant to stay there alone, that's vy I wanted to come vith you and my husband. Once ve bring the baby back to the cabin; the lights vil hav to go out. I not look forvard to that; I hope ve all can sleep until the sun comes up."

Red Johnson could relate to Charlie's wife's accent, and he knew what she was talking about when she complained of the cold. His double-breasted wool pea coat was not totally resistant to the harsh gales that were sweeping down Nassau Street. Together, the trio would try to stave off the cold and keep the conversation going for another half an hour.

CHAPTER SEVENTEEN
ARRIVAL IN HOPEWELL

Nearing the trio's destination, the blue 1930 Dodge touring vehicle cruised slowly, crossing through the tiny town of Hopewell. Darkness had forced its way in. The quaint town seemed desolate and cold with no sign of life. Dried oak leaves that had been protected from the dampness by a window bay were lifted by the north wind, and they flitted and twirled to the last breaths of winter. Other leaves followed closely in procession, crossing the road leading into the sedated town. They too danced with the wind's help and then crashed onto a thin bed of damp leftover snow. The winter had been a cold one and the denizens that lived along the main thoroughfare through Hopewell had remained sedentary inside their cozy houses. Spring was fast approaching, yet it was difficult to tell. The brisk winds were not letting up and they rattled the windows in the town homes and small stores that lined the street. Even Pop Gebhart's Hotel and General Store, the main business on Main Street seemed lifeless. Having crossed over the paved Main Street, the car continued its slow ascent into the Sourland Mountains. Hauptmann steered it down a desolate dirt road, away from the sleepy town. Like a stalking lion, the automobile crept slowly as Hauptmann and Fisch made sure they followed the directions. Just a few more minutes down yet another dark road, and they would be close to their destination. One turn to the left and the unlikely trio would be there.

Hauptmann's hulking Dodge grinded its gears when it came upon the driveway of the Lindbergh's estate. The German coasted down the drive slowly. From this stretch of the driveway the house could not be seen. Dense woods stretched backward to each side of the drive. The car and its occupants continued to crawl up the road. At the house the lights were illuminating, but because of the forest and moonless sky, you couldn't tell. It was 7:30. The car and its passengers were right on time. As they wound around the curvy road, a man raised his hands for them to stop. It was the Great Aviator. He had been waiting for them. Violet was surprised; she wondered what he was up to. Fisch and Hauptmann were unfazed, for they had spoken with him earlier in the day and they knew the plan. Lindbergh approached the driver's side window of the car. He leaned over and gazed into the back seat of the car to make sure Violet had made the trip.

"Since Charlie seems comfortable with you Violet, I thought you wouldn't mind if these gentlemen drove you over to Doctor Mayer's house. He will be waiting for you. The doctor is going to examine Charlie to see if he can help him with his cold. Anne and Betty will be back shortly but I wanted to get the child in to see the doctor. Wait right here; I will go get him. Be patient, it might take a few minutes. I want to make sure the baby is dressed warmly."

Lindbergh knew that Betty had already layered the baby with plenty of clothing. At the foot of the crib she was to leave a blanket. Since Violet had never been to the house before, she couldn't tell how far the walk was up to the house. As soon as the Great Aviator was out of sight from the car, he sprinted directly to the cedar tree to the left of the house. He watched carefully for Betty's signal.

The curvy entry road, like all the other roads near Hopewell was a mixture of gritty cinders and mud from the previous rain. Away from the house's illumination, the sky was now near black. The dark cirrus clouds blackened the driveway like an eerie shroud. The moon would not be visible until the morning. Violet and the Germans peered through the darkness, patiently waiting for the Great Aviator to turn the corner with his young son in tow. Lindbergh had parked his own car up around the bend, just out of sight of the house. He had instructed Hauptmann to remain on the lane, back another fifty yards.

The Great Aviator waited for Betty's signal. It was now 7:40. On the right side of the house the kitchen staff was busy. Ollie Whately had the family dog Wahgoosh cradled in his arm while his wife prepared the evening meal. Ann was doing the usual, writing at her desk, and Betty was following the script, getting ready to signal the baby's father. The layout of the whitewashed fieldstone was perfect for Lindbergh's plan.

In Hauptman's Dodge, the unlikely trio was getting restless and Violet was the worst. She was questioning everything in her mind, trying to make sense out of the evening. "Why in the world is he here?" she asked herself, then spoke aloud. "The staff at Next Day Hill said he had a speaking engagement at the Waldorf in New York."

The two Germans sat quietly, their eyes affixed on the bend in the road. They offered no information and no response to Violet's comment. Hauptmann and Fisch were emotionless; stared through the windshield, waiting for the Great Aviator to return with the baby.

Originally, the Great Aviator was going to have Violet get the baby, but he changed his plan slightly. With the wind blowing strongly, he felt he could get the baby without anyone hearing him. Even though the boy liked to scream whenever he went near him, Lindbergh thought he could cover the sleeping child's mouth if he awoke, and still no one would hear them.

The Great Aviator remained behind the cedar tree. The second floor lights were visible from the side as well as the front. Betty had turned off the lights to the nursery but left her bedroom light on. Lindbergh stared upward at the east facing window; there were no curtains on either side. He stood there waiting and then he saw the light go out. A second later it was back on, and then off again, two more times. Betty was precise with her timing. It was 7:45. After giving the signal, she descended the stairs, and immediately went into the doorway of the living room where she engaged Anne in conversation. The library door that led into the living room was closed. Betty was quick to start the conversation by telling Anne that she washed the baby's nightshirt that he had spit-up on and that the baby was sleeping peacefully. Her screen was working perfectly. Within seconds the Great Aviator took advantage. He entered the front door and quietly ascended the staircase. With his long legs he was at the top step in seconds. Once there, he took one step and carefully placed his tall body in the nursery. He was careful to remain silent so no one could hear him down below. His peripheral vision told him there was no one around; he knew Betty would not have signaled him if the time was not right. With Lindbergh upstairs, she stood in the doorway, continuing to distract Anne. On the other side of the house, the Whateleys were still busy working in the kitchen. They were all creatures of habit, including little Wahgoosh, who continued to sop up the attention that Oliver was casting his way. The plan was working. Now came the hard part, he had to get the baby out of the crib and down the stairs without anyone hearing him. Anne was still at her corner desk talking to Betty. Carefully, he lifted the sleepy child from his crib. The baby did not awaken. Just in case the child did wake up and see his father's face, he gently covered his mouth and then descended the stairs, absent of noise. Quickly, he headed through the foyer to the front door. With one arm holding the baby and the other covering his mouth, he had to use a shoulder to open the door. He made sure the air didn't rush through the house like a vacuum and left the door slightly ajar. By not shutting the door, it also prevented him from making any noise. With the noisy, winter wind rocking the house it would not have mattered anyway. In a flash, the Great Aviator had disappeared from the house; already sprinting for the driveway and angling to the right.

Once Betty sensed that Lindbergh had left, she quietly closed the front door. She would pretend to resume her important duties as the nursemaid. She headed back upstairs and quickly took to wiping the room down one more time to eliminate any fingerprints. Betty thought about the phony scenario of the Lindbergh baby being taken by an intruder who climbed the ladder, made off out the window with the baby, and then ran down the ladder to the ground. She wondered if it would work. She stared down at the empty crib. The Lindbergh baby had been kidnapped. Sadness overcame her, as she realized she might not ever get to see the sickly little child again. She tried to be strong and shifted her thoughts. One thing was certain; there were no fingerprints in the nursery. And as a side-thought, she had made sure there were muddy footprints. Betty paused near the wall and then headed back downstairs to the staff sitting room. She sat down with the Whateleys. Anne was still at her desk and worked on some more of her writings.

The Great Aviator was still running down the drive as it snaked around toward the country lane. He held tightly to the baby; his large hand smothering the boy's face, for fear of him crying. No one would have heard him anyway because the brisk weather was playing accomplice to Charles Lindbergh and his carefully planned abduction. Down the driveway, the trio of conspirators was waiting. Violet Sharpe was pacing around the car despite Hauptmann's insistence she stay put. After getting out of sight of the house, Lindbergh's sprinting shifted to a quick lope. As he neared the car, he was surprised to see Violet walking around. The Great Aviator stared at her and then scolded her with his piercing blue eyes. He was agitated and told her in a stern voice to "Take the boy to Dr. Mayer." He handed the child to the English servant. The young child was awake by this time and he turned away from his father, and then grabbed for Violet with outstretched hands. He stared at both of them but said nothing. After a sleepy yawn he reached his arms around Violet's neck. His short curly blonde hair was matted to his head from sweat and Violet pulled the small blanket up to cover him. The child smiled at Violet, but uttered no sounds. He turned his head back toward his father and then back to Violet, and he ogled her with a puzzled look as they headed to the car. He clutched at the collar on her coat holding it tightly. A frigid gust rocked the door of Hauptmann's Dodge.

The Great Aviator placed his hand on the back of Violet's coat and ushered her to the car. Gently holding her by the elbow, he guided her into the back seat. Violet slid across it with the boy still clutching at her collar. Looking at her, Lindbergh spoke affirmatively but quietly. "Dr Mayer will be expecting you. When Ollie brings Betty and Anne back, I will send the three of them to pick up the boy at Dr. Mayer's. That should be in an hour or so. You, Mr. Hauptmann, and Mr. Fisch can head back up to Englewood where they will drop you off at Next Day Hill. Thank you for helping out tonight Violet, Anne and I really appreciate it. Hopefully Charlie will get better soon."

Lindbergh turned from the car and waved them off without even looking. It would be the last time he would see his son alive. The first phase of his plan was complete. The car made a slight turn to the left. The lights on Hauptmann's Dodge had not been turned on and he carefully steered the car, turning around in the dark driveway. Because of the careful deliberateness of the driver, there was barely any sound at all. Hauptmann kept exactly to the plan and smoothly crawled down the crushed cinder driveway. Like a carefully orchestrated magic act, the car vanished behind the tall hardwood trees.

The Great Aviator turned and walked over to the east side of the house, some fifty feet from the library window, where he had carefully hidden the ladder earlier that evening. He wanted so badly to use the ladder he had worked so hard on back in November, but the wind was not letting up. He knew if he tried to place it against the house it would blow over. It was simply too light. Lindbergh remembered the Minnesota winds of his childhood; he was keenly aware that ladders could easily fall when the winds exceeded ten miles per hour. The ladder barely weighed forty pounds and the extra spacing between the rungs would only create more lift. Risking the entire kidnapping on the ladder was senseless. It would have to suffice as a ruse. The time was now 7:55 He would make his appearance at around 8:20. He stared down at the ladder. From his pocket he took out a chisel that he had found near the briars. He tossed it a few feet from the ladder. "Just something else for the cops to think about!" he thought. "Now, what they will say about the chisel," he mused. "Or the broken rail," referring to the top rail that he cracked last fall. Unintentionally, Lindbergh was already analyzing the crime scene. "Tonight I stole Charlie out the front door, would they think the kidnapper climbed that ladder and descended with him under his arm? Or maybe handed him to an accomplice? Was it the work of a gang? Was the kidnapper too heavy for the ladder and he broke it?" Lindbergh would float the ideas to the investigators and hope that the convolution would steer them away from the real culprits.

With stealth, Lindbergh headed back down the driveway to his car. It was cold and he still had time to burn. He waited in his car another twenty minutes until his watch showed 8:20. Since the car door had not been closed all the way for fear someone might have heard it, he started the car up with it still open. He drove the sixty yards up and around to the right of the house. His foot was partially sticking out beneath the door. Outside the garage, he honked the horn. This time the Great Aviator was quite noisy as he re-entered the house. In his right side trouser pocket, he discovered the white envelope containing the ransom note that he and Doc Condon had worked on earlier in the day. He forgot to place it in the crib. He cursed to himself. "Dammit, I'll have to put it somewhere else."

CHAPTER EIGHTEEN
THE HANDOFF

Meanwhile the odd triumverate of naive conspirators was heading south-east not far from Princeton. Hauptmann was moving fast, in pursuit of easy money but chased by his own guilt. He wondered if he was doing the right thing. Fisch said nothing; he was anxious to get rid of both baby and caretaker and finish the job so he too could collect his share of easy money. Clutching the child, Violet Sharpe's mind was also working overtime. She wasn't thinking about money, she was trying to figure out what the hell was going on.

"Where did Anne and Betty have to go that was so urgent on such a terribly brisk evening? What does Red have to do with all this anyway?" Violet had an uneasy feeling in her stomach as she hung onto the boy. "But Red loves me she thought, he is a good man. Lindbergh on the other hand was his usual arrogant and bossy self, what is he really up to?" Violet was confused and beleaguered about the events that were unfolding. But she did what Red and the Great Aviator wanted. She tenderly held the child to her bosom to keep him warm. Little Charlie grimaced and let out a weak whine. He then turned, first to the left and then to the right. The infant blanket around him completely covered the child's cotton Dr Denton nightclothes and he clung to Violet with a surprised, uneasy expression. She looked at him with a puzzled smile. She clutched him again tightly and cuddled him in the backseat of the Dodge while the two distant men in the front seat said nothing. Inside the car it was pitch black, as it headed down an unlit road on its way back to Princeton. The interior of the car was cold. Tears welled up in the little child's eyes and as they did, he coughed with a slight wheeze. Like Violet, he too was disoriented. It was apparent that the little child was not feeling well and Violet felt compelled out of her maternal instinct to speak to him.

"Why, you sweet little child you do need to see the doctor, don't you?" Again the boy in mild bronchial distress coughed and wheezed, while the thoughts continued to intersect in Violet's mind. The darkness and the child's health just exasperated an already bad situation. She sensed that the boy was fairly sick and wondered why the Lindberghs would want to send their child out on such a crisp cold March evening separated from his parents, and in the company of at least two people the boy did not know. It was a winter night when if you weren't dressed warmly, the cold would work its way into your bones, just like the damp, miserable English winters she endured as a child. In an attempt to keep him warm, she held him tightly to her breast. The unheated car and its passengers were now approaching Princeton.

Leaving the dirt roads, they turned onto the old Princeton Pike for another mile, and headed toward the main street past the Doric pillars of Drumthwacket Mansion. Reaching Nassau Street, they cruised slowly in front of the scenic Princeton University campus, crossing Witherspoon Street on the left. To the right, tall majestic shade trees shadowed flagstone education buildings. In front of them, flickering street lights watched over dancing silhouettes on the sidewalk below. The cold biting air kept the student body inside, diligently working on their studies. On the left side of the street were closed storefronts. It was too late for business. Even the typically busy Baltimore Lunch was lacking customers but for a few coffee drinkers. The only other place that appeared open was the Garden Theatre on Nassau and Vandeventer. There, a young man and woman were talking near the front vestibule. Other theatre patrons were inside, sitting safely within the warm confines enjoying the moving picture show.

Hauptmann drove past the theatre and then turned left onto Moore Street past old Captain Moore's house. He continued, and then he turned left, and then left again on Vandeventer until he was back on the shadowy side of the Garden Theatre. The theatre about twelve years-old, was the only movie house in town and now was directly to the right of the car. Hauptmann stopped and from behind a row of majestic, sycamore trees a gray haired, middle-aged Charlie Schleser with his wife by his side, stepped forward and reached for the door handle. In the car headlights an overactive, black squirrel awake when he should have been slumbering for the winter, scurried toward the car, stood up as if to enter it, and then darted onto one of the safe arms of the sycamore. The nurturing sycamore was its lifeline, providing warmth and comfort during the winter. In the summer, it provided shadowy camouflage and food. The rodent clutched at its flaky bark unwilling to let go, and then turned back to watch Isadore Fisch get out of the car on the passenger side. The lean German was polite as he helped Violet and the baby get out of the car. Violet stared at the Schlesers. Hauptmann from his driver's seat turned sharply, staring at her. He spoke in a strong German accent.

"This is Docta Mayer and his assistant. They vill take the boy into the office to examine him. We vant to be as secret and discreet as possible, the Colonel doesn't vant anyone to know he is here." Violet was hesitant but spoke up through her own English accent.

"Really? What is going on?" she asked. "Where is this office? Red told me we would drop him off at a doctor's office not here near this dark movie house. I don't see a doctor's office anywhere."

Hauptmann became assertive and raised his voice slightly. "You have nothing to vorry about; the boy will be taken gut care of." Violet stared at Hauptmann for more than ten seconds, blinking only once. She was agitated. Defiantly she sighed, and mumbled something under her breath. She held Charlie tightly. She was reluctant and unwilling to turn over the baby to the couple.

Not able to wait any longer, Red Johnson stepped out of the shadows. He called out to the English servant. "Violet, don't worry about it, the baby will be fine. You can come with me. I will take you back to Englewood."

"Red? What are you doing here?"

"C'mon, I'll tell you." Violet hugged the baby and gave him to Dr. Mayer's wife. Red grabbed Violet's arm and walked her towards his car. He whispered to her. "Don't worry, it will be alright."

The bespectacled Dr. Mayer alias Charlie Schleser, along with his wife, got into the backseat of Hauptmann's car with the baby. Mrs. Schleser tried to cradle the Lindbergh boy and just as he was ready to let out a scream, he caught sight of the black squirrel and smiled. For a second that seemed longer than it was, the two stared at each other. The boy shouted something that was indecipherable and then giggled. The boy startled the rodent and he disappeared into the comforting boughs of the sycamore. With no tolerance of small talk or non-business matters, Charlie Schleser quickly uttered, "Let's get out of here" to his partners. The Schlesers along with Hauptmann, Fisch and the baby took a hard right onto Nassau Street and headed back the same way they came. Now the blue Dodge was carrying five passengers. In less than ten minutes, it would arrive at the desolate cabin near Stoney Brook.

Violet was still annoyed and agitated. She said nothing but stared at Red waiting for answers. When he didn't know what to say, she climbed inside his car. She brushed the windblown hair off her rosy face. With the wind still blowing strong from the north, she pulled her wool collar up and pushed her hair down into her coat covering her ears. She looked up and saw that the squirrel had scooted back down the tree. It was as if he too was looking for an explanation of what had just taken place. Confused, it eyed-balled Violet one last time, then looked away. Red got back in and shut his car door. Seeking an egress from the cold, the furry rodent scratched his way up the side of the tree and disappeared into a warm and cozy nest for the rest of the night. The red haired Norwegian drove out of the sycamore's shadows and turned left. He headed north toward Kingston and turned onto a rutted back road where he would eventually meet up with Route One.

"Violet, are you alright? Don't worry little Charlie will be just fine. We should be in Englewood in an hour or so."

"Red, what are you doing here? And what is going on anyway?"

"Didn't Colonel Lindbergh tell you?"

"Tell me what?"

"That I would meet you here in Princeton and drive you back to Englewood." Red knew that the Great Aviator had not told Violet anything.

"Not really, I never really talked to the Colonel. He did all the talking."

"No," said Red. "At the farm, didn't he tell you I would take you home?"

"No, Red. I'm afraid he did not tell me anything. He just kind of glared at me when he was barking out his orders, just like he usually does. Everything seems so strange, including those two strange fellows who drove me here. Who in the hell are the Mayers? And where are they taking that little boy?"

Red was unsure how to go about explaining everything to Violet.

CHAPTER NINETEEN
RED AND VIOLET

———————————————■———————————————

After dropping off the Schlesers, Fisch and Hauptmann turned around one more time and headed back toward Princeton. Because of poor roads they had to go southeast and then head back north. The streets of Princeton remained silent and cold, as the busy dodge changed directions yet again and headed northward in the same path of Red Johnson and Violet Sharpe. Passing the Garden Theatre where they had picked up the Lindbergh baby and his new caregivers, they too rushed toward Kingston. In Kingston, there was still little sign of life, just a few farmhouses where an occasional dim light could be seen flickering in the distance. The strange pair of Germans had to navigate another terribly rutted dirt road until they were able to get out onto Route One. Like Red and Violet, they would be back to their friendly confines in a little more than an hour. After crossing the Hudson River Bridge, they would meet up in the Bronx with the old man who was so anxiously waiting to find out how the operation went.

Violet sat stunned in the passenger side of Red's car hoping to get some straight answers from the wiry Scandinavian, answers that she was unable to get from her German partners. She experienced a feeling of melancholy, as she thought about the Lindbergh baby being shuffled from person to person. The child seemed so confused. She wanted to know the truth. It annoyed her that the sick child was not taken to the doctors by his own parents but she knew that that had been the way it was since the Lindbergh baby was born. He was shuffled from Betty to Mrs. Morrow and back to Betty. Even Anne's strangely jealous sister Elizabeth had watched the child on one occasion, as did Violet. Within the Morrow estate there was a lot of talk about the Lindberghs not being very good parents. But the evening's events all seemed very frustrating to Violet, not to mention Red's involvement. "Why was he here?" Not only was she struggling with the rationale of the Great Aviator and his wife but Red Johnson's role in all of this. She had fallen in love with the Norwegian and now she was casting doubt on him for the first time. As Red accelerated his car onto Route One, Violet's mind was running wild with numerous thoughts. "What was Red really up to?" Before he had showed up, she had made up her mind that when she returned to Next Day Hill she was going to give him a call. She would get to the bottom of this strange and bizarre situation. Now, she was in his car heading back toward Englewood.

"Violet, please listen to me. Colonel Lindbergh does not want the press to find out the baby is sick, or for that matter that you or anyone else took him to the doctor. He told me to tell you if anyone asks you what you did tonight, you are to say nothing. Should the child need to go into the hospital, he doesn't want any snooping, newspaper people violating his privacy."

"Why would anyone be interested in something that I did tonight, Red?"

"Well you never know," responded Red.

"Then what am I supposed to say?"

"Just tell people you were with that friend of yours, Ernie."

"Ernie? I told you he was just some man that I met at the bakery. I don't even know him that well."

"Well, if that is true then fine, but should anyone ask you about my phone call to you this afternoon, just tell them it was your friend Ernie. Lindbergh does not want anybody to know that I am involved."

"Involved?" asked Violet. Johnson realized he just slipped up and was quick to cover his tracks. "I mean involved in tonight's affairs with the baby." Red felt like he had to get himself out of this self-imposed jam.

"You know me being friends with him was just happenstance as they say. I had met him before at Next Day Hill when I was there talking to Betty. He was very friendly; he said he liked Scandinavians and laughed. I told him I was going to go out with you later, so he asked if I could help out for a while tonight. I said I would. Red's tone and his hesitation when he spoke, suggested to Violet that he wasn't telling the truth. But she didn't want to question Red because she did not want to jeopardize an already shaky relationship, even if his voice did sound somewhat defensive as if he was trying to cover up something. But Violet was still curious.

"You know Red, I was not aware of your relationship with Colonel Lindbergh. You never told me that you were friends with him." She let a smile take the edge off the conversation. "What else are you not telling me Mr. Johnson? I mean seriously, Red; I am quite confused about all these things going on around here."

"There are a lot of things that I didn't tell you, Violet, and that is because we have not been together for very long. Violet paused, and then collected her thoughts. She was puzzled by the thought as well as the tone. She felt that since they had been intimate he should not have been keeping any secrets from her. The evening's troubling events, and now Red's involvement, had her more than disoriented. She needed to know the truth but was not going to aggravate the situation or Red. The fact was she loved him, and she knew that he was just trying to help by bringing her back to Englewood. He was a good man. She loved him, and he loved her. He was only trying to help. She did love him. She was sure he loved her.

Red switched the conversation to small talk to avoid difficult questions. But the conversation always seemed to go back to the Great Aviator and his family. They talked about him, neither saying anything too positive. They discussed the baby but not his cold; how cute he was but how indifferent he was to everybody, including his father and how distant the child seemed. They talked about Anne and how nice she was, but they both agreed she was awkward at motherhood. Violet kept to herself the idea that Anne was handcuffed in just about everything she did because of the Great Aviators controlling personality, and the fact that she was trapped by her own naïve adulation for him. Violet also hated how Anne would run to her room to write whenever there was an issue that needed to be resolved, especially if it involved the baby. "Anne should never have had that child," she thought. It wasn't long before Betty's name came up in the conversation. Violet liked her but was unsure of her, saying she didn't think she could be trusted. She did not know that Red and Betty were more than just friends. Red became defensive because Betty was his friend and lover, and he could not have Violet criticizing her. He knew he would have to tell her sooner or later. Before Red defended her, Violet sensed something in Red's demeanor and quickly switched the conversation. With the car seeming to hit every bump she wondered why it seemed like they were speeding.

"Why are you driving so fast?" Red did not answer. He knew he had to get back to Englewood quickly, but he was getting edgy because he knew he had to tell Violet the truth. There was no way of getting around it. Red would have to tell Violet about his and Betty's relationship. She did not know that he had been down to Hopewell on more than one occasion. But he knew that Violet had seen them talking a few times. Red also was aware of her naivety and tried not to bring Betty's name up. He wanted desperately to tell Violet about their relationship, but after thinking it over some more he decided that now was not the time. He would have to wait until the kidnapping of the Lindbergh baby died down, and the little boy was safely in his new home in Germany. He too hoped the boy would be taken care of by someone who loved him; someone who was able to give him the precious time that a young child needed.

The car was fast approaching the outskirts of Englewood. After a conversation that rambled from the evening's events to their relationship, to other relationships that both had been involved in or were involved in, Red knew he had to keep reinforcing the Great Aviator's will that Violet was to not tell anyone about what had happened. Using the same logic of the Great Aviator, he wanted her to understand that the child was better off in a loving environment with two caring parents who had the time to tend to their child. He wanted to say that the mother lacked maternal instincts and the jealous father was often abusive, but he did not. Red and Lindbergh both knew that Violet would be the right one to help take the baby away and if she got caught it would be easy for him to get her out of it because of his power. And Red also knew that Lindbergh was counting on him to take advantage of her naivety because he knew Violet was in love with the Norwegian. The Great Aviator made it clear to Red in no uncertain terms that everything must work just as he planned, or no one would get paid and some people's safety could be jeopardized.

Red found himself repeating his words. "Violet, remember—don't tell anyone about what we did tonight. Lindbergh also said that you should know that what we did was in the best interest of Charlie." Red could not continue the deception and finally told her of the plan to send the baby to Germany. Violet could not believe what Red was telling her. Her nervous energy transformed into anger.

"He sent his only child to live with someone else?" She paused for a second, totally surprised at what she had just heard. "How could he do it? How could a father do that? What about Anne is she aware of all this? Red, I just a have a great deal of difficulty with Colonel Lindbergh doing this to his son, not to mention his wife. But I guess it really doesn't surprise me, we all know he is a bit of a sadist." She stared out through the windshield. "I really don't understand these rich Americans. Do you?"

Red tried to answer several questions at one time. "The boy is supposed to go to some friends in Germany who will take good care of him. You and I probably couldn't do it, but then again you and I would not be flying around the world in some airplane if we were parents. Anne does not know about this, because Lindbergh said not to say anything to anyone. He said the reason he had to do it was because the baby cried all the time whenever he was around, and he feared the baby might have been brain damaged from a loss of oxygen when Anne was pregnant. He also knows that the only person who the baby is really close to at all is Betty Gow. And Betty does not want to be the baby's mother. She told him that. He also fears the child was going to be daft and he did not have the time or patience to deal with it. He also said that there was no way a child of Charles Lindbergh would be mentally retarded."

"Did he really say all of that?"

"Let's just say that what he said was very similar to what I just said."

Anxious to learn what Betty's role was in this; she posed another question. "Does Betty really believe all that stuff?"

"Betty knows that child more than anyone including the boy's mother. And if she goes along with all this than I'm sure it's in the best interest of the baby. You know Violet, there are people who don't want retarded children and they give them up for adoption. You know what happens to them? They end up spending their entire life in a special home for the infirmed where nurses take care of them. Betty thinks maybe in Germany with the right person, he could grow up to be an adult. She hopes that one day she might be able to see the child again over there. You know Violet, Betty really is a good person."

"I never said that she wasn't Red," said Violet.

The Norwegian was quick to protect her but he was not really sure why he did other than because he had strong feelings for her and not Violet. The same thought again entered his mind. He knew that at some time he would have to tell her about his and Betty's relationship. But again the timing was wrong. Right now, he did not want Violet to go on the offensive toward Betty because he knew she could say something that would implicate everybody. And he certainly did not want her singing to the cops because she found out about them. Red quickly switched the conversation back to the baby's parents.

"Look Violet, you and I both know that Colonel Lindbergh does not love that child and his wife is new to motherhood. Beside that boy will be better off in a loving home. Everybody knows how he treats Anne too. He has no respect for her." For the first time he heard himself ridicule the Great Aviator, the man who was counting on him to assist in the scheme to send the baby to Germany.

"I agree with you, Red. I'm not denying what you are saying; I'm just shocked at the whole event. How does this affect you and me? Will we be in trouble?"

"No, the Colonel said as long as we play our cards right nobody will know and we should all get paid. And although he doesn't know this, you and I and Betty all feel the same way about him. The child will be better off somewhere else." Violet responded.

"Even if something comes out what did we do? We took the boy to the doctor. Why should that be such a big deal?" Violet had never heard of Doc Condon but within the week she would. Condon was ready to unleash the second phase of the plan, which would be arranging the payoff. The old man and the Great Aviator were going to make sure everybody got paid, and in the process the police and the general public were going to go for a ride.

Johnson was redundant and he stared straight at her. "Just don't say anything to anyone regardless of what you may hear; what Lindbergh really wants is what is best for the baby, and for all of us to keep quiet. He will take care of the rest. Here take this; the Colonel said you could use it." Johnson handed Violet an envelope with cash in it.

"What's this for?" asked Violet. "I did not do anything and I do not want to be included in this devious plan of Lindbergh's."

"Just take it Violet, Lindbergh won't miss it."

"I know he won't, but I don't want to get caught up in this scheme of Lindbergh's. Violet couldn't help but look into the envelope. There were twenties plenty of them.

"Just take it. There's six hundred dollars there. Just take the money! You're not going to get in trouble."

Violet was confused. "I don't know what to do."

Red got closer. "Listen, what's already been done, you have no control over. If you want what's best for everybody including the baby, then just don't say anything to anybody and go about your business," Red reiterated. "The baby will be better off, trust me. That's what Lindbergh wants anyway."

"Oh sure, Red what he really wants is what is best for Charles Lindbergh. You and I know that and as you said, Betty Gow knows that more than anyone. She takes care of the boy more than anyone else. She sees how he treats that child and what he does to him when he is there. The problem is everybody is scared to death of him. What about the "Hun" and that swarthy Fish character? Where in the world did Lindbergh find them? They look familiar to me."

"They are just a couple business associates of Lindbergh. I think he met them through Bobby one of the young lawyers that works with Henry Breckinridge. There is a group of them that punch the bag down near that German beach near the Bronx, on the other side of Throg's Neck. I know I've seen them myself on City Island. Lindbergh goes down that way sometimes in disguise and hides from all the newspaper people and the crazy kids who look for him. There are even some girls down there." Red immediately stopped talking. He knew he had said too much. By this time he could see the anger in Violet's red face. He suspected her English blood was boiling.

"I hate that arrogant bastard," she shouted, shaking her head.

Red was impressed by Violet's perception of things. He wondered however, if he had said too much, but he wanted to make sure that Violet understood everything so she would not tell anyone about the evening's events. He also wanted to make her feel like she was an accepted member of this "new" inner circle. "Violet, I can't believe how smart you are to understand all of this."

Violet's response was filled with anger and nervous energy, which she transformed into humor. "What do I look like to the Norwegian gentleman—just some English bimbo?"

Red did not know how to take her reply but he could not hide his smile. "I did not mean to insult you," he said with a cautious laugh. He reached over and wrapped an arm around her while still holding on to the steering wheel with the other.

Preparing for when he had to tell Violet about his relationship with Betty, and to make himself feel better about everything Red changed the conversation and projected some guilt back onto Violet. He asked her about her relationship with the butler Septimus Banks.

"I know that 'Ole September' fellow is quite taken by you, do you love him?"

"Oh Red, that's not his name and you know it. His name is Septimus."

"Whatever his name is, do you love him?" Red was also quite perceptive. He knew she wasn't really overly attracted to him and the fact that he drank too much and was a lot older than her gave her strong doubts about a possible relationship.

"Red, you know that I'm not serious with him." Violet reiterated what Red was thinking. "He is old and he drinks too much, and that's all I am going to say about that." She was tired of people trying to make something out of nothing so she really was in no mood to rehash her relationship with Banks. There weren't a lot of hard feelings there but there certainly were plenty of rumors. The gossip even though it was trivial, troubled her. The truth in her mind was that he was older, and not really very caring of her. She felt she had been used by him, and didn't want to talk about Banks at all, especially with Red Johnson. Violet wanted to move ahead in her life and for once, she felt that she was heading in the right direction. She had developed a strong fondness for Red, and at least he seemed to care about her. He was even closer to her age. But she couldn't help sound a bit too defensive to Red's insinuation of a serious relationship with the butler and couldn't let it go.

"Why did you bring his name up so suddenly?" She paused for a few seconds. "I think some of the other staff, especially Emily, are making more of it than I am. They talk too much anyway. Septimus is a good fellow but he is more worried about his ego, he thinks being the Morrow butler is like being an ambassador or something. I personally don't want to live the life as the wife of a damn butler, Red. Beside I can't seem to get him to stop his drinking. I'm sure you can understand that. I mean who wants to be trapped in that type of lifestyle for the rest of their life. I have dreams too." Violet then tried to turn things around.

"What about you and Betty? Word around Next Day Hill is that you two are quite the item."

"Violet, I told you more than once that Betty and I are merely friends. We spent some time together up in Maine last summer but we're really just friends. Red couldn't help but lie. He and Betty had become more than just friends. He hoped Violet didn't suspect his deception.

She didn't. She turned toward Red and in a soft voice spoke. "I don't love him, Henrik. I love you." She smiled, stared into his eyes, and then looked out the passenger window. Red hesitated but gave her a weak smile for two reasons. One reason was he had to hide his guilt when Violet said she loved him. The other reason was it stunned him when she called him Henrik. He hated it, and he wished he had never confided to her his real name.

CHAPTER TWENTY
CONDON PLACES CALL

D oc Condon had explained to his friend and business partner Al Reich that there were a couple houses for sale across the river in Englewood. After driving around for a while, he told his buddy that he needed to stop at the drugstore to get some snuff so he could clear his head. He told Reich that he would be out in a minute. While inside the store, he stepped into a phone booth and dialed the number of the Lindbergh estate. Following the plan, he was going to establish the alibi for Betty's boyfriend Red Johnson. It was 8:30, and the phone rang in the servant's quarters. Ollie picked it up. Doc Condon used his best Red Johnson imitation but did not say it was Johnson. Whately did not recognize the caller. The Englishman was polite and said "one minute," and immediately sought out his Scottish co-worker. Betty expected the call and came quickly to receive it. Ollie handed her the phone-cup.

Condon flirted with the Scottish nursemaid. "And how is my pretty Scottish lass doing on this chilly evening? Is everything going well on your end darling?" The old man was attracted to Betty and thought himself quite the lady's man. He could not, however hide his obnoxious self.

"As far as I know," she responded.

"I know you can't talk right now so I won't say much more other than your boyfriend's alibi has been established. What a lucky young man that Norwegian sailor is, I wish I was forty years younger. You and I would be quite the couple my dear."

"I would like that, Red. That sounds like fun."

"Okay, my dear. Good night." Condon hung up the telephone, tipped his hat toward the young lady at the counter without really looking at her, and strolled back out into the cold air. An extremely fine rain with minute ice particles was barely visible as the weather gods struggled to make up their mind. The old man shivered then groaned, as he plopped his large frame down into Reich's Ford coupe. He pulled out his snuff can. He took a tiny pinch between his thumb and index finger and snorted the fine tobacco up his nose. Al Reich laughed, shook his head, and drove off. He was going to cart the old man back to his house and head home for the evening. He didn't know that Condon's evening was not quite over. After the drop-off, he would catch a late night trolley down to Jerome Avenue where he would wait in the vacant house for the Germans. Anxious and pensive, the old man couldn't wait to hear them describe the evening's events.

In Hopewell, things were going as planned. With Condon's call having been made, Betty waited for the Great Aviator to come back downstairs for dinner. Like a well-planned stage production he did just that, exiting the bathroom, descending the steps and then nodding to her as slipped by. Her smile served as an obscure signal to let him know that everything was going just as they had planned.

CHAPTER TWENTY-ONE
CRISIS IN HOPEWELL

B ack at the Hopewell estate, Lindbergh readied himself for the evening. He stuck exactly to his plans and they were falling in place. He checked the house out including the people. Everything was the same as usual, and that was exactly what he wanted. After feeling secure that his meticulous but sinister plan had not been detected, he sat down for a few minutes to eat a light meal with Anne in the dining room. They talked about their child only briefly with most of the conversation consisting of small talk, as Lindbergh was not one to discuss business with his wife, especially business that included a dark shady plot to relocate his son to Germany. In his mind, things were going a mile a minute as he repetitiously went over the plan, but he continued to carry on his meaningless conversation with his wife. The Great Aviator was not about to give any clues as to what he was thinking. He did not tell her about a four-hour meeting he had with four other men about kidnapping their baby. And he did not want to slip up, and tell her that he had been in Hopewell on the estate grounds for the last three hours, making sure that all the components to the plan were just right. This included relocating the ladder from where he hid it in the field to the proper place near the house, and also all the little things that he had set up in advance. He did not tell her that he had been worried about making too much noise driving up the entrance road, for fear that "Wahgoosh" would start barking and then everybody would be waiting for him to enter. He did not tell her that he drove around through the dirt roads surrounding the estate several times, or that he was toting a ladder around in his car. And the Great Aviator did not tell her how rattled he had become, when a young man in another car stared at him down near the mailboxes as he drove past. He never mentioned that he had to coyly dip his head down under his fedora or that he had to look the other way when he drove past. Or that he checked the young man out in his rearview mirror. And he never mentioned that he failed to show up at the Waldorf Astoria where he was supposed to be a special guest and address a crowd of anxious admirers. Or that he didn't even bother to notify the folks at the Waldorf or NYU to say that he wasn't going to make it...... By now his mind was racing out of control.

"Charles you seem far away anything wrong?"

"No," he stated as he looked up at his wife. "No, no.... I'm just tired." His restless mind almost got in the way.

At about 9:15 they went into the living room where they continued their conversation. Lindbergh sitting in a favorite armchair lunged forward and cocked his ear.

"Did you hear that, Anne?" Anne looked at him startled but said nothing. "It sounds like limb broke from a tree or a crate slat snapping." He hesitated for a few seconds. "I guess it was just the wind," he said.

Anne never gave it a second thought. "I'm going to go upstairs and work on my writing. Are you coming upstairs anytime soon?"

"Yes, I have to get something out of the bedroom. Then I still have to finish some work in the study. I'll follow you up." The two ascended the stairs. The Great Aviator wanted to make sure his wife did not enter the nursery. If she went in that direction, he would have to either head her off or divert her attention. When Anne entered their bedroom without checking on the baby, Lindbergh proceeded down the hall to make contact with Betty who had been in her room showing Elsa Whately a new dress that she had purchased. Lindbergh gazed at her and nodded slightly when Elsa looked the other way. Betty stared back coyly and gave her own subtle nod, assuring the Great Aviator that everything was all right. Elsa had not picked up on anything. Seeing that Anne appeared to be busy in her bedroom, Lindbergh went into the bathroom and stared at himself in the mirror. His icy blue eyes peered back at him. He wanted to say something to himself, but he just splashed cold water on his face. Anne heard him and thought nothing unusual, as she too prepared for the evening. He slipped into some comfortable clothing because he knew he would be up all night, joining the search for the baby. The time was now 9:30. The Great Aviator exited the bathroom and went downstairs to the study, where he waited for another crucial part of his scheme to take place.

On the outside, Lindbergh remained cool and collective. But because it seemed like the ten o'clock hour would never come, he sat on the edge of his desk chair pensive. He worried about the potential for things to go wrong. Sitting there behind the desk, he went over the plan again and again in his mind. By 9:40 everything was still going smoothly. He wondered though why Elsa had not come down the stairs yet. Lindbergh knew he could not afford to make any mistakes. If everything was going as planned then the baby was already with the Schlesers, Violet was back near Englewood with Red Johnson, and Hauptmann and Fisch were cruising over the bridge to New York City, where they would check in with Doc Condon. So far, the Whateleys had detected nothing. They had not said or mentioned anything that was questionable. It was also of vital importance that Betty played the actress role well. At ten o' clock she was to ask who had the baby, at which point, the Great Aviator would run up the stairs and announce to Anne that, "they have stolen our baby."

Again, he checked his watch. It was 9:45. He could hear the door to Betty's room open. Elsa descended the stairs and went to the back rooms near the kitchen. She said nothing, and did not bother to look into the library when she walked by. The Great Aviator leaned over his desk with the illusion that he was working. He assumed that Whagoosh was still in there with Ollie.

As worried about things as he might have been, the Great Aviator did not appear nervous as he was just counting the minutes waiting for Betty to make the next move. The concern for the baby was not top priority; he felt that the baby would be fine with the Schlesers. Charlie Schleser's wife ensured him that she would take good care of him, and they were certain the child would be placed in a stable home in Germany where he could grow up into adulthood. By then he will have established a new identity; no longer would he be the missing Lindbergh baby. The Great Aviator remained calm, but he fixated on the minute hands of the wall clock. It was closing in on the 10 o'clock hour. His own watch was showing 10 o'clock. He heard Betty walk down the hall into the baby's nursery. Seconds later, she exited the room and knocked on Anne's door. He could hear her ask Anne if she had the baby, but he did not hear his wife's reply. Seconds later, Betty came rushing down the stairs.

"Colonel Lindbergh do you have the child?"

"Why, no," he replied. The Great Aviator leapt from his chair and sprinted up the stairs. Without looking in the child's room he reached for his rifle in his closet. He then turned toward the nursery and shouted, "Anne they have stolen our baby!" Following the script he entered the nursery, turned on the light and immediately noticed the muddy footprints. He turned to Betty who was now entering the child's room and said "Call Ollie. I need him now!"

The Scottish nursemaid quickly ran downstairs to get Ollie Whateley. Anne entered the nursery looked around for a few seconds, swallowed and stared at her husband. She wondered if this was just another one of his practical jokes.

"Charles, stop this foolish game. What did you do with the baby?" When she saw that her husband had pulled his gun from the closet, and he wasn't smirking, she felt a lump in her stomach. In a panic, she raced down the stairs to the first floor, to join Betty in the search for the missing baby.

"Ollie, stop. Come with me. Let's go back down the steps and head outside. Do you know if there's a flashlight downstairs anywhere? We may need to go out and get one if we can't find one." Lindbergh pushed past the butler who was heading up the steps but he still kept an air of control about him. At the same time, he knew he had to play the role of a nervous, distraught father. He didn't realize nor did he think it mattered that it was ten o'clock and the local hardware store was closed. There was no way they could get their hands on a flashlight at 10 o'clock. Ollie was passive and played the role of subordinate to the Great Aviator. He did exactly as Lindbergh said, and followed him down the steps.

The two men headed out through the foyer to the front of the house. Meanwhile, Anne joined Betty Gow and Elsa Whately and the three of them were turning the whole house upside down looking for the baby. Each room was frantically searched. Lindbergh cautiously circled around the house with Ollie by his side. After a few minutes, they hurried inside asking if anyone had found the baby. When the response was negative, Lindbergh immediately told Ollie to get to the phone.

"Call the police in Hopewell. Tell them someone has stolen our baby." The Great Aviator ran back up to the nursery. He looked around the room and then back toward the doorway. With everyone downstairs, he pulled a handkerchief out of his trouser pocket. Wrapping it around his hand, he lifted the sealed envelope that contained the ransom note from his shirt pocket. Because he had forgotten to place it in the crib, in his hurry to get Charlie out of the house earlier, he decided to place it on the radiator cover near the windowsill. He charged back down the steps.

"I found a ransom note on the windowsill. No one is to touch it." For a few seconds there was silence. Overtaken with fear, Anne and the Whatelys did not ask how he knew it was a ransom note. They were amazed at the Great Aviator's ability to think clearly. He had a calm demeanor and spoke as if he knew exactly what to do. While the progression of events was overwhelming for most of the Sorrel Hill residents; the Great Aviator was cool, as he guided the puzzle pieces into place with clear precision. No one had noticed a note. Betty Gow said nothing; she knew what it was. Lindbergh had not eyeballed her one time and she too was impressed with the Great Aviator's ability to act rationally even if he was the person straddling the line between perpetrator and victim.

Ten minutes later, with the local police on the way, the Great Aviator continued the plan. He called up his lawyer Henry Breckinridge and told him what had happened. Breckinridge said he and his wife Aida were on their way back. (They had just left Hopewell on Sunday after visiting). Lindbergh called the New Jersey

State Police in West Trenton. Lieutenant Daniel J. Dunn answered the call. The officer was unsure if what he was hearing was a prank or whether the person calling really was the Great Aviator. After a minute, Dunn called back and when the same voice answered he asked if he was speaking to Colonel Charles Lindbergh.

"Yes this is Colonel Lindbergh."

"Sir, the New Jersey State Police are on the way." After the local and the state police assured him that they were sending people out to the farm, and with his attorney Henry Breckinridge on the way, Lindbergh took a deep breath and waited for the night to play out. He smiled as he thought, "So far, so good!"

CHAPTER TWENTY-TWO
RED AND VIOLET PART

I t was a few minutes after nine o'clock when Red pulled his car off of Lydeker Street and into the driveway of Next Day Hill. He had sped all the way from Hopewell. The night watchman George Marshall didn't see Red drop her off. He kissed Violet goodbye and said he had to go visit his brother up in Hartford, even though he wanted to stop at Johannes and Marguerite Junge's house to reestablish his alibi. Not wanting to complicate things, he refrained from saying, "I love you" to Violet, but promised to give her a call as soon as he could. Violet walked inside the grounds and couldn't stop thinking about the evening. She knew that as soon as the press found about the baby, it would be real hard for her and Red to see each other because people were going to ask questions. Questions would surface not only about what they knew about the baby, but also their relationship. As Red cruised down the street, Violet remembered she had promised to go out with a man named Ernie Miller. Walking toward the house she saw his car pull up the drive. She stopped and walked back to the car where there were three other people. She decided she could use a drink and got inside the car. They sped off to the Peanut Grill in Orangeburg, New York where she would get her mind off the evening's events. It was a thirty-minute trip along the Hudson. Without explanation, Violet again found herself in the company of people that she knew nothing about. She wondered why her life had become so complicated.

It was only a short drive to the Junge's house for Red Johnson. He, like Betty had grown fond of the Junges. Marguerite's husband was disabled, and needed help getting around, so Red didn't mind driving him around on occasion. They all became good friends in a short amount of time. They were new immigrants to America and lived in a local apartment house. Red thought making an appearance at their apartment was a good idea, even if there was a four and one half hour gap between the time he saw William Boland and the time he arrived at their apartment. He had been paid a thousand dollars and more was coming his way as soon as Doc Condon was able to deliver the ransom money. To be safe, he was going to leave the money at his brother's house in Hartford.

Red was such a likeable guy, Violet believed him when he said he and Betty were just good friends. But Violet needed reassurance. She was troubled about the evening, especially the role she played in getting the Lindbergh baby from Hopewell to Princeton. She felt sad about the inability of the Lindberghs to bond with their only baby. She worried about the boy's future and she knew the only parent the boy ever knew was his nursemaid Betty. If Betty felt comfortable with the boy going to Germany, than she had to agree with it. People respected Betty; she was nice and seemed responsible.

The car with Violet, Ernie Miller and another couple pulled into the dirt parking lot of the local Orangeburg roadhouse bar that everyone called Peanuts. Like most speakeasies during prohibition, it was frequented by all the different ilk of the local population. Violet had been there before, and she had promised this new friend Ernie that she would go out with him for a drink. She did not tell Red that a man named Ernie Miller had asked her out to the roadhouse. She really didn't care because she knew the relationship wasn't going anywhere. But she told Ernie she would go, and she wanted to get something to drink, to clear her mind of all the restless thoughts. She was fixated on Red Johnson when Ernie asked her what she wanted to drink. She told him, "coffee without cream or sugar." "No alcohol?" he asked.

"No, I just want a cup of coffee." She thought a stiff cup of Joe might clear her head of the evening's cloudy events Ernie Miller was agitated and introduced Violet to another man who took a seat next to her. She was in no mood for chit-chat. She knew she needed to give Ernie some attention but she had trouble focusing. He seemed nice enough; he just wasn't her type. In her pocketbook was the cash Red had given her. She thought of the money and the baby. "Why did she keep the money?" She was willing to place her trust in the Norwegian but like most of the staff at Next Day she had her doubts about Lindbergh. He was no good. She made up her mind to give the money to her sister Emily so she could return to England.

Violet remembered what Red had said to her over and over. "Whatever you do Violet, do not tell anyone about tonight or any of the things we talked about." Red was stern, "I mean it." "Okay, okay I won't" Violet had replied.

Violet finished the coffee she started. She sat with Ernie and his friends for a few minutes before telling him she felt ill. Embarrassed, she asked him if he would take her home. Ernie seemed disappointed that the young lady he had met a few days earlier, who appeared so full of life, now seemed so quiet and uninterested. Violet was grappling with too many things that were weighing heavy on her mind. The short time she had spent at the roadhouse seemed like an eternity. In reality she had stayed only twenty minutes, but little did she know she had established an alibi that could be confirmed by at least three people. She had indeed been in Orangeburg when Charles Lindbergh's baby was taken, at least according to the report the Great Aviator had given to police. Roughly forty-five minutes after the abduction had supposedly taken place, she had made it to her bedroom at Next Day Hill.

Red stopped by the Junge's house to do as the Great Aviator had suggested, reinforce his alibi. After spending a few minutes, Red, Marguerite, and her husband went out for coffee. They took a scenic drive along the palisades before Red dropped Marguerite off at Next Day. He then took her husband home and headed up to Hartford, Connecticut to his brother's house.

CHAPTER TWENTY-THREE
THE GERMANS HEAD NORTH

H auptmann's dodge had rattled through the dirt roads that led to Kingston and up to the old Brunswick Pike. They were now speeding as fast as they could up to Route One into northern New Jersey. Able to make good time up the main highway through New Brunswick, they were already north of Edison's Menlo Park. Hauptmann's dodge barely touched the ground as the two men discussed their compensation for their roles in the abduction. Hauptmann was discussing ways to parlay the money into something bigger in the stock market, perhaps he and Anna could make a return trip to Germany. Doc Condon had already distributed the six thousand dollars with Fisch, Hauptmann, Johnson, Schleser and his wife, each getting a thousand. Condon also gave Red another six hundred dollars to give to Violet, with the hope of keeping her quiet. The rest of the money was to be used for expenses. After a few days, Condon would get the fifty thousand dollars of ransom money and distribute it amongst the four Germans who had the principle responsibilities. Hauptmann and Fisch had to pick up the baby, get supplies to the Schlesers who would be the caregivers, and then handle the ransom payoff. Once everything had settled, Fisch was to leave for Germany and then meet up with the Schlesers in Germany where they would tie up any loose ends with the adoptive parents. Richard Hauptmann would remain in the states with his wife until everything had blown over. Anna Hauptmann had no idea of the scheme. She held down her bakery job while her conniving husband was an active member of a kidnap scheme. Condon and Lindbergh had promised everyone they had it all figured out and the only thing they had to do was keep quiet and complete the job. Condon had devised a way to communicate with them through the local Bronx newspapers and then they would set a date for the payoff, which was going to take place near the old dock at Throg's Neck. To do this they had to make sure the police were not involved in the payoff. They would use Lindbergh's power to keep the police far away from the payoff scene. Throg's Neck would be dark and quiet; the perfect place for the payoff. The Great Aviator was confident he could fully control the investigation and the payoff. He had promised to pay with unmarked money. But Fisch and Hauptmann both had trepidations about what would ensue regarding their role in the kidnapping, even if Lindbergh had assured them that he would take care of everything as long as they did their job. Since they were always dabbling in schemes they wanted to make sure their bases were covered. But overall none of the conspirators realized the scope of what they were involved in, nor did they anticipate the intense public fallout that might follow. And they certainly weren't expecting any massive media onslaught. For Fisch, it was another scheme to make some quick cash, simple as that. If someone as powerful as Charles Lindbergh was in charge, he would keep everybody safe. Although at times he looked uptight, Fisch seemed carefree about his latest scheme. As soon as everything calmed down, he would be heading back to Germany on a steamer. Lindbergh wanted him to assist in any way necessary to keep everything secret. But Hauptmann knew Lindbergh was extremely powerful and it scared him. Lindbergh had more to lose than anyone and he was not so sure. He didn't want to get into any trouble because he was not a citizen, and he did have a criminal record back in Germany. And he had Anna to worry about even if his marriage was on shaky ground because of his sexual promiscuity. Financially, he was doing okay, making some money here and there, some of it legitimate and some of it not, but he knew he could make even more money in America than back in the totally stagnant economic mess of post-war Kamenz, Germany.

CHAPTER TWENTY-FOUR
BACK IN HOPEWELL

After notifying the police and speaking with his attorney Henry Breckinridge, the Great Aviator now waited for the rest of the world to find out that his son had been kidnapped. The first officers to arrive at the Lindbergh estate were Hopewell Borough Police Chief Harry Wolfe and Constable Charles Williamson. They entered the house and were immediately led up to the nursery. The first thing they noticed was the faint, muddy footprints that Betty had made around the room. Even though the footprints were not real obvious, the officers detected them immediately. They were not however in the Great Aviator's master plan. Betty had taken it upon herself to doctor up the crime scene, and the prints were the only real bit of evidence that suggested an intruder. Lindbergh and Betty had made sure there were no fingerprints found anywhere, but now there were footprints. It didn't coincide with Lindbergh's plan of confounding the police. The officers also noticed that there was a dab of mud on a leather suitcase that was directly beneath the window. And then Lindbergh pointed out the ransom note on the radiator cover beneath the right window. He was quick to add to the confusion. "I didn't want to touch it because I thought there might be fingerprints."

"Colonel, we should not touch anything. There may be fingerprints all over this room."

The Great Aviator expected the reaction and quickly took over the conversation. "I know that; no one has touched anything. I will have someone come in and do the fingerprints. I have been in touch with the state police. I'm sure they have experts." The Great Aviator's control of the police investigation had begun.

In no time the Great Aviator was making decisions about how the investigation was going to be conducted. And as he expected, the people around him couldn't hide their awe and reverence. The officers said nothing else about the fingerprints. They were unaware that Lindbergh had relied on Betty Gow to go over the room with a damp cloth to remove all fingerprints. The lack of fingerprints would be the beginning of a crystal ball of confusion. The more you gazed into it, the more frustrated you became and that was exactly what the Great Aviator's plan was designed to do.

The two officers carefully stretched their necks closer to the window so they could see the ground below. It was obvious because of the wind pushing beneath the window, that it might not have been totally closed. The wind also rattled the shutter but it appeared to be secure against the house. Officers Williamson and Wolfe didn't say much, but they turned away from the window and continued to peruse the room. With gut wrenching courage they gazed down into the crib. For a moment they paused simultaneously, and then the Great Aviator invited them to take a look outside. The three men exited the room. The officers nodded toward each other as they descended the stairs and on to the outside of the house. They were closely following behind the Great Aviator as he took the lead.

In no time Lindbergh had led the men around the corner of the house directly beneath the window and then over to where he had placed the ladder a couple hours earlier. The officers stared at the ladder almost as if they were in shock.

"They climbed this ladder?" asked Constable Williamson, shocked by how narrow it looked. Looking at it closer, he noticed something else. "Looks like whoever came down that ladder might have snapped it, there's a crack near the side rail, near the top. It appears to be broken." Lindbergh was very calm as he remembered back in November when he was testing it, the rung and the rail cracked almost immediately. Williamson continued. "He could not have weighed very much, I mean, geez, there's no disturbance on the ground. It doesn't appear as if this little cat-walk around has been disturbed either." Williamson was referring to the builder's temporary boardwalk. It was placed around the house in order to keep the Sourland clay off of people's shoes and out of the house.

The men centered themselves beneath the window. They looked closer at the ground beneath the window to see if there was anything, possibly indentations from a fall. Off to the side, they noticed several slight marks one half-inch deep, where the ladder had pushed into the soft clay.

With little emotion Lindbergh interjected. "I hope the kidnapper didn't drop the boy."

The Great Aviator had floated two possible theories. The first theory suggested that the kidnappers used the ladder to snatch the baby and the second one proposed the idea that they might even had dropped the baby. The three men stared upward in disbelief at the second floor nursery window. With a mix of bewilderment and intimidation the officers redirected their stares at Lindbergh, and shook their heads. Across the top of the hardwood trees the freezing north wind howled.

CHAPTER TWENTY-FIVE
THE GERMANS REPORT IN

F ish and Hauptmann like everyone else involved in the kidnapping, were anxious for the evening to end. Methodically they crossed the bridge toward the City, where they deceptively slipped into the massive but sleepy metropolis. The strange duo immediately drove to the vacant row house at the end of Jerome Avenue where the whole group had met earlier that morning. They parked the dodge in the front and seeing no one around because of the biting weather, they entered through the front door. Condon was in the sparse living room waiting for them, trying to keep warm. There was an old coal fired furnace in the basement; it took the chill off the house but the night was growing colder. Steam whistled as it crept through the radiator pipes, squeaking along the way and mixing with the cooler air in the room. Condon had been playing solitaire with a set of German playing cards that had been left from an earlier meeting. The old man fingered the cards, flipping them back and forth between his fingers and then pulling them all together, he banged the deck on the table. He rose up tall from the table, and looked down on the two men as he faced them. He held on tightly to the cards.

"I have not seen the bell bottom, the Norwegian," he said. "Hauptmann and Fisch looked at each other with a look of surprise. "He said he vas going to stop and see Marguerite Junge and then drive to Hartford to see his brother." Hauptmann mumbled Connecticut because he couldn't pronounce it. "You von't see him tonight. He's gone," he said, recovering nicely.

"Red said Lindbergh told him to make sure he checked in with somevone to verify his alibi and then go back to his brother's house."

"Oh, uh I uh, forgot he changed that part of the plan," said the old man resembling an absent minded college professor. He banged the cards on the table as if he was going to reshuffle, but he was more interested in details. He was excited about the kidnapping and anxious to find out if all their planning had been successful.

"Well, now gentlemen, please tell me how it went," the old man prodded. "I need to know if everything went as we had planned." It was Fisch's turn to speak and he too seemed excited. He spoke in his broken English with a Yiddish inflection.

"The maid went along and did her job just like Lindbergh wanted. As far as we know there was nobody who knew what we were doing except Gow and Lindbergh. Ve never even talked to Schleser and his wife, ve just vanted to get the hell out of there before the cops started looking. The Norvegian picked Violet up in Princeton by the Garden Theatre on Nassau Street and drove her back to Englewood, to Next Day Hill. Well at least that's vhat he was supposed to do. We left for the motorway before them and did not see them since then. Ve did not see them and they did not pass us." Fisch was still excited, he had said more in one minute than he had throughout the entire morning meeting. Hauptmann was more reserved and tired. He was anxious to pick up his wife and head home to his house in the Bronx.

Sometime after eleven o'clock, Condon found himself alone as Hauptmann and Fisch went about their business. Like he usually did, Hauptmann would pick his wife Anna up at the bakery and grab something to eat there. Before he headed in that direction, he dropped his German partner off in downtown Manhattan. Fisch was his usual self not telling anyone where he was heading. He melted into the steely shadows of the city's busiest borough. As the night wore on, there were fewer cars traveling through the city and Jerome Ave was deserted. Condon walked up Jerome, grabbed a trolley and headed over to his favorite nightspot, the Bickford Restaurant in Fordham Square. He wanted to deliver his slanted orations of jaded philosophy to the small groups of young college students he would encounter. Many knew the old man from his teaching days and part-time lectures at Fordham, or his classes at the College of New Rochelle; others had heard his patriotic ramblings before at the restaurant. Sometime during the discussion, the word had reached the restaurant that the Lindbergh baby had been kidnapped. Condon went into an emotional and obsequious rant. He couldn't hide his passion, as he described the anguish the parents were experiencing and the 'Little Eaglet', who was now caught in the dirty grip of unpredictable underworld figures.

"How could they do such a thing to such a sweet little child and his wonderful and courageous parents? Colonel Lindbergh is such a great man; he has changed the course of history." Condon continued as he and his company offered potential profiles of the kidnappers. For Condon it couldn't have been more obvious. It was a crime perpetrated by the mafia. He couldn't help but criticize "those wops," those Italian immigrants who were usurping the laws and contributing to moral decay. After an hour Condon became cautious, as he didn't want to give away his involvement in the kidnapping. Sometime around one o'clock, he headed back to his residence on Decatur Street. He would have to meet up again at least one more time with Fisch and Hauptmann before he entered the case as the go-between. Then he hoped he could finalize plans to distribute the payoff. The three men would return to the vacant house on Jerome Avenue in a few days to assess what they needed to do. Once the ransom money was paid out and little Charlie was on his way to Germany, there would be no reason to meet again. To do so would only invite trouble.

Fisch's plans included him going back to Leipzeg, Germany his hometown. Germany was still reeling from the Great War and was ravaged from economic depression. Although the ten thousand dollars he would make from the kidnapping wouldn't make him the richest man in Leipzeg, it would allow him to live comfortably for a while. As the night wore on, Fisch was feeling tired and his stomach felt queasy from not eating, but unlike everyone else that was involved in the evening's events, he had not shown much worry about how things had played out. For him, it was just another crazy scheme to make money. Shortly after Hauptmann dropped him off, the frail German went back to his apartment and quickly fell into a deep sleep. Hauptmann had other plans, and was anxious to get to the bakery. There were always tasty morsels of food lying around that would vanquish those hunger pangs. The day had been long and he needed to replenish his body with nourishment. For Anna and him, it would be a typical evening after a long day's work. He felt confident she wouldn't interrogate him about his whereabouts or ask why he was running late, but he knew if he had to, he could conjure up a credible excuse.

The Hauptmanns returned to their quiet Bronx home. Anna had already fallen asleep and unlike everyone else, Richard struggled to get to sleep. His mind weighed heavy, as he kept thinking about the little Lindbergh baby, wondering where he was on such a cold, windy night. He prayed someone wouldn't put the finger on him for the role he played in the child's abduction.

CHAPTER TWENTY-SIX
VIOLET RETURNS TO NEXT DAY HILL

Violet did not bother to speak to anyone as she made her way to her bedroom. She was tired and confused from a stressful evening. Frustration interfused with anger seemed to be taking its toll on the English serving-maid. Her fair complexion turned pasty; her wholesome demeanor now gone. She felt angry about the Lindbergh boy. Her heart ached for the child. She knew he had become a burden to the Great Aviator, and now she feared he had become a pawn in a dangerous game. For the first time, Violet wondered if she too had emerged as a pawn to one of the world's most powerful men. Stress and fatigue had made her eyes swollen and red. Constricting blood vessels called out, contrasting her puffy, white face. Still, Violet was determined to get to the bottom of the events that had transpired, and had made up her mind to call Red during her morning break, if she could reach him.

She shed her clothes and washed off her heavy makeup. She brushed her black, wavy hair. On her nightstand, a gold wind-up Westclox read 11:13. She crawled beneath the covers of her bed. Her mind would not stop replaying the evening's events. It was all about Red and the baby. Her body grew tired despite the uneasiness and a racing heart. She closed her eyes. She let her body go and drifted off into the first stage of sleep. It only took a couple minutes for her body to go limp. A commotion downstairs startled her, and she pulled herself up in the bed. She checked the clock again. This time it was 11:19. Not realizing where she was for a second, she widened her eyes to the familiar surroundings. Confused, she thought that she had been asleep for a long time. Her body's rhythm was off-kilter, as she heard muffled voices in the rooms down stairs. Lifting herself out of the bed, she walked over and opened her door to a crack. She could hear Mrs. Morrow sobbing in the downstairs sitting room.

"Someone has taken my grand-child, little Charlie has been stolen. My poor daughter, I need to talk to my daughter." Violet listened as the staff was gathering in the parlor to console her. She could hear her friend Emily trying to show some empathy. And she could hear Septimus too. All the people that seemed to care for her were doing the same for Mrs. Morrow. Violet was overcome with guilt. She knew the real story, but what was she supposed to do?

Violet looked at the clock again out of habit and it was now half-past eleven. She continued to listen to the cacophony of voices, all of them trying to do their best to consul the matriarch of the Morrow family. Discerning the voices, she knew something was ringing hollow. Now she wondered if she might have been duped that evening. Motionless she sat, listening to opinions and perceptions as she remembered what Red had said to her. "Just don't say anything to anybody regardless of what you may hear." She thought to herself. "Did Anne or Mrs. Morrow have any idea of what the Great Aviator was up to?" She leaned in toward the doorway listening to the downstairs conversation. Again, she interrogated herself. "What were Lindbergh and Red up to? "They better not pull me into this scheme" she thought. Before too long, she could hear the local police entering through the main door of Next Day Hill. Immediately, they started asking difficult questions and she could hear Mrs. Morrow's anguished responses. She knew Anne and Mrs. Morrow had no idea of what the Great Aviator was up to. She was telling the police that" her son in law was sitting in the living room with Anne, when he heard a noise outside." He said "he ran up to check on the baby and the window was open and a note had been left on the radiator cover. The note was demanding ransom." Mrs. Morrow repeatedly told the staff and the police what her daughter had told her. She kept repeating the word kidnapping. She had taken the information from her daughter and condensed into just a few sentences.

Violet stayed up stairs keeping an ear to the cracked door. She listened intently. The local police were now asking Mrs. Morrow a great deal of questions about the staff. Was there anyone on staff who could have been involved?" Mrs. Morrow responded swiftly. "Oh no I do not believe that is possible. My servants and staff are all good people. I don't think they could do something as sinister as that."

Violet was asking herself some questions of her own. Who were the Mayers anyway? Were they really going to take the boy to Germany and care for him or was someone else already in place to do that? Were the police already considering her a suspect? She quickly gathered her thoughts. She had to call Red in the morning. Surely he would tell her what was going on. She decided not to say anything to anyone and she broke into a nervous cry. She wondered about the

Lindbergh boy. She went over all kinds of scenarios in her mind. Where was that baby? Was Red involved? Was he a kidnapper? Suddenly she went back to a previous thought. Was she being set up? She pondered that question. Was she the one the police were going to point the finger at? Were the two Germans the real culprits? Her thoughts ran wild and Red was in the middle of them. She had to see him to find out was going on. She loved Red. He would help her. He loved her. They were lovers and he would save her from all this mess. It would all work out. Violet composed herself. With a tissue she wiped her eyes and nose; then quickly descended the steps.

"What is the commotion, Mrs. Morrow?" She asked.

"The baby, the baby, someone has taken the baby," Mrs. Morrow cried.

Violet responded. "Charlie? Someone took Charlie? Where was Betty or Anne? Weren't they there?" She found herself taking part in the deception. She certainly had an idea where the baby was but she did not lead on. She remembered what Red had told her and said nothing about the evening's events.

One of the local detectives who had arrived with the police, immediately started asking Mrs. Morrow and her staff a great deal of questions. After about ten minutes of their interrogation, they turned towards Violet. The heavier detective asked Violet if she knew anything about the baby's whereabouts. Violet acted surprised. "Who, me? Why, why I don't know anything about the baby's disappearance." She sounded nervous and unsure of herself.

"Just asking Miss. Sharpe," responded the detective.

Mrs. Morrow was anxious and uptight, and offered an idea that seemed to give her some sense of assurance. "I bet that son of law of mine is playing a trick on everyone"

"That's a dirty trick to play on someone Mrs. Morrow, would Colonel Lindbergh really do something like that?" asked the detective.

"Oh yes, he does that kind of thing all the time."

"Hmm, that's surprising for someone like him," replied the detective.

Mrs. Morrow shook her head. "If only you knew." The two detectives looked at each other and raised their eyebrows. It was not response they were expecting. Mrs. Morrow called back to the Hopewell house with the hope that it was all a big joke, but she could not get through to speak to her daughter. The phone line was busy. Violet sat on the couch. She felt paranoid as well as guilty, as she watched the people in the room trying to make sense out of everything. Her body remained still except for her head, as she turned in all directions listening to everyone. She thought about what she knew, and she was taken aback by the questions posed by the detective. As if he was trying to antagonize her, he interrogated her some more. He turned toward the serving maid.

"Have you been here all day?" Without even waiting for an answer the other detective went on to the next question. "Was anyone beside you, and the staff, and Mrs. Morrow of course, aware that Mr. Lindbergh and his wife were staying in Hopewell instead of here in Englewood? You did say that Mrs. Morrow didn't you, that they were not supposed to stay in Hopewell tonight?"

"Yes, that's right. They usually stay here during the week and go to the farmhouse on the weekend?" Again he turned toward Violet, "Miss Sharpe, is that right?"

"Yes," replied Violet, again not sounding too sure of herself. The detective pressed on.

"Did you talk to anyone today, or tell anyone that Colonel Lindbergh was going to be at the farmhouse?"

Violet's face flushed. Her puffy eyes glanced away from the detective. For a second she hesitated then spoke. "I did talk to someone on the phone that I had met at the bakery in town, a man named Ernie."

"Did you say anything about the child to him? Is Ernie your boyfriend?"

"No, of course not. The child's name never came up. You really have no right getting into my private life." The detectives were actually asking questions of everyone, but Violet felt like she was being interrogated unfairly. It was obvious in her tone.

"Why do you keep asking me questions?" She asked. "Why don't you ask some of the other people around here the same questions?"

"Miss Sharpe, this is routine procedure."

Mrs. Morrow interjected. "Violet, they're asking all of us questions. We have to find out what happened. However, it seems to me you should be asking these questions in Hopewell. We have an excellent staff here at Next Day Hill, and Miss Sharpe is an especially good person who would never be involved in such a terrible crime." Mrs. Morrow lost her composure, and she started to sob again. Looking at the policemen with a trembling voice, she pleaded. "Please find our little baby."

Violet felt guilty. She did know something about the boy and his disappearance. She felt like she was betraying the woman who had just complemented her. But she remembered what Red said to her. "Don't say anything to anyone about what they did. For the baby's sake Lindbergh doesn't want anybody at all in on what was going on." She still couldn't fight the guilty feelings, even though she thought the child would be better off with two parents that acted like parents and gave him the time and attention that he needed. Above everything else, she knew the boy needed to be loved.

"Miss Sharpe, we would like to talk to you some more, maybe you could think back, recall what you did this evening. Could you call us?" the detective asked.

Violet started crying and could not stop. She kept repeating herself. "I don't know anything, I don't know anything. Why do you need to ask me all these questions? I feel so bad for little Charlie."

"Miss Sharpe, this is just routine procedure. Maybe the child will be found tonight and all this will be over."

Trying to take the attention off of Violet, Mrs. Morrow called the Hopewell residence again. It was now after midnight and this time she was able to get through. She spoke with her son in-law. "Charles, did you hide the baby somewhere?"

The Great Aviator was quick to respond. "Of course not, you know I would not do something like that, this is serious." His demeanor on the phone was cool and collective. "I will call you when I find something out." He hung up the phone.

CHAPTER TWENTY-SEVEN
THE GREAT AVIATOR TAKES CONTROL

Lindbergh wore a pair of dark trousers and a brown, leather, flying jacket. Having the 'Officer in Charge' status fed his ego and quest for power. He was non-stop, roaming around the house and grounds barking orders, taking over like an army sergeant in a foxhole. He was comfortable with his new role as overseer of the kidnapping, but the constant swarming of people was overwhelming. Questions were coming at him fast and furious. It was imperative he control the investigation, so he could keep his end of the bargain with the Germans, but he wondered if too much attention would complicate the situation. For the first time, he also seemed unsure if the child would be able to leave the country without being noticed. Having Charlie's golden locks trimmed would help disguise the boy, but it could also bring about suspicion. Doubt and uncertainty came with the kidnap operation, and Lindbergh channeled his energy as a way of dealing with his anxiety.

Anne sat on the couch watching her husband with tremendous respect and awe as she tried to hide her despair. The situation however, was beginning to wear her down. Not wanting anyone to see her, she lifted herself off the couch and walked up the stairwell. Charles excused himself from Officer Williamson and followed her up the stairs. Anne needed a quick respite from the increasingly stressing situation. She sat on the bed holding back the tears. Charles took a seat right next to her. He was not the type to hug her, but he assured her that everything would be okay.

"How in the world did they know that we would be here? And how would anyone find us out here in these mountains? I mean to get here you have to travel a lot of dirt roads in the dark." Anne seemed desperate, as she waited for the right answer. When her stoic husband did not respond, she left the question unanswered.

One would have expected the crime scene to be filled with trauma and panic, but the Great Aviator and Betty Gow remained cool and collective. His wife, considering the circumstances also handled the situation calmly. The Whateleys appeared to be more distraught than the parents and the nursemaid. Anne as she usually did in stressful situations, hid within the confines of her upstairs bedroom. She really wanted to be alone, away from her husband. Deep down she thought her husband was up to his old tricks, and was playing a prank. She pulled out some stationary, and composed a letter to her mother in law that started out by saying "Charles has done it again, hiding the baby from me." She hesitated and then stopped. After some thought, she decided against writing for the moment. Again she suppressed the tears. "What if the baby really was kidnapped by some group demanding ransom money?" She wondered how her husband could continue the prank, since the house was now invaded by police officers. So many people were visibly upset. Deep down Anne was about fed up with her husband's callous jokes, but this time he had gone too far. She remembered once before; he had hid the baby in the clothes hamper for an entire hour. There was no way he could continue such a joke since the police had been notified. This time it was real. He had not produced the child like he had done before, and now there were people from all over the community out searching for her only child. Investigators were asking questions of everyone especially the Great Aviator.

"Go over it again Colonel Lindbergh, what you heard and what you did."

Lindbergh responded to the officer. "As I already told you gentlemen, we were sitting downstairs in the parlor. I heard a crack or a popping sound like a stick or a crate getting crushed. I ran up the stairs looked in on the child, and he was not in his crib. I immediately noticed the letter on the radiator cover and the muddy footprints on the floor. I called Anne, and told her they had taken our boy. We ran downstairs, looked around and proceeded to call the police."

"Was there anyone who was angry at you or your wife? Did you know anyone who would have taken the child?"

Lindbergh's response was quick. "No, no one at all."

At about midnight, there was some commotion. The head of the New Jersey State Police was making his way through the front door and into the growing crowd of people. Not an overly tall man but stocky with a solid build, H. Norman Schwarzkopf made his presence known as he walked over to meet the Great Aviator. A West Point graduate and a political appointee, Schwarzkopf walked upright and proud. He was clad in the Jersey blue uniform of the state police. His dark blue riding pants were adorned with a yellow cavalry stripe down the side, and they were tucked into shiny black boots. The uniform was neat and impressive. His blue woolen overcoat had the triangular state police patch on the shoulder; a black belt crossed his chest. His hair was military as was everything else about him, but he had an air of sophistication about him. Unfortunately like everyone else, he seemed to tense up when the Great Aviator stuck out his hand and introduced himself. When he did, Schwarzkopf nodded as if to say "I'm sorry," but he immediately went to work, asking Lindbergh to give him the details surrounding his missing child. He too asked Lindbergh to go over everything again, including him hearing the snapping sound outside the window. After listening to the Great Aviator for a few minutes, Schwarzkopf explained that he was putting some of his best people on the job. Buster Keaton would be the chief investigator and Frank Kelly would be checking for fingerprints all over the bedroom, on the ransom note, and also on the ladder outside. They would check the footprints in and outside the house, and they would begin questioning everyone in the house with the exception of the parents, who he assumed would be too distraught and unable to endure any painful questioning. In addition, there would be inspectors at the Morrow residence asking some questions of the staff. The two men walked outside, and immediately Lindbergh took over the conversation and told him what he wanted the New Jersey Police to do. Schwarzkopf, like everybody else listened in agreement. The Great Aviator had placed himself in charge of the investigation.

The men walked swiftly over undecipherable footprints in the muddy ground. In the dark, without a flashlight, Colonel Schwarzkopf let Lindbergh deliberately lead two of his troopers around the estate to the ladder. Lindbergh looked at the troopers to see what response this would evoke. All three men stared at each other, shrugged and then said nothing. The Great Aviator called for Colonel Schwarzkopf. Quickly, he walked toward him. Now all the men were staring at the ladder. Schwarzkopf immediately gave the order not to touch it, hoping to be able to lift some prints when Frank Kelly the finger-print man arrived. Schwarzkopf hoped he could lift some fingerprints from the side rails of the ladder or possibly the rungs. Next, the men walked closer to the house, and looked up toward the baby's nursery. There in the damp ground was the weak indentation that Lindbergh had made earlier with the ladder. Schwarzkopf looked at Lindbergh.

"Why would they move the ladder? If they had the child in hand, moving the ladder would slow them down. Wouldn't you say so, Colonel?" Lindbergh was surprised by Schwarzkopf's question. He had not thought of that. It would be one of several things that Lindbergh had not thought of.

Still, Lindbergh was not intimidated by Schwarzkopf's presence. His insight and military bravado did not impress him. The Superintendent seemed tentative and so far, had seemed to go along with everything that the Great Aviator had said.

Lindbergh perceived him to be unsure of himself about criminal investigations; he did an unusual amount of nodding when he spoke to him, and the man in charge had quickly figured out that Schwarzkopf could be manipulated.

As Lindbergh discussed the ladder, he worried that he might have gotten a little carried away when he built that ladder a few months back, but he knew as long as he was in charge of the investigation that wouldn't be a problem. He had used his engineering skills to devise an extension ladder that would work and be long enough to reach the second floor window. The actual craftsmanship from a carpenter's perspective may have been weak, but one could tell quickly that the ladder was not created by just anyone. It would be a piece of evidence that would confuse the police, and now that's exactly what it was supposed to do. But Lindbergh also knew that Hauptmann was a carpenter by trade, and he knew that if he had to, he could point the finger at the German immigrant. The Great Aviator had thought of different backup plans should something go wrong, but he hoped it would not come down to that. He had also keenly scanned over the cast of Germans and concluded that Hauptmann would be an easy target. The immigrant was a carpenter, acted arrogant, but in many ways he seemed naïve. During their meeting Hauptmann appeared to be nervous around him. Lindbergh always kept a backup plan stowed away for just about everything he did.

Colonel Schwarzkopf ordered Officer Keaton to examine the ladder in an attempt to extract any possible evidence. This evidence in his mind was huge. But the leader of the New Jersey Police had no idea that Charles Lindbergh had made sure that everyone who was there had already placed their fingerprints on the ladder. It was now Norman Schwarzkopf's turn to be deceived.

The two men walked together into the house. Schwarzkopf asked Lindbergh if there was a room where the two of them could talk. He then asked the Great Aviator if he could see the ransom note that he had found on the windowsill. Lindbergh grew a bit nervous, as he got up and led the leader of the New Jersey police up to the nursery. He pointed to the radiator grill beneath the window.

"As I said, we have already sent for our fingerprint man Colonel, he should be here shortly." Schwarzkopf looked around to see a neat room with the exception of some very faint, light orange footprints under the window. As if Lindbergh hadn't already noticed, Schwarzkopf pointed out pieces of evidence.

"These prints are not that obvious, but if you look closely you can see them. I noticed there is a smudge of what appears to be yellowish clay on that suitcase beneath the window and the same type of faint smudges on the child's bedding as well. This mud or clay seems to be in just a few places and it's barely visible. It's interesting; the kidnapper did not leave any large clumps or deposits of the clay anywhere, just smudges. I wonder if there is any of the stuff on the ladder.

Schwarzkopf was using his store detective experience to try to find the perpetrator of a kidnapping. At about twelve-thirty when word of the crime was trickling out across the country's media conduits, the first onslaught of media people was navigating those same dirt roads up to Sorrel Hill. Since the Great Aviator was calling the shots, he was counting on them to completely destroy the outside crime scene, which meant they would stomp over any footprints and run their fingers and palms up and down the homemade ladder obliterating any trace of his own prints. Even though he had taken the time to disguise his footprints and had wiped the ladder down, he still worried he did not get all of his own prints off the ladder. But he knew that the fingerprints and footprints of hundreds of reporters would add to the confusion, and would serve to frustrate the investigators even more. Since the fingerprint man had not yet arrived, his plan of compromising the crime scene was going to work perfectly.

By one o'clock in the morning the Lindbergh's estate was crawling with not only local newspaper people but also anxious sightseers. Some of the curious had traveled from the local towns and cities, once word had spread to the radio. There were the gritty local folks who shared the same hilly terrain as the Lindberghs, and then there were the outsiders. People from obscure villages around Hopewell like Ringoes, Lambertville, and Pennington. City slickers from Trenton and more sophisticated townspeople from Princeton even attempted to make their way up to scene of the kidnapping.

From New York City a slew of reporters were en route. The Hearst International news organization was already sending a dozen of its best reporters. The United Press and the Associated Press were also on their way with another dozen people each. Despite the darkness, the lights on Sorrel Hill shone brightly; like a beacon they pulled people towards the crime scene. A steady parade of automobiles was clogging up every road that led to the Lindbergh estate. In fact, it had become easy. Follow the car lights in front of you; they will lead you to the scene of the crime.

Inside the deceivingly tight fieldstone house, things had become claustrophobic. There were state policemen, detectives, reporters, the staff who were huddled in the back serving quarters, the Lindberghs and Henry Breckinridge and his wife. Breckinridge, whom Lindbergh befriended shortly after marrying Anne, was not only his attorney but also his personal advisor. Unaware of the Great Aviator's master plan, he was committed to serving him with his great public relations skills. With previous experience in Woodrow Wilson's administration, he knew a great deal of people, and he was determined like everyone else in the inner circle to do whatever he could to ensure the safe return of the Lindbergh baby. But unfortunately like everyone else, he too would be exploited. In essence, he had become the Great Aviator's right hand man and he was going to 'orchestrate' as Lindbergh fed him the 'sheet music'.

The police looked on as the two men organized a makeshift press conference for a select group of newspaper people that Charles Lindbergh knew and trusted. He liked them because they had written flattering articles about him after his flight. Now the Great Aviator was giving them the first jaded bits of information; he was putting the spin on his deception in the crowded confines of his living room. With two other colonels by his side, Attorney Breckinridge and Superintendent Schwarzkopf, the Great Aviator began to implement his strategy.

"Gentlemen, we believe a syndicate group of gangsters has taken our child. Outside, there is a ladder that we suspect was used to take the child from his crib. Anne and I are pleading with these kidnappers to respond and inform us as to what they want. We will negotiate and follow whatever steps they think are pertinent to the safe return of our child. It is extremely important that we follow a plan that must be executed in secret so that Charlie is not harmed. We appreciate your cooperation."

The two men had said nothing of the ransom note, as the Great Aviator wanted to proceed with caution when it came to making the payoff to the Germans. He had to wait for Condon to make his appearance, and then the two men would follow the script they had laid out. The diverse aggregate of people nodded in agreement, as the father of the missing child displayed his concerns. But he also made broad assumptions about who the kidnappers were and how they would proceed to get the baby back. Anyone attached to the investigation may have wondered what exactly their role was going to be in the investigation, but they stood back in awe as the Great Aviator ran the show.

The Hopewell house was turning into a scene of mass confusion. Beside the local police and the state police, there were reporters who entered the house with Lindbergh's permission. The same people that Lindbergh seemed to avoid were now permitted to enter his house on the very night of the supposed kidnapping. Lindbergh wasn't struggling to be polite as usual. Instead, in a total reversal of his typical behavior, he asked Ollie Whateley to fix sandwiches for the intrusive crowd. The scene was a convolution and a diversion; it was like a party; people were eating and interacting with one another. It was exactly what he wanted.

Throughout the night, determined troopers worked feverishly looking for clues, on and off the grounds. The house on Sorrel Hill was ablaze, with every incandescent light bulb glowing brightly. Wide-eyed and still alert, the Great Aviator moved about with unlimited energy. With his rifle in one hand and a trooper by his side, he played the role of an anxious father waiting for his missing son to come home. He was never frantic and always collective, which supported his shrewd ability to deceive. Showing little emotion, he reviled in the attention and savored the role as the 'Officer in Charge'. Five years after his famous flight, Charles Lindbergh had once again reclaimed the world spotlight. And now with that light shining on him, he took the helm. He called every shot and delegated orders. With little experience in criminal matters, Colonel Norman Schwarzkopf and his likewise inexperienced band of state troopers tap-danced behind the man in the spotlight.

At daybreak, just ten hours after the Great Aviator handed little Charlie off to Violet Sharpe, he was at ease sitting at the breakfast table. All night long Ollie Whately had been providing coffee and sandwiches for everyone, from reporters and lawmen to the staff. Now he was making a hearty breakfast for the Great Aviator. His ability to eat at a time of crisis surprised many of those present. Most people ten hours after having their child abducted; would have found eating a difficult chore. Such was not the case for the man behind the abduction. He consumed a robust meal of bacon and eggs. His demeanor was calm. He laughed. He ate. More than once, he nonchalantly joked with Colonel Schwarzkopf. This odd behavior had surprised the New Jersey Police Chief, as well as a few other lawmen who had earlier observed the collective Lindbergh conducting his son's search with a casual indifference.

By late morning, the state police had successfully evicted the media from the estate. The newspapermen had unknowingly completed their destruction of the crime scene. Now they were shuffling back and forth from Sorrel Hill to the Gebhart Hotel and Lucheonette in downtown Hopewell. When the press got too close to the driveway, the state police would give them the boot. Those that did get close, (merely a handful of reporters) had become pawns of the Great Aviator. He used them to disseminate his gangster strategy. That morning and afternoon, troopers had dispersed themselves throughout the area, asking people what they heard and what they saw. Some neighbors admitted hearing dogs barking unusually loud, but mostly everyone responded by saying 'they didn't see or hear anything unusual.' One person had witnessed an interesting event the day before, throwing up a red flag for the investigators. Much to the displeasure of the Great Aviator, the young man he watched collecting his mail the day before, told police early that morning, that he saw a man with a ladder in his car on the day of the kidnapping around six o'clock. High school student Benny Lupica casually mentioned that to a trooper before heading off to Princeton Day School. Later in the day, the state police went to his house; asking him to recall the incident. When he told them what he had seen, they asked him if he could ride over to the Lindbergh house for a few minutes. Lupica told them he didn't mind. Lupica had not even heard about the kidnapping until he got to Princeton Day School. He then figured out why there were so many people milling around the dirt road near his house, asking questions of everyone, including him. He departed for school having no knowledge of the kidnapping involving Charles Lindbergh's son. But at his school everyone was talking about it. Students even asked him if he ever saw Lindbergh and he said he had not. As a matter of fact he told them, he wasn't really sure what he looked like because he didn't read the papers. Benny Lupica was a typical teenager. But he thought about the man he saw with the ladders. He was well dressed and his face was well hidden; all he really noticed was the ladder. There was one thing however that Benny Lupica was sure of. The car that he saw with ladders protruding from the passenger side window had New Jersey plates.

Lupica rode on the running board of the police car up the winding driveway to the house. He was led into the garage, where the investigation team was assembled. The Great Aviator was summoned from the house and walked tall into the garage.

"Colonel Lindbergh, this is Ben Lupica. He is the young man who claims he saw a well-dressed man with ladders in his car yesterday afternoon." The Great Aviator stared straight into young Ben Lupica's eyes. Lupica didn't seem to recognize him. Lindbergh took no chances. He nervously dismissed the young man.

"Look, I need to take care of my wife. I'm more worried about her right now. You can send the boy home, it is nothing. Thanks." The Great Aviator quickly went back to the house and climbed the stairs to see his wife. Before he entered their bedroom, he stopped in the bathroom. He flushed his face with some cold water. Looking into the mirror, he saw his reflection staring back at him. He flared his nostrils, closed his eyes and gathered his thoughts. He mumbled at his reflection. "Damn kid! I am surprised he didn't recognize who I was." He shook his head toward the mirror. "That boy better keep his big mouth shut." Walking out of the bathroom he took a deep breath, and then went in to check on Anne.

Downstairs, the police were equally baffled by Lindbergh's departure. They told young Ben Lupica that they would be back in touch. They wondered what brought on Lindbergh's behavior. The one trooper shrugged his shoulders. "He must be getting tired—the man's under a great deal of stress."

That evening the Great Aviator, Anne, and Henry Breckinridge had decided to send a message to the kidnappers, to inform them that the baby had a special diet that he needed to stick to. They described it to the reporters, who were allowed up the driveway to the command headquarters. On the morning of March 3rd, splashed across the front page of every major newspaper, were the child's diet and his desperate mother's appeal to the kidnappers.

Mrs. Anne Lindbergh asks that the baby's diet be adhered to, as follows:

A half-cup of orange juice on waking.

One quart of milk during the day.

Three tablespoons of cooked cereal morning and night.

Two tablespoons of cooked vegetables once a day.

The yolk of one egg daily.

One baked potato or rice once a day.

Two tablespoons of stewed fruit daily.

A half cup of prune juice after the afternoon nap.

Fourteen drops of viosterol, a vitamin preparation, during the day.

The Great Aviator did not want Anne to say anything about the viosterol because he did not want anyone to find out that his child was sick and needed extra vitamins—especially vitamins used to treat rickets. After some thought, he let her state the need for the viosterol. For once, he held his tongue and let it pass. What bothered him most about making the appeal was that he, the great American icon—a man known throughout the world as the Great Aviator, inferred to the world that he had a son who was in need of medical attention. He hated the presumption that his son seemed physically disabled.

On the afternoon of March 4th under Colonel Breckinridge's advice, the couple issued another appeal to the kidnappers. With the Great Aviator hovering over his shoulder, and assisting him in writing the statement, Henry Breckinridge addressed reporters before he gave them the press release. There was no law enforcement involved in the preparation of the statement. Breckinridge prefaced the edict by stating that, "Colonel Lindbergh will meet the kidnappers anywhere, under any conditions they may wish to lay down, even to going into the underworld itself, to meet the men who have his baby and arrange for his return." He then handed out the message, which was to be circulated amongst the reporters. The statement the two colonels had prepared said:

Mrs. Lindbergh and I desire to make a personal contact with the kidnapers of our child. Our only interest is in his immediate and safe return and we feel certain that the kidnappers will realize that this

interest is strong enough to justify them in having complete confidence

and trust in any promises that we may make in connection with his

return. We urge those who have the child to select any representatives

of ours who will be suitable to them at any time and at any place they

may designate. If this is accepted, we promise that we will keep what-

ever arrangements that may be made by their representatives and ours

strictly confidential and we further pledge ourselves that will not try to

injure in any way those connected with the return of the child.

Charles A. Lindbergh Anne Lindbergh

Upon the release of this statement, law enforcement people raised their eyebrows. New Jersey's Attorney General William A. Stevens was furious. In his opinion, it was audacious of the Lindberghs to usurp the law, regardless of the fact they were distraught parents. Within hours of the press release, he issued a statement of his own in disagreement. "Although the Lindberghs in effect had said they would not prosecute, we (the state of New Jersey) will."

Also on Thursday afternoon, Doc Condon had his friend Al Reich drive him over to Brooklyn in his Ford coupe, where he pretended to be looking at some property. He told Reich that he wasn't overly fond of Brooklyn, but there was a piece of property he thought he could make some quick money on. Unable to find it after driving around several blocks, he told Reich to forget about it. However he did ask Reich to stop at a mailbox so he could send some information to the owner of the property. Reich obliged. Condon did not tell his good friend that he was mailing a ransom note. It was the same note he and the Great Aviator had drawn up on the morning of March first, the day the Lindbergh baby was kidnapped.

March 4TH would be an eventful day. At the command headquarters in the Lindbergh garage there were more than several people going through the thousands of correspondence sent from all over the country. Most were sympathy notes, or letters offering support to the distraught couple. Throughout the morning/ the Great Aviator had worked closely with the detectives sorting through the mail. He was focused, searching through it, eyeballing any envelope that had a Brooklyn post-mark. There were many, but he was quick to toss away sympathy cards and notes of support from thoughtful Brooklyn residents. Shortly after lunch, Lindbergh called for a detective. He had uncovered Condon's second ransom note. There was a familiar marking, and the text appeared very similar to the first note. It appeared to be written by a person of Germanic origin. The Great Aviator showed little emotion, but he was relieved that the second ransom note had arrived on time. The few men privy to the actual note, noticed that the writing was not quite as sloppy and that it was somewhat different. Even the signature or "singnature" was more defined but there was no mistaking it. Lindbergh sat down at the table with Henry Breckinridge and Colonel Schwarzkopf. The first thing he mentioned was the first two sentences of the note. "Dear Sir. We have warned you note to make anything public also notify the police now you have to take consequences——means we will have to hold baby until everything is quite."

"Gentlemen, this is a warning. We cannot try anything funny. Colonel Schwarzkopf, we are going to have to be very careful we don't antagonize these underworld characters or they are going to harm my son. The last thing I want to do is to piss them off." The thirty-seven year old Great War veteran was in agreement. He nodded but said nothing.

On March the Fifth, another note arrived. Condon trying to keep the police from getting their hands on it, thought that if Henry Breckinridge received it first, he might be able to have more control on arranging the payoff to the Germans. He sent it to Breckinridge's Broadway office. Condon was now operating by himself, and would be in total control of writing the rest of the ransom notes.

The third ransom note was accompanied by another note requesting Breckinridge to hand it to Colonel Lindbergh. The old man continued the deception in the ransom notes. He wanted to keep the police out of the investigation so he and the Great Aviator could keep their end of the deal and pay off Fisch, Hauptmann and the Schlesers. Condon's third note mentioned the police four times. Again, he made it appear that the kidnappers were Germanic. He was deliberate in making it sound that way, so much so that it was becoming obvious to some law enforcement people who saw the notes, that it sounded like someone merely pretending to be German. They wondered if was a group of immigrants or an underworld group who was deliberately trying to mislead them. But it was the shrewd Doctor Condon, masterfully feeding the deception. He knew everyone would scratch their heads and wonder, but he and the Great Aviator kept up the propaganda that the kidnapping was the work of the underworld. The two notions of a Germanic group and an underworld group were ingenious in Condon's mind, because it would keep the investigation going around in circles. And he always led people to believe that there was more than one person behind the kidnapping. In the new letter he made it sound like the kidnappers were angry at the police, even accusing them of intercepting the mail. He went on to say the police could not be trusted.

Keeping them out of the picture would give the 'distraught father', more control because he was 'so worried' the kidnappers would harm his child. In keeping up the deception, Condon issued a warning:

WE WARN YOU NOT TO MARK ANY BILLS.

The third note read:

> *Dear Sir: Did you receive ouer letter from March 4. we sent the mail in one off the letter—near Boro Hall, Brooklyn. We know Police interfer with your privatmail. How can we come to any arrangements this way. in the future we will send ouer letters to Mr. Breckinridge at 25 Broadway. We believe polise capturet two letter and tit note forwardet to you. We will not accept any go-between from your sent. We will arrang theas latter. There is no worry about the boy. He is very well and will be feed according to the diet. Best dank for information about it. We are interested to send your boy back in gut health.*
>
> *It is neccisery to make a world-affair out of it, or to get your boy back as soon as possible. Why did you ignore ouer letter which we left in the room the baby would be back long ago. You would not get any result from the Polise because our dinaping was pland for a year allredy. But we were afraid the boy would not be strong enough. Ouer ransam was made out for 50000 but now we have to put another to it as propperly have to hold the baby longer as we expected so it will be 70000$ 20000 in 50$ bills 25000 in 20$ bills 15000$ in 10$ bills and 10000 in 5$ bills we warn you again not to mark any bills or take them from one ser. No. We will inform you latter how to deliver the mony but not before the polise is out of this cace and the pappers are quite.*

The Great Aviator didn't have to coerce his advisor Henry Breckinridge into involving more underworld figures. This time, the other colonel suggested to the Great Aviator that they should use two of Mickey Rosner's associates as go betweens in dealing with the payoff. Even if the kidnappers said in the letter they didn't want go-betweens from the Lindbergh side, Breckinridge thought it still might be worth a try to use Rosner's connection to the underworld. Of course Lindbergh was just waiting for Doc Condon to enter the scene, but that was still two days away. Until he did, using two more mobsters might help influence others into believing the gangster theory. Lindbergh and Breckinridge issued another statement with the press being the conduit.

> *If the kidnappers of our child are unwilling to deal direct we fully au-*
> *thorize 'Salvy' Spitale and Irving Bitz to act as go-between. We will*
> *also follow any other methods suggested by the kidnappers that we can*
> *be sure will bring the return of our child.*
>
> *Charles Lindbergh Anne Lindbergh*

Once again the newspapers printed the parent's request on the front page. Soon after the announcement, Colonel Schwarzkopf had showed concern over using Rosner's connections. It was clear; he did not like Mickey Rosner. The Superintendent had expressed his reservations earlier about Rosner and the underworld, but again he found himself forced to go along with the distraught parents and their lawyer-advisor Colonel Henry Breckinridge. Spitale and Bitz set up residence with the rest of the crowd in the Lindbergh garage. With Rosner providing the twisted information, and Spitale and Bitz preparing to be go-betweens, there were now three mobsters involved in the negotiations to bring back the Lindbergh baby.

The time had now come for Dr. Francis Condon to place his ad in the Bronx Home Journal. His old friend James O Flaherty was the editor, and although the paper was more concerned about Bronx events than world events, it would still serve Condon's purpose. It was his favorite newspaper; most importantly it was convenient. Although Condon seemed to enjoy his involvement in quirky enterprises such as writing editorials in the Journal under alias names, and giving obnoxious orations at New Rochelle, his family remained skeptical about most of the things the old man involved himself in. His wife and two sons kept their distance. The sons were well aware of their Dad's strange tendencies. His daughter Myra protected her father and tried to keep an eye on him. But even she wondered what the old man was up to this time. Condon was now totally submerged in his plan to help the Great Aviator, and he followed it with precision. His letter to the editor of the Journal was dramatic:

I offer all I can scrape together so a loving mother may again have her
child back and Colonel Lindbergh may know that the American people
are grateful for the honor bestowed upon them by his pluck and daring.

Let the kidnapers know that no testimony of mine, or information
coming from me, will be used against them. I offer $1000.00, which
I've saved from my salary (all my life savings), in addition to the sug-
gested $50,000.

I am ready, at my own expense, to go anywhere, also to give the
kidnapers the extra money and never utter their names to anyone.

If this is not agreeable, then I ask the kidnapers to get any Catholic
priest, with the knowledge that every priest must hold inviolate any
statement which may be made by the kidnapers.

Knowing that the letter from Condon was in the Journal, the Great Aviator had Bobby Thayer conveniently pick one up in the city and bring it down to Hopewell. To hide his real intention, he told him "Get every newspaper you can find including the Bronx Journal." Inside the command center, eight troopers were busy sorting and reading the mail looking for clues. Once Lindbergh got his hands on the papers, he pretended to be looking for clues, searching every paper. He grabbed the Journal and upon finding Condon's heartfelt letter, he casually mentioned it to one of the eight troopers. The trooper said he didn't think much of it, that he had seen similar offers of help. He then handed it back to the Great Aviator. After generating little interest, and without anyone noticing, he placed the paper in his back pocket and went back inside the house.

Inside the house sitting at a table were two treasury agents. Earlier, Lindbergh had shown them the first ransom note. The two men, Elmer Irey and Arthur Nichols, had been brought into the case through Lindbergh's friend Ogden Mills. The Great Aviator walked over to Irey who was discussing ways of coordinating a ransom payoff. Irey was reiterating the importance of using gold certificates to pay off the kidnappers. Nichols, who came up from the Philadelphia office was nodding in agreement. This was troubling to the Great Aviator and he had already gone round and round with Irey over paying with marked bills, saying he

was not going to jeopardize his son's life. To show that an unknown and uncon-
nected go-between would be best in negotiating with the kidnappers, he pulled
the paper from his back pocket, and placed his index finger on Condon's letter.
He told Irey to read it.

"What do you think of this fellow?" asked Lindbergh. Wouldn't the kidnappers trust someone like this, someone who is neutral? He seems caring."

"No Colonel, you don't know who these people are, for all you know they may
be the kidnappers. You just can't trust anyone at this point." Irey didn't seem
intimidated by the Great Aviator, and was all business. He spoke like a true federal
agent, so much so that Lindbergh was beginning to dislike him. He worried about
Irey's determination to pay with marked money, and he had to do everything he
could to dissuade him from doing so. He felt Condon's letter might evoke some
emotional reaction that might change their mind about using marked bills, and
also to use a neutral go-between. Unfazed by Lindbergh's interest in the Condon
letter, Irey and Nichols told the Great Aviator that they would do everything they
could to help bring his son back. But he had a responsibility to find the kidnappers
as well as getting the baby back safely. They got up from the table.

"Look Mr. Irey, I only have law enforcement people on this case, I sure would
like you to stay on."

"Okay, Colonel. We will be back tomorrow."

The next day Condon received a response to his own letter. The old man was
now controlling all the correspondence. The note from the kidnapers read:

Dear Sir: If you are willing to act as go-between in Lindbergh cace
pleace follow strictly instruction. Handel incloced letter personaly to
MR. Lindbergh. It will explain everything.

Don't tell anyone about it. As soon we found out the Press or Police is
notifyed everything are cansell and it will be a further delay.

Affter you gett the mony from Mr. Lindbergh put these 3 words in the
New York American.

     MONY IS REDY

Affter notise we will give you further instruction. Don't be affrait we
are not out fore your 1000$ keep it. Only act strickly. Be at home
every night between 6-12 by this time you will hear from us.

After Condon gave himself permission to be a go-between, the Bronx Home Journal issued a disclaimer saying that Condon was acting on his own initiative. But the old man cared little about that. He was prepared to take a walk on the world stage. And the world would finally get to meet the distinguished Doctor Condon, the great educator and philosopher, the man with charisma and charm, and the man who would do anything for his new friend Charles Lindbergh.

CHAPTER TWENTY-EIGHT
JAFSIE MAKES HIS MOVE

N ow that Condon had heard from the kidnappers, he needed to make contact with Lindbergh. Up until this time, the vociferous Condon was an unknown to the law enforcement people on the case. Within one half hour that would change; in the next twenty-four hours they would all know him. He was ready to place a call to the Great Aviator's command center. He would tell them he had received something very interesting. It was from the kidnappers of the Lindbergh baby and it had a distinctive marking. To help in the deception, his first move was to involve a few other people and to get their opinion on the kidnapper's reply. He took the trolley over to 188th street and the Grand Concourse to one of his favorite restaurants Max Rosenhains. Condon with his thick mustache and large shoulders was physically impressive for a man of seventy-two, and he carried himself with an air of confidence. He swaggered up toward the restaurant, looked around and could not find his friend Al Reich's Ford. Condon then saw a cab crawling up the Grand Concourse toward his hack stand. Quickly, he flagged him down.

"Hey there Mac, can you drive a long distance?"

"Mister, I'll drive you anywhere you want to go as long as you pay the fare."

"Well. I'm not sure if I'm going but here's a dollar, if I'm not out in thirty minutes, it's all yours."

"You got it Pop, I'll be right here."

The old man dressed in a wool overcoat and derby hat, entered Max Rosenhains still hoping to find his best friend Al Reich. He twisted his head and looked around the restaurant. He did not see him. Finally realizing Al was not present, the old man took a seat at a table next to another younger friend named Milton Gaglio.

"Milton, have you seen Big Al?"

"Can't say that I have, Doc. What is the professor up to tonight?"

Doc Condon was in a hurry as it was getting late. Since Al Reich was not there, he figured he might have to use the cabbie to get down to Hopewell. But then he changed his mind; using some quick thinking, he saw Reich's replacement sitting at the bar. When he saw an opening he was going to bring up the kidnapping and see if Milton Gaglio would be a good substitute. Gaglio, a clothing salesman, would often sit around with Condon, Reich and Max Rosenhains the owner and talk philosophy, with the attention seeking Condon always dominating the conversation. This night he was going to use Milton Gaglio, and give himself another opportunity to blow his own horn. He wanted to portray himself as an altruistic retired educator who had this overwhelming feeling of generativity. He was the caring, fatherly figure who wanted to give something back to society. He would involve himself in the kidnapping because he cared so much about America, and its daring hero Charles Lindbergh, and now his missing baby boy. And he was going to need help carrying out his plan. He hoped maybe Milton could give him a ride to Hopewell. Immediately, the sycophantic old man went into a melodramatic rant about the kidnapping and his hero Lindbergh.

"Well, Milt, I am very troubled by this abduction. I cannot for the life of me understand how someone could do such a troublesome thing, as to steal that beautiful little child from his mother's bosom. Why must a father, a great man indeed, with so much already given to the world, to have such a precious gift stolen from him, endure such pain, such agony? At what depths will man go to satisfy one's own desires and self-interests? I ask you, is this how we repay such an undaunted, ambitious hero?" Condon was setting the stage, so he could tell everyone that he had communicated with the kidnappers, and he the Great Doc Condon was going to do everything he could to help the Great Aviator and his emotionally distraught wife, bring back their missing son.

About this time, Max Rosenhain walked over to their table. It was getting close to eleven o'clock.

"Rosie, let me show you and Milt something. You fellows may not believe this, but I have been contacted by the kidnappers." Milton Gaglio and Max Rosenhains turned toward each other. They had the same look of doubt on their face.

Max laughed as he spoke. "Doc, you are crazy, you're making this stuff up."

Condon wasn't amused by Rosenhain's comment. "I beg your pardon, sir. Let me show you this note I have received in the mail." Condon placed the letter on the table. Rosenhains and Gaglio read the note together and finished at the same time. This time they both turned sharply toward the sly, old timer.

"What are you going to do?"

"I don't know yet. What do you think I should do?"

Rosenhains was quick, "Doc, you need to call up Lindbergh!"

"Why, I don't know his number, but I guess I could find it by dialing the operator down in Hopewell."

"Go now" replied Gaglio. "Go over to that phone booth and start calling."

Condon planned to call anyway, but he took the advice. His two friends took the bait. The time had come. Condon would now make contact with the Great Aviator. Condon carried the long, white envelope over to the phone booth. Inside he had placed a smaller, sealed envelope with a special note addressed to Colonel Lindbergh, Hopewell. Within minutes, Condon had gotten through to the operator in Hopewell, who was already working overtime. In no time a man answered the phone. The old man found himself getting edgy and nervous from excitement. He was now interjecting himself into the Lindbergh kidnapping, where he, not the Lindbergh child, would become the center of attention, and the entire world would want to know all about him, the wonderful Doctor Condon.

"Yes sir, my name is John Francis Condon. I am a professor from the Bronx, New York. I have received something you might be interested in." The man who answered the call was Bobby Thayer.

"Yeah, go ahead. Read what you have there in front of you"

"Yes sir." Condon began.

"Dear Sir, If you are willing to act as go-between in the Lindbergh cace pleace follow......he read the letter through to the end.

"Is it signed in any way?" asked Thayer.

"Yes, it is secantal, like the sign of the mafia." Condon slipped. He suddenly realized there was no signature on the letter he had just read. He had placed the signature on the note to Lindbergh that was still in the sealed envelope. Immediately, without Maxie and Milt seeing him, he opened the envelope that was addressed to Colonel Lindbergh."

"Open the envelope that says to Colonel Lindbergh, Hopewell and read it as well," commanded Thayer, his voice now raised. He did not know Condon had just opened the envelope.

Quickly he read it.

Dear Sir,

Mr. Condon may act as go-between. You may give him the 70,000$. Make one packet the size will be about there is a drawing of the proposed packet.

We have notified you already in what kind of bills. We warn you not set any trapp in any way. If you or someone els will notify the Police ther will be a further delay. After we have the mony in hand we will tell you where to find your boy. You may have a airplane redy it is about 150 mil. Awy. But before telling you the adr. A delay of 8 houers will be between.........

"That is it," said Condon.

"Once again, and this time describe the signature for me," instructed Thayer.

"Well, there are three strange shapes and different colors," replied Condon.

"Okay sir, what did you say your name was?"

"Doctor John Francis Condon."

"Doctor Condon, you need to tell me where you are located, because we need to talk to you right away."

"Look I know you are busy Colonel Lindbergh. I can come to Hopewell."

"No, no this is not Colonel Lindbergh; I am just helping him out. Do you know how to get here Doctor Condon?"

"I will figure that out sir." Condon smiled. He knew where Lindbergh's estate was.

"Look, bring your letters and we will have someone waiting for you at the gates to the estate. They will lead you up to the house. If you get lost, stop at the Baltimore Lunch in Princeton. You can call us back from there for directions or ask someone there, they should be able to tell you how to get here. It should take about two hours from the Bronx."

"I will be there in two hours," replied Condon.

"Yes, sir."

Condon knew he was not talking to the Great Aviator, but he wasn't sure whom he was talking to. Thayer hung up the phone and seemed puzzled. He thought to himself. "Why does that fellow sound familiar to me...Doc Condon... who is Doc Condon? Even his voice sounded familiar." Thayer shrugged off his thoughts and hustled in to the house to inform the Great Aviator of the news. Lindbergh would act excited even though he had been waiting for the call. Condon meanwhile, asked Milton Gaglio if he was up to driving his car to the Lindbergh estate in New Jersey.

"I'd be glad to," said Gaglio.

"Gentlemen this is exciting! I would like to go as well," said Maxie Rosenhains.

"Well, let's go," said Condon. Rosenhains and Gaglio went to get their coats. Condon stepped outside and waved the waiting cab driver away. Within minutes, the three men were heading out of the Bronx on their way to cross the newly constructed Hudson River Bridge into New Jersey and then down to Hopewell.

CHAPTER TWENTY-NINE
THE OLD PEDAGOGUE GOES TO HOPEWELL

———————— ▬ ————————

After a dark bumpy ride in Milt Gaglio's car, the trio arrived in Princeton. When they made it to Nassau Street, they could see the lights from the Baltimore Lunch Diner. Condon had just been there the day before with Richard Hauptman and Isadore Fisch. They took the old man to the cabin, where he dropped off a few more supplies to the Schlesers. Condon wanted Charlie Schleser to give him an update on the baby's health.

It was almost three o'clock in the morning when Condon and his two associates finally reached the Lindbergh house on Sorrel Hill. As had been the case since March the first, there was an unrelenting bustle of activity around the estate. NJSP manned the entrance to the driveway; their cars formed a wall fifty yards up the cinder track. Maxie tried to break the uneasiness of his company by asking what he thought they would say when a harp, a wop, and a Jew came sauntering into the Lindbergh mansion. Condon laughed, and told the men not to fret, that Lindbergh was a great American.

The old pedagogue met his escort Henry Breckinridge at the gate. He had never met Breckinridge before but he was well aware of who he was. Breckinridge gave the troopers the okay to let them through. Lindbergh's tall, distinguished advisor crouched on the running board of Milton Gaglio's car as it snaked its way up the driveway toward the house.

Upon entering the command center, Condon was amazed at the number of people actively working to find the Lindbergh baby. There were at least eight troopers manning the phone lines and reading mail. Breckinridge guided the three men through the garage into the house. Coming out as they were entering was Bobby Thayer. He looked at Condon and immediately recognized him. He remembered meeting the old man several weeks back at Throg's Neck. Thayer said nothing, but he was taken back. New York City was a huge place with lots of people. "What are the odds of him being the man the kidnappers contacted?" he thought. As Condon was led up the steps to meet Colonel Lindbergh, Thayer thought that it would be a good idea to talk with Colonel Lindbergh about this new person who was entering the investigation. He made sure to schedule some time with the Great Aviator, after his meeting with the old man. Until then, he remained serious but polite as he watched the old man climb up the steps. Colonel Breckinridge led Condon to the Great Aviator who was lying in bed awake while his wife slept. His interlocking hands cushioned the back of his head, as he sat patiently waiting for his accomplice. After seeing the two men disappear upstairs, Thayer paced about the command center. He was confused.

Lindbergh and Condon were anxious to update each other on what was happening from both sides. They were sticking to the same plan of paying off their co-conspirators with unmarked money, and to continue with the premise that the kidnapping was perpetrated by the underworld. At the same time, state troopers under Colonel Schwarzkopf were still combing the countryside searching for clues and interviewing locals. All over the country people felt the anguish of the Lindberghs. In the state of New Jersey there was a relentless energy. People were willing to inconvenience themselves, to do anything to assist in the finding the Lindbergh baby. Reporters were already drawing up their own theories. One Hearst reporter claimed that the kidnapping was really a hoax with one of the culprits being someone named the 'Pig Woman'. The reporter claimed it was a diversionary tactic intended to take the attention off of the economic crisis. She was told not to write the story but did anyway. Hearst fired her immediately.

CHAPTER THIRTY
A SICK CHILD

L ess than ten miles from Hopewell in an obscure wooded location, things were getting serious. Trying to care for the boy was becoming more difficult for Mrs. Schleser, and her restless husband was growing tired of living in such a secluded place away from the city of New York. Young Charlie's health was quickly deteriorating. Pneumonia was plaguing the boy causing bronchial spasms; his every breath was becoming a struggle. The child who cried often, could not even cry at all now because when he did, it exasperated his condition. His lungs were working overtime. He was wheezing, and a crunchy sound of desperate bronchial tubes expelling air was alarming to the caretakers. Aside from the concern for the baby, it was keeping everyone from getting restful sleep. Little sleep and uncertainty kept the Schlesers on edge. And even though everyone was feeling miserable in the old cabin, what Charlie Schleser was really worried about was having his name attached to a murder case. There was no doubting the fact that the baby's health was declining fast. Schleser was a convicted felon. For him being involved in the potential death of the Lindbergh baby meant the possibility of life in prison or even worse, a death sentence. Charlie wasn't eating, his color was pale at best, his fever had gotten worse and he was desperate for someone to show some loving care. His new caretaker was trying her best, but she was a stranger. The baby did not respond well to anyone but Betty and only recently his own mother Anne. What the baby really needed beside immediate medical attention was the tender loving care of his parents.

CHAPTER THIRTY-ONE
MEETING IN THE NURSERY

————————————————————◼︎————————————————————

The nursery was the same as it was on the first of March, with the exception of the sunlamp that the Great Aviator removed because he didn't want anyone to think that Charlie's ill health had required it. The fact was that it was used to combat the baby's rickets by replenishing needed vitamins. The rest of the room was virtually the same as it was. The baby's toy-box was still beneath the French window, a smaller box stood beneath the southeast corner window, the fireplace mantel still had the same figurines on it, a porcelain rooster with two little birds. On the floor near the hearth was a kiddie-car. The folding pink and green screen with farm animals shadowed the crib.

"The nursery is down here, Doctor Condon. You can sleep on the floor if you don't mind." The Great Aviator was speaking loud enough so that everyone down in the living room could hear him. That would include all law enforcement people, and the three staff members who were in the kitchen area but still within earshot. His wife heard her husband tell this stranger that it would be okay to sleep in her missing son's room. She was surprised at what her husband had said to the old man who was now standing near the doorway of her missing son's bedroom.

Lindbergh spoke softly. "Anne, this is Professor Condon. He has some valuable information about the ransom notes. He could be very helpful to us."

Anne looked at Condon with a sense of surprise, gave her usual smile, and said nothing. Condon seeing this uneasiness, immediately introduced himself to the distraught mother and then held out his hand. He could not resist the temptation to display his sycophantic personality.

"I will do everything in my power, Mrs. Lindbergh, to bring your son back as soon as possible." Before he could continue into a typical, melodramatic oration, Anne walked away.

She nodded toward the old man, and walked back into her bedroom. She gently called for her husband. "Charles, can I speak to you for a minute?"

Condon slipped back into the nursery as the Great Aviator went into their bedroom.

"Charles, do you really want that old man in the baby's room? We don't know anything about him, for all we know he might be some crazy person," Anne whispered.

"Anne, there is no other place to put him and I need to talk to him about the ransom notes. He has received a letter from the kidnappers with the same coded signature."

Anne's reply was one of surrender more than anything else. "Okay, Charles, if you say so. But like I said, we know nothing about this guy; for all we know, he might be the kidnapper."

"Who? Doc Condon?" The Great Aviator caught himself as he began to defend a man he supposedly just met. The sly Lindbergh recovered nicely.

"Don't worry, Anne. I'm going to talk to him for a while in private. If I suspect him to be a fraud, or someone who may be involved, I will bring up some state troopers. They will have him taken away to be interrogated." Lindbergh left the bedroom and went back to the nursery. He left the door open so people could hear their conversation. Ollie brought up two chairs so the two men could sit down to talk.

"They have taken fingerprints, Doctor Condon, but so far they have been unsuccessful in finding anything unusual. As you can see by its contents, this is the typical child's room. We believe the kidnapper entered through this window and descended the ladder that you saw downstairs." Lindbergh was cool and collective as he gave the old man a private tour of his missing son's bedroom. Condon on the other hand was more dramatic and seemed to be astonished that someone could commit such an evil act.

"Such a travesty Colonel, that someone could be so audacious and without the slightest sense of values, and would knowingly perpetrate such a heinous crime. Is there no morality left in this world Colonel?"

Condon was great at playing the game and Lindbergh liked that in the old man. The two men eyeballed each other, waiting for each to say something. Lindbergh then got down to business with the old man. He closed the nursery door quietly. He lowered his voice to a soft whisper.

"We have to speak softly. As you can see, this place is crawling with cops. The reporters are back down at the entrance to the driveway. I did as you said. I let them run roughshod over the grounds on Tuesday night and they destroyed a lot of evidence. I never thought there would be so many people involved in this thing." He paused. "Alright, our next step is to figure some way to deliver the money to Fisch and Hauptmann before they mess things up."

"Have you seen the baby?"

"Yes, I have seen the baby Colonel. I had Hauptmann drive me down on Saturday. There was still a great deal of traffic on the weekend but we managed to get down to the cabin. Hauptmann dropped me off and I walked through the woods. I spoke with Schleser for about twenty minutes and walked back to the road where Hauptmann picked me up. I'm afraid the boy is quite sick with a bad cough. That old cabin is cold and drafty, and the smoke from the fire is probably not good for his respiratory system. I do believe that Mrs. Schleser is doing everything she can for him. She really seems to care about him, but the boy is miserable.

"Doc, the boy is always miserable. He has been that way since he was born. That's why he should go to Germany where someone can give him the proper care and attention." Lindbergh spoke with little emotion. In his mind, his two statements were mere matters of fact.

"But they are scared, Colonel; afraid to take him to New York City because of the tremendous amount of attention this thing has created. The departure date may have to be moved back even further from the original date. I know they are getting nervous and I tried to reassure them that things will work out, that they needed to sit tight. They are also worried they aren't going to get their money because of so many cops snooping around. They think they might have to stay in that old house for longer than we originally planned."

"Doc, things are getting complicated. But we have to figure everything out logically and get the boy out of the country. The Schlesers are right; there are just too many cops around."

Condon shifted the conversation. "How did those other few newspaper people get in here?" He asked.

Lindbergh answered the question indirectly. "I know them. I thought we could use them to our advantage, to make things confusing like you said, but I could not believe all the damn reporters on Tuesday night. I don't know what the hell I was thinking. I never estimated the amount of attention. I think however we can use them to our advantage because there will be so many misleading reports it will keep that sense of confusion that you had talked about."

"Exactly, Colonel," responded the old man.

"Well, Doc, we have to figure out the ransom money situation. You'll need to tell Fisch and Hauptmann they will have to meet us down by the water to deliver the money. They will have to give the Schlesers their share as well. Betty has already been paid so that won't matter. The Schlesers , Johnson and the two Germans are going to want their money as soon as possible. I think they're going to deport Red Johnson from the way it sounds. He has no papers and there is not much I can do about that. We should get him his money though before he does leave. The police will have to understand; I need to do this alone so the kidnappers won't hurt the child. So far they have let me run the show. I think they understand where I am coming from about the child's safety. However, I'm worried because they want me to mark the ransom money. That means we won't be able to pay off Fisch and Hauptmann with clean money. Obviously the other two Germans, the Schlesers will want clean money as well. Doc, I just can't pay them with marked money. What are we going to do, what are our options?"

"If they do force us to use marked money, Colonel, those two Germans will spend it and get caught and that sir will really complicate everything. Our plans will be compromised, and the cat will be let out of the bag. We must prevent that from happening."

"Exactly, Doc. I agree with you. So what is our next move?"

Condon thought about it for a while and then came up with an answer. "I don't think we have much room here, Colonel. You will have to make sure the cops keep their big noses out of the ransom negotiations. I know you said before you cannot take any more money out of the bank without the cops finding out somehow. What if the kidnappers upped their ante at the last minute and you could only get some of the money marked? We can increase our demand in the ransom note."

"We already upped it, Doc. I don't think we can go over seventy. We will still end up using marked bills. If I pull more money out of the bank, I will create suspicion. I just need to keep the Treasury guys out of the picture. The Germans have done their part and I respect that. I will fight the T-men the best I can, but I can't implicate anyone."

Condon smiled. "Don't worry, Colonel Lindbergh. We will figure this out." Confident in their abilities to deceive, the two men shifted to optimism.

The Great Aviator got excited. "I can't wait until the baby is in Germany. Everybody will have been paid and then Anne and I can get on with our lives. The new baby will be here by early summer. All this will be over."

"Now, see Colonel Lindbergh, with our two minds, we shall get everything straightened out in no time. Not to place a damper on your enthusiasm sir, but

I do have another concern. I too am a bit worried. Now that you have enlisted my help to negotiate the ransom money, the cops are going to try to keep a close eye on me as well."

"Yes Doc, but maybe we can maintain a sense of secrecy for the time being. I will protect you don't worry."

Lindbergh changed the subject nonchalantly. "Let's see, we told the Germans we would set up the ransom payoff near the water. They will be waiting for our signal. There are plenty of places down there where we can hide and keep the cops out of it. I wonder if I would be able to get someone to keep the cops away, you know tell them we need to keep the coast clear so the baby is not in jeopardy."

"That would be the best scenario yet, Colonel. I know the Bronx like the back of my hand and it would be advantageous as well to keep all law enforcement out of the borough. Hauptmann also knows the Bronx. We could say we are going to do a drop off in the cemetery; it would divert attention away from the real handoff. Wherever we do this, it must be dark. The darkness could help us should anyone try to watch us." Condon looked upward for a second and then shook his head. He wobbled his black derby against his thigh slightly. "We will tell everybody after the payoff that we took care of business in the cemeteries. But our best move would be to meet at the old dock." Condon kept thinking. "You know, if no one really knows where we are, we could just go to my office at City Island, and pay the ransom money there."

"We can't do that Doc. There still may be some nosey newspaper people or New York City cops anticipating this. They might just stake out your office."

"You're right, Colonel. Maybe we could go to the boathouse over there. It's usually deserted at night and if we disguise ourselves we might be able to pull it off."

"Let's just stick to the old dock near Throg's Neck. But we need to have a backup plan just in case we see anyone. I will need to get assurance from the police that they will not interfere. I hope I can get them to stay away from the Bronx totally so we can negotiate the release of the baby and make the payoff."

"Well, let's just wait until I meet with Hauptmann and Fisch one more time, and then go from there. What is most important Colonel is that we follow our script closely. Let's hope the government guys stay out of it. We need to keep the money clean."

"Sounds like a plan, Doc. Just put the information in the ransom notes. Also, you might need to write a few more notes. I don't care how many you write, just keep the cops guessing.

"Actually, Colonel, I have several ideas. It will all depend on how the ransom negotiations play out. My notes will reflect all pertinent information. You have nothing to worry about Colonel. Also if you remember sir, I used the table template on several pieces of stationary so they are all uniform."

"Just make sure you mail them in different locations so they can't draw a bead on you. And you need to continue to keep the police guessing with that handwriting. Doc, remember the kidnappers are German."

Condon smiled at Lindbergh's concern. "Colonel, you will not have to worry about that. You forget that we are partners here. When I get done with those coppers, they won't know if they are coming or going."

Lindbergh loved Condon's attitude. He almost seemed to gloat in the fact that they were toying with the police, or the cops as he liked to call them in an almost derogatory way.

The Great Aviator continued to whisper, "We will need to contact Hauptmann. He is much easier to find and he'll be able to locate Fisch. They are waiting for our next move." Not quite ready to end the meeting, the two men debated the location some more, then went back to the ransom and the police.

"Yeah, I really like the idea to get more money out of the bank just in case the cops make us mark the original amount but I know that will be impossible. I am sure the cops will let me call the shots. So far they have. I mean, Doc, I have a damn gangster living downstairs trying to set up a deal with Al Capone and they really haven't said anything about it." Lindbergh was talking about Mickey Rosner, a New York City gangster who claimed he could help the Great Aviator find his kidnapped son. Condon knew Thayer's friend Rosner, but he did not know that the Great Aviator had the gangster living in his house at Sorrel Hill. Lindbergh went on.

"Henry Breckinridge and Bobby Thayer brought him down from the city. Henry did not know anything about him, but Bobby and his boss Colonel Bill Donovan know him and they told him he could help us find the baby. Bobby assured me he would keep a close eye on him. Two other mobsters are going to help as well. The police did not like the idea but they basically said nothing. Rosner told everyone that he was working closely with Al Capone and a few other Chicago underworld figures who could definitely bring the boy back. Hey, I don't care how much it costs me because it is all part of the diversion." Lindbergh and Condon thought it was hysterical, but were careful not to show it. The Great Aviator was hoping to keep the underworld theory going for as long as possible because it would help to divert attention away from him and Doc Condon. The police had to go along with it because, like everyone in the country, they too thought Charles Lindbergh was a desperate father willing to do anything to get his son back. Consequently, they allowed him to call all the shots.

With the exception of the sunlamp, Little Charlie's nursery was exactly as it was on the night of March the first. Surrounded by the toddler's toys, it had now become the new planning headquarters for the Lindbergh-Condon kidnapping operation. Condon asked Lindbergh if he could take a few toys from the nursery to make it look good, and the Great Aviator obliged.

"Take whatever you need Doc, I am going to get some shuteye. You know what you need to do. I will have Henry accompany you back to your house tomorrow. At some point I will have to tell him the truth, and since he is my lawyer he will keep things confidential. Besides, he knows about the baby. He was here this weekend; he saw how unhappy the child was. Sending him to Germany where he can get the proper care is not really a bad thing and he will understand this. If we don't get to talk any more tomorrow, I will call you at your house. I hope these blankets are comfortable for you, I know you might not enjoy sleeping on the floor but there are no more rooms available unless you want to stay at the State Trooper barracks in Wilburtha. I will see you in the morning." The Great Aviator shut the door to the nursery and strolled back to his room.

The next morning Condon was treated to a large breakfast prepared for him by the Whatelys. Betty Gow, with nothing to do now that her main responsibility was gone, helped serve the breakfast. The topic at the table was very light with Condon trying to be the center of attention. Thayer, who was also present at breakfast, was suspicious. The Great Aviator had agreed that Colonel Henry Breckinridge would accompany Doctor Condon back to his home in the Bronx where they could prepare for the payoff as they waited patiently for word from the kidnappers. Lindbergh knew at some point he would have to tell Breckinridge and possibly Bobby Thayer the truth. For now, they would be pawns in the game, the same as the rest of the people at Sorrel Hill.

Once Breckinridge departed in his car with Condon, Thayer approached Lindbergh near the kitchen. "Slim, I need to talk to you."

Lindbergh knew what Thayer was going to say; he knew it was about Doc Condon. "Yeah, I know the old man is the same guy we met back in November or December, whenever it was. The fact is I trust him, I believe the kidnappers have contacted him."

"But Slim, maybe he is one of the kidnappers. How do we know this guy is sincere and legitimate? Why, we don't even know if Colonel Breckinridge is safe."

"Bobby, Bobby—he's a fine fella. There's no way possible that he would be involved in this."

"Yes, but how do you know?"

Lindbergh's expression changed. He didn't want to give his involvement away but he was getting perturbed at his friend's persistence on the matter. "Look Bobby, I appreciate your concern but you will have to trust me on this. Doctor Condon is going to help us get the boy back. The gangsters who have taken him have for whatever reason contacted this guy, and he seems very competent. We must be careful we don't lose this opportunity. The old man is the break we have been waiting for."

"Ok, buddy. I just want to be sure who we are dealing with." Bobby Thayer still had his doubts.

CHAPTER THIRTY-TWO
A CHILD'S DEATH

For ten days little Charlie Lindbergh struggled in his new surroundings. His caregivers were struggling as well. The baby's whining and his inability to breath, kept the Schlesers up at night and even though the baby was not theirs, they were upset and worried. The March weather was not very helpful; it made the cabin drafty and uncomfortable. This worsened the baby's cold, and turned it into a predatory infection attacking an already weakened immune system. Like the steady March winds, the cold that settled into his fragile body on the weekend of February 26th was unrelenting. Despite being surrounded by strangers in a cold cabin, the toddler fought hard against the disease that transformed into an overwhelming bacterial infestation of his lungs. The young child had struggled for two weeks, fighting to inhale and release air from his atrophied lungs. At first, he screamed for maternal care and someone to protect him. Since that was impossible, he turned to his new caregivers. Out of desperation, he looked to Mrs. Schleser. She tried to provide him with everything she could, but what he really needed had never really been there from the beginning of his life. The boy was alone, and had been alone for some time. His unconscious desire for a parent's love had grown complacent. On occasion, he found that love from Betty and when she was around, his mother. But Betty grew tired of being the 'mommy', and she supported the Great Aviator's plan, hoping the outcome would be positive. Without the love needed to help fend off a disease like bacterial pneumonia, it was inevitable that he would lose the battle. Being alone, his struggle became more difficult.

In his last few days the baby's bronchial tubes grew louder. A muffled, crunching sound followed by a whistling wheeze had resonated from the makeshift bed of woolen blankets. Every time the boy took a breath of oxygen, he had to force himself to expel it out, sending his bronchial tubes into spasm. He coughed violently as his body worked overtime. But it wasn't the spasms that were killing him. With a burning fever ravaging his body, he was dehydrated. He lacked enough energy to sustain life. When his lungs were unable to process enough oxygen his circulatory system started shutting down. And then the seizures came. His shoulders and neck would tighten causing jagged pain to his head.

Charlie's lungs had been overrun with bacterial demons, and they cried out. Squeaky little voices emanated from his body when the air in his lungs forced its way up the bronchial tubes, like escaping air in a tight balloon. In his last minute on earth his little body convulsed. The sound of wheezing now changed to something else, a death rattle. His lungs in a last desperate attempt to expel oxygen screamed out like a blaring trumpet summoning him to enter a new place. When he breathed his last, the boy's expression turned from one of agony to a sense of relief. His pale face was now gray. His lungs had stopped. His heart's valves shut down. With two strangers staring down at the lifeless body, the ordeal was finally over. No longer would he seek the light of his mother's bosom or the fiery rage of a father protecting his young, his search was now over. The little boy was now free of pain and his wayfaring soul would no longer have to float over such an ocean of uncertainty. He was at peace. The Schlesers however, were in disbelief. They wondered how they got themselves into this situation.

Without a car, Charlie Schleser would have to walk or hitch a ride to Princeton where he would place a call to Isadore Fisch at his boarding house. There was no other option and no one else to call at this stage of the operation. Since Hauptmann did not have a phone, Fisch would tell him the news. But Schleser had to be careful. Now that Lindbergh and Condon were assuming the roles of the opposition, they were in on the hunt, looking for the kidnappers. And Charlie Schleser was one of them. No one would believe a convicted felon that this was a plan hatched by the Great Aviator himself. He had to tell Hauptmann to come and get the baby. But he wondered if they should just end the game, and give the dead child back to his father. After all this was his plan; they were just helping him out. But Schleser knew that the Great Aviator would not see it that way. The dynamics had changed. Charlie Schleser was smart. He felt he couldn't trust Lindbergh because of his iconic status and he was unsure of Richard Hauptmann because he was a hustler like himself. He, Hauptmann, and Fisch were all willing to make money. But he would urge the carpenter to dump the body quickly. And he needed his share of the money. Would the Great Aviator pay up? Would he hold up his end of the bargain? How was this going to play out now? Would he still head back to Germany as planned? He wasn't sure. But he knew it was not he or his wife's fault that the baby died. The Lindbergh baby was sick, he needed medical attention and they could not provide that. The famous pilot should not have carried out the plan with his son being stricken with pneumonia. Schleser hitched a ride to Princeton and placed a call to Fisch, who would get Hauptmann to drive his car. The next day, under the cover of darkness, the two men would pick up the child's body.

It was four o'clock in the morning. The two Germans were dressed in suits. They looked polished and dapper. It made them less conspicuous and made them both feel important. The drive down to Princeton was becoming routine and Hauptmann knew the way with no problems. But there was nothing routine about this trip. Both were anxious and worried. Now their roles had turned more sinister. The Great Aviator's plan had fallen apart. They had to pick up a body, a child's body and dispose of it. What else could they do? What if they told the truth? What if they took the body to the Lindbergh estate and gave him back to his parents? But they knew they couldn't do that. The baby had been dead for over a day now. They couldn't just go rambling in and say "Here, Colonel, here's your boy. It just didn't work out." The cops would be all over them. And what about their money? They wanted those thousands of dollars. Hauptmann and Fisch went round and round discussing the possibilities. It wasn't supposed to happen like this. They had been involved in several shady deals that required them to carry a weapon but none involved the disposal of a dead body.

The sun had not yet risen when the pair arrived at the cabin around dawn on March 11th. The Schlesers had placed the boy's body in an old burlap bag from Doc Condon's basement. It had been used for supplies and had been folded and tossed in the corner of the cabin. The March air was crisp; it's wind steady. Richard Hauptmann navigated his way through the woods to the obscure shelter. Isadore Fisch was nervous and cold as he waited in Hauptmann's unheated Dodge. With Fisch having breathing troubles of his own, they agreed that it would be best if Hauptmann picked up the body and carried it through the woods to the car. It was obvious to Hauptmann that the Schlesers were exhausted. With only a candle to illuminate the cabin, a silhouette of the couple smothered a crumbling brick wall. They were holding on to each other, waiting pensively for Hauptmann. Mrs. Schleser held back her tears as her husband handed the boy's body to the stoic Hauptmann. Emotionless, he took the burlap bag from him. Because he didn't want to look suspicious with four people riding in the car at five-thirty in the morning, Hauptmann thought it best if they remained in the cabin. He told them he would return shortly to pick them up and take them back to New York City. When Hauptmann got back to the car, Fisch was nervous and antsy.

"We need to take care of this fast. I am scared driving around with his baby's body," he said.

"Well, I don't like this either," replied Hauptmann. They said nothing else. Hauptmann turned his car right onto the dirt path and drove away from the cabin to a main road. He was worried; he didn't know any other roads except the ones he had traveled back and forth on from Princeton to Hopewell. He knew he couldn't head back to Princeton, so he turned his car in the direction of Hopewell. When he got out on the Wertsville Road, Fisch was getting excited.

"We have to get rid of this body, Richard. It will be getting light soon." Suddenly, a car was visible in the rear view mirror.

"Oh, shit!"

"Don't get nervous," shouted Hauptmann to his accomplice. "Ve must be strong and not panic. Vatever you do, do not turn around and look at the car. Just remain seated and act normal."

The trailing car kept a steady pace behind them as they drove toward Hopewell on the only road Hauptmann was familiar with. When they got within five miles of the Lindbergh estate, the other car veered off down a dirt road. Hauptmann and Fisch tried to regain their composure. They drove another mile and then stopped. Hauptmann got out quickly, opened the back passenger side door and pulled the burlap bag from beneath the seat. He tripped and then ran into the woods about twenty yards from the road. He tossed the burlap bag beneath several tall trees. Leaves and undergrowth cushioned the body as it dropped to the ground. Hauptmann did not look back to where he placed the body and within seconds he was back in the driver's seat of his Dodge. He turned the vehicle completely around, reversing directions, and headed back toward the cabin. They were through with the baby's body. Neither said anything on the five-mile trip back to the dirt road that ran along the cabin. Near a gathering of winter bushes Charlie and his wife were waiting. They had packed up their measly belongings in the woolen blanket. In the Great War barracks bag that Doc Condon had given them, they placed a few of the baby's belongings. They got into the back seat.

"What took you so long?" asked Charlie Schleser.

"We had to find the right place because there was a car trailing us," said Fisch.

Charlie Schleser shouted, "They didn't see you, did they? " Nervous, he repeated himself. "They didn't see you drop the body off, did they?"

Schleser's wife was also nervous, but Hauptmann was strong and business-like. He was vehement in his response.

"No," said Hauptmann. "Ve have nothing to vorry about, except getting our money. That is the only thing ve need to do now. No one saw us."

The journey back up to New York was for the most part silent. The four Germans were uneasy about the child's death and although all of them had criminal pasts, they couldn't help but feel bad about the Lindbergh baby. The trip back into the city lasted less than two hours, as the unemotional Hauptmann had pressed hard on the accelerator. Charlie Schleser and his wife didn't really know Hauptmann that well and they had some reservations about him. His business-like approach worried them that he was not trustworthy. Fisch however, understood Hauptmann and grew fond of him, as they were now partners in various schemes. The four Germans stopped at the Horn and Hardarts automat, where they sat down for a late morning breakfast. They decided that they had to contact Doc Condon to tell him that the baby was dead. They all agreed that Richard Hauptmann should call Condon.

Mrs. Schleser told Richard that she had something for him to do before he spoke with Condon. "Richard, you need to stop by our house and get the baby's belongings so you can give them to Doctor Condon. I vill vash the baby's clothing so Condon can give them to Lindbergh. I don't know if he still vants that stuff but I couldn't leave it at the cabin or throw it out because someone vould find it. The baby's outfit was filthy." She held her hand up to her mouth.

"I felt so bad for him" A fast stream of tears raced down her cheeks. Charlie put his arm around his wife.

"It is okay, the boy is in a better place now; he is no longer suffering." She kept visualizing the child in her mind, remembering the terrible condition he was in, sweaty with fever and his little body resisting the strangling clumps of mucus. The men said nothing else. Bruno Hauptmann lifted his ivory colored mug and gulped some more black coffee. Charlie Schleser again tried to consul his wife.

"It wasn't our fault, honey. It was Lindbergh's fault. He should have known the boy was in such a sick condition. The son of a bitch is responsible, he just better pay up, that's all I can say. We deserve more than ten grand for what we went through. If anyone is to blame, its dat son of a bitch Lindbergh."

Richard agreed to pick up the bag of belongings and give them to Condon while they continued to discuss the payoff. They had endured eleven nervous days after the abduction, and they all wanted their money. At about eleven-thirty they went their separate ways. It was just before noon when Richard Hauptmann returned home. His wife had gone out. He would drive down to the Woolworth's Five and Dime Store and call Doc Condon. He was going to tell him about the baby and that the 'gang of four' was getting antsy and they wanted their money.

CHAPTER THIRTY-THREE
HAUPTMANN CALLS CONDON

t Doc Condon's house, his wife wondered when her husband was going to return. She was sure he was going to assist with the Lindbergh kidnapping because of the letter he wrote and the response he received from the kidnappers. But Myra Condon didn't always know what her husband was up to, and was well aware of the fact that his unique personality had led him into situations that were not always positive. But she wasn't aware that her husband had a dark side, keenly disguised by his eccentric nature. Her grown children especially her sons, had been skeptical of their father since he wriggled out of pedophilia charges a few years back. But his wife thought of him as just being different, and tolerated him for their daughter's sake. She supported him through most of his endeavors.

At a minute before noon the telephone in the Condon home rang. On the other end was Richard Hauptmann. Mrs. Condon did not know him and he never gave his name. Hauptmann as usual was all business.

"Is Doctor Condon at home?"

"No, he is lecturing. He will be home around six o'clock. If you would like I can leave a message for him. What did you say your name was?"

"No, just tell Doctor Condon to stay home after six o'clock, I vill call again at seven." Hauptmann said nothing else and hung up. He wanted to tell the old man that the baby was dead, and he needed to know what the plans were for the payoff. Mrs. Condon suspected the caller was not American born probably either Scandinavian or German.

Condon and Breckinridge had actually taken most of the day discussing the way to make a payoff. Breckinridge was also fascinated with the old man and like everyone else that spent time with him, became an audience to the old man's ego-satisfying antics. They stopped at Breckinridge's Broadway office where the always, loquacious Condon sat at an expensive walnut table in a leather chair enjoying having his ego stroked. He was now a principle player, in fact, he thought of himself as the great hero who was going to help the Great Aviator bring the little Eaglet back home.

A little after six, he invited Colonel Henry Breckinridge back to his house to meet his wife Myra. Since the old man did not drive, Breckinridge became his taxi. The polished Breckinridge was tolerant, and since the Great Aviator had asked him to keep an eye on the old man, he felt he was just doing his job. Breckinridge's services were out of loyalty. He had not been informed of the Great Aviator's real plans.

Mrs. Condon remembered that her husband had received a call earlier in the day from a foreigner. She informed her husband of the call while everyone was within earshot. A small group had gathered at the Condon household. It included not only Condon, but also his wife, their daughter Myra, Colonel Henry Breckinridge, Milton Gaglio, and Al Reich, Condon's ex-prizefighter buddy who was becoming a frequent visitor. Condon's wife told him that the caller said he would call back after seven. She didn't say anything else about the call, not thinking much about it. With so many people present, Condon was on edge. He knew this was not supposed to happen; he and Lindbergh were the only ones who were supposed to make contact. He did not want the Germans destroying the plans because if they did, everyone, including him and the Great Aviator, would find themselves in a tough predicament. But after a few minutes, he thought of why Hauptmann, (he assumed it was Hauptmann) had called. The baby; it was the baby. He needed medical attention. How were they going to pull that off?

By seven o'clock, five people were awaiting a call from a foreigner, whom only four people assumed was the kidnapper. Condon knew he would have to be extremely careful when the call came in. It would be impossible for him to answer any questions with so many people present. They had one telephone and it was in the hallway. Because there was more room in the back parlor everyone had assembled there waiting for the call. Breckinridge was hesitant to say so, but he didn't want a big audience involved in such a serious matter. Condon didn't seem to mind. It made him feel important and he wanted everyone to notice his role in the negotiations with the kidnappers of the Lindbergh baby. At 7:04 the phone rang. Condon answered.

"Yes, who is it?"

"Dr. Condon? This is Richard Hauptmann. Ve have to talk, are there other people there vith you?"

"Why, yes. Where are you calling from?"

"I am at a public phone. Ve need to talk. I need to know vhat to do. Be home tomorrow same time, I vill contact you. I vill send you a note. Ve can meet at Woodlawn Cemetery."

Condon could not engage Hauptmann in conversation and wasn't sure what to say. "Yes, I sometimes write articles for the papers."

"It sounds like you can't talk, Doctor Condon. Try to be home tomorrow or next day. I vill send an important note to you. Make sure no von else sees das note." Hauptmann was unsure of how to communicate.

"I shall stay in," replied the old man. Hauptmann hung up the phone. Condon waited for several seconds as he tried to think of something to say and then hung up. He turned towards the others.

"It sounds like they were speaking in Italian. I heard someone in the background shouting Italian. The one voice said 'statti citto'."

"What the hell does that mean, Doc?" asked Al Reich.

"It means to shut up in Italian."

"That means we are dealing with a gang," said Breckinridge. "Probably part of the mafia, or maybe some of Capone's boys."

Condon had escaped without getting himself in trouble. He told Breckinridge that the caller would be in contact the next evening. But he worried that Hauptmann might mess things up the following night. Henry Breckinridge promised to return the next day and retired to his New York City apartment.

Eleven days after the kidnapping, the late winter weather had yet to break. But the chilly afternoons were getting longer, and there was still sunlight left when Colonel Henry Breckinridge returned to Condon's house the next evening around six o'clock. Before driving over to Decatur Avenue, he had spent the morning and part of the afternoon at his Broadway office working. Doc Condon had thought of trying to locate Hauptmann or Fisch down near Throg's Neck, but he was wary that someone might get suspicious of him if he started snooping around. Instead, he had spent part of the afternoon putting the trademark signatures on several more blank notes. Carefully, he lined up the edges and checked with his ice pick to make sure they all lined up perfectly just like all the other notes had. He was now ready to set up an elaborate plan for the exchange of ransom money, even though he and the Great Aviator had already decided to meet at the old dock on Throg's Neck. He was hoping the Great Aviator was able to stave off the treasury men and keep the money clean. By four o'clock he had finished, and he waited patiently for his new friend Colonel Henry Breckinridge.

With a March sun setting over the Bronx, Joseph Perrone was waiting for a fare in his taxicab not far from his hack stand. With no customers in sight, he cruised into the intersection of Knox Place and Gun Hill Road when a well-dressed Richard Hauptmann approached his cab from behind. He was wearing his fedora and a brown overcoat, and didn't bother to hide his identity for fear the cabbie might get suspicious and take a mental picture of him. Initially, Hauptmann had planned to drop the note in Condon's mailbox, but he worried that it would be too risky. Instead, he decided to pay a cabbie to drop the note off, with the hope that Condon would meet him according to the time specified. Hauptmann asked the cab driver if he could take a note to 2974 Decatur Avenue. A white envelope had Condon's address printed on it. Hauptmann told him he would pay him for taking his time to drive over there. Before the cab left, Hauptmann gave the man a dollar and then wrote down the taxi's license plate. Perrone, a little uneasy, pocketed the bill but left his cab running.

The normally garrulous Condon was subdued and nervous. He did not tell anyone he was expecting a note around six o'clock, he merely said he was expecting a call from the kidnappers that evening. With Breckinridge safely planted on a sofa in the back parlor, talking with Gaglio and Reich, he was able to intermittently sneak away to check on Hauptmann's status. He kept pensively poking his head out the front door looking for the communication from Richard Hauptmann. Finally, he saw a cab crawling up the street counting the house numbers. When the cabbie got out of the car, Condon acted surprised, but quickly intercepted him at the door. He told him to wait on the veranda near the stoop; he wanted to ask him some questions. Condon took the envelope. With everyone still talking in the back parlor and the grand piano screening him, he was able to pocket the note and climb the steps to the back bedroom where he had earlier set up his ransom note operation. He took out one of the already signed notes that he had hidden earlier and slipped into the bathroom. He took a seat on the toilet and read Hauptmann's note. It was not like any of the ransom notes; the retired educator was actually impressed with Hauptmann's printing and writing ability. There were no misspelled words, and it did not appear as though it had been written by a German immigrant. The note said:

CROSS THE STREET AND FOLLOW THE FENCE FROM THE CEMETERY DIRECTION TO 233RD STREET.......I WILL MEET YOU THERE.

Condon knew the area where Hauptmann wanted to meet; it led to the entrance of Woodlawn cemetery. He would have to devise a way to meet him without anyone seeing them and it would have to include a few diversions. The old man suspected that Hauptmann wanted to talk about getting the ransom money and also update him on the baby's health. In less than three few minutes, he had written another note that included the same language and signature. With the usual misspellings and grammatical errors, Condon's new note said:

Mr. Condon

We trust you but we will note come in your haus it is to danger. even you can note know if police or secret servise is watching you. follow this instruction. Take a car and drive to the last supway station from Jerome Ave. here 100 feet from the last station on the left seide is a empty frankfurter stand with a big open porch around. you will find a notise in senter of the porch underneath a stone. this notise will tell you were to find uss.

Act accordingly. After 3/4 of a houer be on the place. Bring mony with you.

The old pedagogue had become adept at improvising the ransom notes. Making several notes that bore the trademark signature ahead of time allowed him to write new notes much quicker. In order to maintain the deception, he knew how important it was to continue writing the notes in the same format. His latest note would include a graveyard rendezvous with not only Hauptmann but also Isadore Fisch. They would meet at Woodlawn cemetery at nine o'clock. The creative scheme included an elaborate schedule of events that would include a potential ransom payoff. Condon held his new ransom note in his hand and placed it with Hauptmann's directional note inside his jacket pocket. Making sure all his ransom note materials were carefully hidden away in a secret hiding place in his off-limits, back bedroom, the old man descended the stairs.

The cabbie Joe Perrone was still hanging around the front of the house. Condon entered the kitchen to inform everyone that a cab driver had just dropped off a new note. Acting excited, he held his hand up with the one he had just written He then sent Milton Gaglio to go talk to the cabdriver to see if he could get some information out of him. Gaglio nodded and went out to the veranda and began interrogating the surprised cabbie. His first question was an obvious one. "Who gave you the note?"

Condon, Reich, and Henry Breckinridge read the new note together as Condon put it on the dining room table. Breckinridge started to panic when he noticed that the kidnappers wanted him to bring the ransom money. He knew even though Lindbergh had given Doc Condon permission to deliver the ransom money, they were not quite ready because the bank still had the money and the treasury agents were still trying to work it out so they could pay with marked bills. Breckinridge was unaware that the Great Aviator was desperately trying to delay the payoff by fighting tooth and nail to avoid paying with the marked money in order to protect his accomplices and his own ass. And he was running into trouble because treasury agent Elmer Irey was extremely adamant about marking the money using gold certificates, which would be easy to trace. To complicate matters, President Hoover and Treasury had been discussing the replacement of gold certificates during the economic uncertainty which would make it even easier to capture the kidnappers. But Lindbergh and Condon wanted to get the payoff completed soon, so he figured it was at least time to discuss a possible payoff even if they weren't ready. He would tell Hauptmann that the real payoff would be executed near the old dock on Throg's Neck as soon as he could workout the date and pay with unmarked money.

Henry Breckinridge called the Great Aviator in Hopewell to inform him of the communication with the kidnappers, and asked him what he thought the next step should be. Lindbergh told Breckinridge to let Doc Condon handle the kidnappers by himself. Lindbergh reiterated that too many people getting involved in the payoff or communication could bring harm to his child. Since Condon didn't drive, Al Reich would have to drop him off at the last subway station on Jerome. Condon's inability to drive annoyed the Great Aviator, but he was sure he could work around it because he relied on Condon's insight and criminal mind. He allowed Reich to drive him as long as he stayed away from the negotiations. Condon would make sure Reich remained in the car. Lindbergh also knew he had to keep Breckinridge away from the meeting as well. He was confident that Condon was savvy enough to keep both men out of the scheme. Condon was in a class of his own when it came to deception and manipulation.

Al Reich savored the intrigue and was worried about Doc Condon meeting in a cemetery with a shady gang of kidnappers. Although he was loyal to his old friend, Condon reassured him that he would be okay. Together, the two men took off down the deserted street. They were heading toward the dark shadows of Woodlawn cemetery.

Condon had Reich stop on Jerome in front of the old frankfurter stand. He instructed Reich to remain in the car, and then crossed the street. He remembered the porch with the old rock as he had passed this area many times. In fact, the old man had lived in the Bronx for so long he had a mental blueprint etched in his mind. He jogged over to the frankfurter stand. He crouched down by the rock and pulled out Hauptmann's note from his jacket. It told him to: "Follow the fence down to the cemetery". Condon came back to the car, showed Reich the new note and they cruised down to the entrance of the cemetery. Again, Condon told Reich to stay in the car. He walked around for a few minutes looking to see if Hauptmann or Fisch had showed up. Inside the cemetery, behind the granite tombstones, Condon could see the silhouette of a person. Through the darkness, he struggled to see if it was one of the Germans. He walked over to the cemetery gates and waved Reich off, to let him know he was okay. The old man entered the cemetery. He could now make out the person hunched behind the stone memorial. It was Richard Hauptmann.

"Where's Fisch?" asked the old man.

"He's around somewhere," replied Hauptmann. "Doctor Condon, das baby is dead."

"Dead? What do you mean dead?"

"Doctor, the Schlesers did everyding they could for the boy. He vas very, very sick. Das boy vas sick on Tuesday night, when ve took him to the cabin. Are ve going to get in trouble for this? It vas not our fault." The old man was stunned. A monkey wrench had just been tossed into the master plan. He fingered his budding walrus mustache; for once he didn't know what to say. He waited a moment before he spoke.

"Where did you put the boy's body?"

"Ve dropped him on the road from Princeton to Hopewell. Ve didn't know what else to do." Obscured by the eerie shadows of the cemetery, Isadore Fisch's small frame could barely be seen. He leaned on a tombstone and listened to the conversation. Condon noticed him but said nothing. On top of one of the grave markers Fisch placed a large, brown paper bag. Feeling the impulse to involve himself in the conversation and without the slightest hesitation, he changed the subject from the baby to the payoff.

"Ve will get our money right, Doctor Condon?"

Condon glared at the skinny little man.

"Vould I burn if they find about the baby, Doctor Condon?" Hauptmann ignored Fisch's question and asked a question of his own.

"Both of you must be silent for minute. Let's take this one at a time. Where are Charlie Schleser and his wife?" asked Condon.

"They drove back to New York with us. Ve drop them off at their house on Andrews Avenue."

"Okay, they must keep this quiet. First of all, I have to figure a way to inform Colonel Lindbergh about his son's death. We cannot let anyone find out about this or you will not be able to get your money." Hauptmann's demeanor shifted. His voice was angry.

"Yes, Doctor Condon. Ve must all be quiet because you and Lindbergh also have something to lose here."

"What do you mean?" said Condon, now raising his voice and sensing that the scheme was falling apart.

"I mean, this was you and Lindbergh's idea, you came to us with this plan. Ve all could burn."

"No one's going to burn Richard, I just hope no one finds the baby's remains before the payoff because then it would not make sense to pay you now would it? And if we still took money out of the bank then people would want to know what we were going to do with it." Isadore Fisch then stepped forward from the darkness with his package.

"Here, these are the baby's clothes." Fisch threw the paper bag at Condon's feet.

"What are you doing with these? Don't you realize the damn cops would nail you to the wall if they caught you with these?" Hauptmann then raised his voice again; his English was bad.

"There vas no place to put them, if someone found them too ve vould not get our money eider." Condon knew the Germans wanted their money and from the sounds of things they had gone through a stressful situation with the death of the child. He also knew that Hauptmann and Fisch were not about to become stoolies for the Great Aviator and he wanted to make sure he came up with a solution to the problem.

"First of all, are you absolutely positive no one will find the baby's body?" Hauptmann answered quickly.

"The spot where ve dropped him off is very shady road. It's on a hill. There are lots of trees and covering, I don't thing anyvone vill find the body. But it vas dark and I couldn't see everyding."

"When did he die?"

"Schleser called Fisch yesterday morning. He valked all the vay near Princeton to make das call. And I picked up Fish. I told my wife I had vork at the apartments and then ve drive to Princeton. "When did he die? Condon asked Hauptmann a second time, his voice raised.

"So I guess the date is March 10th. The baby died yesterday... that's right it vas March 10th." Hauptmann was nervous with his response.

"Well, this is a travesty. The poor child—it hurts to know he had to suffer. I will figure a way to tell Colonel Lindbergh. Look gentlemen, we will figure a way to pay you your money. Colonel Lindbergh is fighting with the authorities because they want him to mark the money. It might be that he can only pay with marked money, I don't know for sure. We will arrange to pay you as soon as we can, but you will have to be patient as we get the T-men off of our backs. I don't know what the hell to tell you if we have to pay you with those damn gold certificates."

Condon's thoughts were disjointed as he tried to do everything. The dynamics had changed with the death of the baby and the overwhelming pressure to pay with marked money. He wanted to make sure that this thing did not blow up in everyone's face because of the obvious repercussions. The old schoolmaster was determined to do everything he could to not let that happen. He continued his discussion with the two Germans.

"I guess there is no reason for you to go to Germany now. Look, Colonel Lindbergh wants to hold up his end of the bargain. I will continue to write more notes and more responses in the newspaper. I want you to buy both the Home Journal and the New York American, so you can be assured you get the signal. I may even use both papers at the same time. Just make sure you buy both. But as I said, it will take some time clearing up the money situation and you absolutely must be patient."

The two Germans said nothing. They weren't overly excited about Condon's response, especially about the marked money, but they believed him that the Great Aviator was doing everything he could to help them. They would have to tell the Schlesers about the payoff situation. They too deserved their money. Things were deteriorating and everyone was getting nervous.

"Look, I have an idea. You must hide that package for a day or so, wait for me to signal you in the paper and then send it through the mail addressed to me. What clothes do you have any way?" asked the old man.

"It is the baby's sleeping suit and the baby blanket. Charlie's wife washed them by hand with soap. Why don't you take it and give it to Lindbergh?"

"I can't do that. Besides I have a man waiting for me in the car. Even though he is a good friend, I would not want him to become suspicious of me. Richard, I want you and Fisch to drive to Connecticut and mail just the sleeping suit, go up north of Greenwich to Stamford and mail it so no one gets suspicious. Keep your fingerprints off of it. When I receive it in the mail, I will put another ransom note inside about the payoff. But I want you to write more directions about meeting me." Condon held up the directions that Hauptmann wrote earlier that he gave to the cab driver. This time instead of Woodlawn, let's say we will meet at St. Raymond's cemetery. Say something like you did here in this note. I will say I found the note beneath a rock near the nursery. I will open it up and it will say something like you know, cross the street follow the road down to the corner, something like that. Come alone and bring the money. I will do exactly the same with this one like I did before. This helps to keep the police guessing. Got that? Put the directions in with the sleeping suit."

"I got it Doctor."

"Look fellas, this is getting too complicated; there are already too many people involved. I understand that the police are trying to deport Red Johnson because like a lot of you people, he doesn't have any legal papers. And there is a cloud of suspicion over him. We paid him some money for carrying Violet back to Englewood and promised him more, but there's enough cops buzzing around him I don't know if we will get to see him again. We will try to eradicate the suspicion around him, and Betty as well, providing we can. Lindbergh promised the both of them that he would protect them from the police. We knew it would get complicated but we also figured that we could have paid you boys by now and little Charlie would be in Germany. We will now have to confront this new challenge with the baby's passing and the treasury department's insistence on marking the money. Once again, I must reiterate to you gentlemen the importance of being patient."

"What about Violet?" asked Fisch.

"She had been questioned the night of the kidnapping, but as far as I know she has not said anything. Remember, Red said she was fine with the idea of taking the baby somewhere where people could take good care of him. She absolutely cannot find out about the death of the baby. She would get pissed off if she finds out the baby died. I'd like for Red to get in touch with her, to soothe her feathers a little bit, but that probably isn't going to happen now."

"Well, ve von't see Violet anymore so you don't have to vorry about us saying anyding. Beside vonce is enough for me, I think she vould drive me crazy," said Hauptmann.

Condon smiled and then changed the subject. "Listen fellas, let's do this. When you see my advertisement in the papers asking you to send it, then you must mail the sleeping gown. I will ask the kidnappers in the note to the newspapers 'to show me that you really do have the baby by sending the gown through the mail.' Throw away that blanket or better yet burn it somewhere where no one will see you. And try to be cautious when you mail the sleeping suit even if you are in Connecticut. Put the directions in there to keep the police guessing and to make it look like we are working together on this. Besides it will buy more time so Colonel Lindbergh can straighten out the money situation and keep it clean. Gentlemen, I am sorry for the delay and tell the Schlesers not to worry. They have done their job well. We will arrange a payoff on Throg's Neck back by the old dock, and afterwards I will tell everyone we made the payoff in St. Raymond's Cemetery. It will be as soon as we get the money together. Do not listen to anything in the newspapers other then my ads. As you know they are signed by my code name Jafsie. The newspapers only write things that are not true. When you see the word 'YES' in the ad we will meet that night at nine o'clock at the old dock. That will be the cue, and you gentlemen cannot make any mistakes. Remember look for the word Y... E... S...." Condon spelled it out for the two Germans. I will continue to place the ads in both newspapers just in case you don't get one or the other for some reason. You MUST get both papers and only look for MY ad. We will get this straightened out and you will get your money. But you have to be patient. Don't forget to write the little directional note and send it with the sleeping suit." The old man was in a rare mood. He was not eloquent nor was he his usual braggart self. But he was efficient, as he thought about the best way to follow the plan through. He knew he needed to talk to the Great Aviator immediately to not only tell him about the baby's death, but to get some sense of assurance that no one would get caught, including himself and America's favorite son, Charles Lindbergh.

Doc Condon returned to Al Reich's Ford coupe. He was excited about his mysterious rendezvous with the kidnappers. He identified the man he talked to as a Scandinavian named John. "He was about five foot-ten inches and had a strong accent." The pair had to get back to 2974 Decatur so they could tell Henry Breckinridge that the Great Doc Condon had finally met with the "despicable kidnappers" of Charles Augustus Lindbergh's 20 month-old son. Condon's description to his friends, and later to the police of who he was now referring to as 'Cemetery John', seemed to include a little bit of everyone. At some point in his description of the man he met, he would mention a Norwegian sailor (RED JOHNSON), a man with tuberculosis (ISADORE FISCH), and a carpenter with a pronounced thumb and chiseled features (RICHARD HAUPTMANN). Condon would also try to clear the Great Aviator's friends Betty Gow and Red Johnson who were getting accused by police and newspaper people. With the Great Aviator's encouraging him, the old man claimed the kidnapper stated more than once that the police should leave Red and Betty alone because "they are innocent, they had nothing to do with it." Condon would give his account of the meeting in the cemetery to investigators repeatedly. And it seemed to many people that every time he did, he added more information that only seemed to convolute everything. In the annals of criminal history, the old man's shrewdness was unmatched and he knew it. The most sinister thing about it was that he loved what he was doing.

That same night in Englewood, Violet Sharpe was giving police investigators the runaround deliberately evading questions about the kidnapping. Unaware of the baby's death, she worried about the investigation and the possibility of being implicated. She wanted so bad to tell the police that the baby's father was the one responsible for the baby's disappearance. "Why don't you go ask the Great

Aviator?" She wanted so bad to just say that to the police but she held her tongue. The investigators were sure she had something to say by her coy expression, but she felt that it was most important to remain quiet and act stupid. What she was really trying to do was protect Red Johnson from being implicated.

CHAPTER THIRTY-FOUR
HOPEWELL TWO WEEKS AFTER
THE KIDNAPPING

Near the once sleepy town of Hopewell at the Lindbergh command center, Colonel Norman Schwarzkopf was doing a good job of keeping the FBI out of the picture by not being forthcoming with information. Despite J. Edgar Hoover's offer of help, Schwarzkopf was determined to let the New Jersey State Police go at it alone. They were pursuing several leads, some out of state, but none connected to the real kidnappers. Schwarzkopf, with assistance from Bobby Thayer was also trying to get rid of the mob connection, which seemed to be going nowhere fast. Mickey Rosner, who had camped out at Sorrel Hill for almost two weeks, claimed he was in touch with the real kidnappers and the baby was doing fine. Realizing he was a fraud, Thayer had to tell him his services were no longer needed. Lindbergh too, realizing the mob angle was losing steam, gave him the okay. Rosner, like most attention-seeking criminals, hated giving up the spotlight. The case was generating all kinds of scams from all kinds of people, everyone claiming they knew the whereabouts of the baby and who the kidnappers were. Even the real Chicago mob was trying to negotiate the release of Al Capone, in exchange for the Lindbergh baby. The Great Aviator found it rather interesting since he was the man behind the baby's disappearance, but it thrilled him because it diverted attention from what was really going on. Schwarzkopf's men worked diligently pursuing every possible lead, but most led them down the same dead-end road. But the Superintendent remained loyal to the Great Aviator and although he was kept out of the ransom negotiations, he did whatever the man asked of him. Bobby Thayer without Lindbergh's knowledge did some investigating of his own. He was trying to get some background information on the old man that he had met last fall near Throg's Neck. It seemed old man Condon was indeed a part time educator at Fordham and New Rochelle but apparently had been accused of improper behavior with children. He had been fortunate enough to get those charges dismissed. In Thayer's mind, there were too many things that seemed askew with the mysterious Doctor Condon. It was too convenient for him to just appear on the scene as an intermediary in such a high profile kidnapping case. His personality was odd and he seemed to know too much. Especially, when he said the ransom note he received with his communication from the kidnappers had the sign of the mafia. How did he know what it was? And now he was a cog in the Great Aviator's inner circle? Thayer wanted to trust the Great Aviator but he had a strong feeling something wasn't legitimate about the whole thing. Even though he spoke with him when Condon first came to the house, he felt he needed to talk to Colonel Breckinridge as well. When the right time came up, he would do just that. Thayer was smart and he had his doubts about the whole situation. But he didn't entertain the thought that he was a pawn. Both he and Colonel Schwarzkopf had no idea they were being exploited by the Great Aviator. By calling every shot, Lindbergh kept the Superintendent of the New Jersey State Police out of all the discussions, and all the decision-making. Bobby Thayer was the most competent person at the command headquarters, and the Great Aviator was confident he could use his abilities to keep the plan intact. Lindbergh would always reiterate the importance of keeping his son safe, while he arranged the payoff. For Thayer and Schwarzkopf, that was exactly what they were trying to do. It was the focal point. They had to safely bring home the Lindbergh baby. But the Great Aviator had a strong grip on Schwarzkopf. The Superintendent had pledged himself and his men to the distraught father and was willing to do anything to bring the child home. Thayer was also willing to do anything to bring the boy home, but unlike the Superintendent, he was uneasy about Doc Condon and the way Lindbergh was conducting the investigation. The Great Aviator was equally frustrated with the Treasury Department. He found a real roadblock with Elmer Irey and his two officers Arthur P. Madden and Frank J. Wilson, who resisted strongly to Lindbergh's intentions of keeping the money clean.

CHAPTER THIRTY-FIVE
WORKING THROUGH DIFFICULTY

On March 16th the baby's sleeping suit arrived in Doc Condon's mailbox. The Germans did as they were told. Hauptmann even took a chance by having it weighed and sent it from a Stamford, Connecticut post office. Also inside, was the directional note that Condon had asked for. Condon was alone when the package arrived and opened it immediately. He then added another note from the kidnappers. With great concentration he had penned a 260-word communication along with the same trademark signature. Again, it was all part of a delay while they worked out the payoff. In the note he mentioned not to involve the police, that the kidnappers wanted their money, and to make sure the payoff happened; he said the baby was fine. He put it in his pocket with the directional note. The last statement in his ransom note about the baby was difficult, but the old man felt he had to give some sense of assurance to everyone involved in trying to get the baby back. But he had made up his mind to tell the Great Aviator the truth about his son. It was imperative that he tell him that Charlie was dead.

It was after lunch, when Condon gave a call to Henry Breckinridge. The Colonel said he would be right over to examine the sleeping suit, and added he needed to call Lindbergh. Breckinridge drove up from his Broadway office. Within thirty minutes, he was there examining the suit and the note.

"Well, I am not the one to make the call on whether this is Charlie's suit. My first inclination is to say that it is, but Colonel Lindbergh will have to make this identification. I called him before I left the office, and he said that the farm was crazy with newspaper people and investigators. From the way it sounded, it might be a while before he got here. He said he would never be able to leave without someone seeing him, and that he would have to come over later on"

"Yes, Colonel Breckinridge, I think it would be best if the Colonel takes care of this. It will be difficult for him to see this sleeping suit, but he is the only one besides Anne and the staff at Sorrel Hill who would be able to identify it."

Breckinridge had informed the Great Aviator of the package. He told him the kidnappers did as they had said. The two men waited all afternoon and evening for the Great Aviator to arrive. It was an hour past midnight when the Great Aviator arrived at the Condon residence on Decatur Ave. Lindbergh looked like a goofy, college student wearing circular amber glasses and a hunting hat. The disguise proved to be effective as the Great Aviator had made it all the way to the Bronx without anyone seeing him leave or arrive. As comical as that might have seemed, the night was going to get more complicated and serious. Tonight, Condon had decided to tell him that his son was dead.

Condon had to find the right moment to inform Lindbergh about his son. Colonel Breckinridge had taken on a more important role as big brother to the Great Aviator while he supposedly struggled with the kidnapping of his son. Carefully, Breckinridge watched as he pulled the wool, sleeping suit out of the package. Lindbergh showed little emotion as he examined the clothing. Henry Breckinridge wondered how a father could be so calm and collective knowing his son was in the hands of a band of evil men. For the first time, he wondered what was really going on.

"This is Charlie's. I am sure of it. It appears as though the kidnappers washed it. Now why they would do that?" Condon reached out his hand.

"Here is the note that accompanied the sleeping suit," said the old man. A subdued Breckinridge continued to eyeball the 'distraught' father, who remained consistently undaunted, and with the same demeanor. Doc Condon kept quiet, waiting for Lindbergh's reaction to the new ransom note.

"It appears they have the baby and they want their money. It is still the same situation. I just wish I could pay them with clean money and get my son back." Condon spoke up.

"Colonel Lindbergh, what is the latest news from the home front?"

"The Treasury men have basically stated that they will not involve themselves in Charlie's return unless we use gold certificates. Apparently, they feel gold certificates would be much easier to track down. Using regular currency means it would take forever to find out who the perpetrators of the kidnapping are. There is also talk within the government that they will pull all gold certificates at some point and people will have to turn them in or face penalties. As you gentlemen know, I don't want to use any means of marked payment, but Treasury is bent on catching the kidnappers. If they issue a deadline, it will be quite difficult for anyone to turn them in without someone getting suspicious as to why they didn't turn them in sooner. I worry that if the kidnappers realize this, they will not cooperate and I will not get my son back." Lindbergh pretended to be a distraught father so his advisor Henry Breckinridge would not get suspicious. But Breckinridge felt his stomach squirm when his mind began to question the events that were transpiring. He couldn't help but think that things seemed rehearsed.

The three men discussed the payoff together with Condon and Lindbergh still hoping to avoid paying with marked money. They all agreed that if they got rid of the Treasury department, they would never catch the kidnappers. For the first time, Breckinridge began to approach things differently, mentioning that it would cast a cloud suspicion on the father if he vehemently refused to cooperate with law enforcement. He stared at the Great Aviator watching for his reaction. But neither Lindbergh nor Condon flinched, and it was still obvious to them that their dilemma had not been resolved.

After an hour, Breckinridge announced he needed some shuteye and retired to the upstairs back bedroom where he had been hunkering down for the last week. With Condon's wife and daughter already sound asleep in the front bedrooms upstairs, Colonel Breckinridge would follow in their footsteps. Laying his expensive suit down carefully on a chair; he dropped his tall frame into the bed. He stretched out wondering what the truth was, as things just didn't seem right. Who was this old man Doc Condon? And why was he sleeping in his house? He made up his mind. Henry Breckinridge was going to approach his friend the Great Aviator the first chance he got. He closed his eyes and quickly dozed off.

Now that Condon and Lindbergh were alone, the opportunity opened for the Great Aviator and the old schoolmaster to discuss their plot. The most pressing issue that Condon wanted to address was the fact that the baby had succumbed to pneumonia. The house grew quiet with the early morning. Condon wasted no time. He still spoke in a whisper.

"Colonel, now that we have a moment alone I cannot defer this important and tragic news. Sir, your child has died. Apparently his condition became exasperated by pneumonia and he succumbed from seizures. The Germans were quite upset, almost angry."

The Great Aviator said nothing as he studied the old man.

Condon's heart palpitated and he took a deep breath. "I am sorry Colonel; I know this is not the outcome we had planned."

The stoic Lindbergh played it off. "Doc, it wasn't our fault—the boy was weak. His bones were soft, his body was weak, I doubt if he would have been able to sustain a normal life anyway. Why, he had not even learned to talk yet. I don't know if it was because he couldn't hear or something else. The Great Aviator was saddened by the news, but he was quick to make excuses. In his mind, he wondered if all the miles he made Anne fly during her pregnancy contributed to the physical problems. The rickets and the weak bones probably were caused by a genetic disorder. But the Great Aviator was not about to mention either reason to his new friend and accomplice. He quickly composed himself, and changed his focus to the next challenge, and that was to deal with the Germans who seemed perturbed and wanted their money. If Henry Breckinridge was amazed by Lindbergh's cool demeanor, when he inspected the sleeping gown, he would have been in shock if he saw his response to the baby's death.

"Doc, there is nothing we can do about Charlie now. But we still have to pay up. The Germans might get vindictive if we do not pay them. They could slander the both of us and although a great deal of people wouldn't believe that because of our reputations, we can't take that chance. We must pay them their money and be done with this. Where did they put Charlie's body anyway?"

"Hauptmann told me they placed it in the woods on the road from Princeton to Hopewell. He said it was in the same burlap bag I had used for supplies and he didn't think anyone would find it." Condon had to do a little pretending because he knew Hauptmann didn't seem too sure about whether there was a possibility of the body being found.

"Doc, I guess the best thing to do now is to continue writing the communications between yourself and the kidnappers. Keep it going until we can arrange the payoff. If we have to pay with gold certificates, we can get some of them in smaller bills, which would be harder to track down. My greatest fear is that the Germans will be stupid and get caught passing the marked bills."

"Surely, they are smart enough to know that if they do, they will run the risk of getting caught." Lindbergh shrugged his shoulders at the old man's reply. He realized after he said they were smart enough, that maybe they weren't.

"But if they do get caught it will be real hard for me to do anything to bail them out. I just have a bad feeling the T-men will not allow us to do things our way. The police will let me do what I want, but regarding the ransom money they want to mark every goddamn bill."

"Colonel, we have tried to hold up our end of the bargain. They must understand the perilous, predicament we are in and the tremendous implication that could result if we continue to try to pay with unmarked bills. Schleser is a smart guy, the other Germans I'm not so sure about. They are shrewd characters. But it is understandable sir that we be assertive. They certainly cannot get caught passing marked bills." Lindbergh agreed.

"I agree Doc but I don't know what other options we have. Let's just continue the plan with the notes and newspaper ads, and maintain the deception."

That same evening without Condon's knowledge, a neighbor of Doc Condon's announced to a newspaper reporter, that he knew whom the mysterious Jafsie was who was sending in the ads to the newspapers. Several reporters appeared to be hanging around 2974 Decatur Avenue. They were looking for a scoop.

Also that night an important meeting took place in Manhattan as the Great Aviator tried to defend his stance of paying with unmarked bills. He had a strong argument that he was worried the kidnappers would harm his child. And he knew he had to defend this stance even after knowing his son was dead. Dominating the meeting were Lindbergh's Achilles heel, the Treasury Department's law enforcement wing of the I.R.S. Elmer Irey, Frank Wilson and Arthur Nichols were intent on paying the ransom with the gold certificates. Before they even discussed the details, everyone except Lindbergh and Breckinridge was questioning the usefulness of Doc Condon. With Condon not in attendance, they had labeled him a sycophantic publicity hound. The newspapers were planning to divulge his identity to the public, and the lawyers, the bank people and the T-men thought it would be best if they dismissed him from the negotiations with the kidnappers. The Great Aviator found himself sinking in quick sand, but he was determined to keep his wily accomplice in the fold. Lindbergh argued that it was his son, and he had the right to pursue whatever mode of negotiations he wanted. But the payoff however, was different. He argued that he and Anne were not interested in prosecuting the kidnappers. Their main goal was to get their child back safe and sound. On this issue Lindbergh had struck a nerve with Elmer Irey. He arose from his chair and stormed out of the meeting. Irey believed strongly that it was his responsibility to apprehend the kidnappers so they didn't do it again. After several minutes of seething, he re-entered the meeting room and threatened to remove his assistants and permanently dismiss his office from the case if Lindbergh continued to argue against marking the bills.

"Colonel Lindbergh, I am impressed by your extraordinary ethics, but we cannot sir compound a felony. We cannot be part of this unless we use marked money. We simply can't let these filthy animals get away with such a despicable crime. Simply stated sir, it is our responsibility to prevent this from happening again. You must look at this from our perspective. We have talked about this before." Elmer Irey's words were stern and serious. The Great Aviator said nothing. He knew he was defeated on this issue. He pursed his lips and said nothing. The Great Aviator simply could not keep fighting for clean money without casting an air of suspicion upon himself. Irey went on to say "the Justice department had been working with the Morgan Bank to set up the payoff with gold certificates." The meeting ended with the Great Aviator agreeing to use the marked money. There was nothing else he could do except call Doc Condon.

Upon returning to Hopewell, Lindbergh obtained a private line to Condon's Bronx home. He told the old man to continue sending in the ads and writing the ransom notes, but it was becoming increasingly clear that the Justice department was winning out. It didn't seem there was a way out of paying with marked money. It was a standoff between two powerful men. Lindbergh was unwilling to give up on the idea and Irey was not going to compromise. The Great Aviator, desperate, was seeking any excuse to keep the money clean, and Irey was resolute and determined to find the kidnappers of his baby. In the end it was Irey who won. The Great Aviator had no options left. As soon as he was ready; they would go ahead and make the payoff. Later during his conversation with Condon, Lindbergh admitted to being defeated on the issue. As they worked on a plan for a payoff, they had to be careful not to say too much for fear that Irey and those pesky T-Men might be listening in.

Still Doc Condon continued to flood the papers with communications. On March 13th the Bronx Home News printed: *BABY ALIVE AND WELL, MONEY IS READY, CALL AND SEE US. JAFSIE.* The next day it said: *MONEY IS READY, NO COPS, NO SECRET SERVICE, NO PRESS. I COME ALONE LIKE THE LAST TIME. PLEASE CALL. JAFSIE* The paper ran the same ad again on the fifteenth and on the sixteenth the ad said: *NOTE?????*

On March 18th the Bronx Home News ran another ad: *I ACCEPT, MONEY IS READY. JOHN, YOUR PACKAGE IS DELIVERED AND IS O.K. DIRECT ME.* In preparation for the payoff, he had a wooden box specially made. He had called for this in an earlier ransom note. Even if this seemed overly dramatic, the old man thought that it was the best way to carry the money to Throg's Neck. Hopefully, the box would be big enough to hold the ransom money. But he was anxiously waiting for the final nod of approval from the Great Aviator; knowing the Germans were getting restless.

A persistent Condon continued flooding the Bronx newspapers. On Sunday March 20th Condon placed another ad in the Home News: *INFORM ME HOW I CAN GET IMPORTANT LETTER TO YOU. URGENT. JAFSIE*

On Monday the 22nd, he tried to hurry up the payoff in a desperate attempt at keeping the bills clean. In the usual disguised writing, he asked why the Lindberghs had to wait so long to get their baby back and that it was the fault of the police that the pay off had not happened. Condon then responded again the next day in the Home News saying he needed to see the baby before delivery: *THANKS. THE LITTLE PACKAGE YOU SENT WAS IMMEDIATELY DELIVERED AND ACCEPTED AS REAL ARTICLE. SEE MY POSITION. OVER FIFTY YEARS IN BUSINESS AND CAN I PAY WITHOUT SEEING GOODS? COMMON SENSE MAKES ME TRUST YOU. PLEASE UNDERSTAND MY POSITION. JAFSIE.*

While Lindbergh was still desperately struggling to keep the money clean, Condon was doing his part. He waited five days and responded again: *MONEY IS READY. FURNISH SIMPLE CODE FOR US TO USE IN PAPER. JAFSIE*

He was ready to send in that final ad to the American before the payoff to let the Germans know that "Yes everything was OK" but he did not want to give in just yet. On Wednesday March 30th, Condon wrote another ransom note. This one claiming that if they didn't hurry up and make the payoff they were going to add another $30,000 more bringing the total to $100,000 and he wanted to know why Mr. Lindbergh was taking so long to make the payoff. At the end of the note he went so far to say they would even double the amount if they didn't hurry up. Condon sent yet another response. *I ACCEPT. MONEY IS READY. JAFSIE*. It was obvious to anyone involved on both sides that this couldn't keep up. Something had to give.

But even as March was coming to a close, a desperate Charles Lindbergh tried one more time with Irey. His personality would not allow him to lose to the Treasury men. This time he tried to elicit sympathy by using the child's sleeping suit as motivation to pay immediately with clean unmarked money. Elmer Irey would not go for it. He even tried to lay some blame on the press with the hope that he would say "Go ahead pay with unmarked money." But Irey was no newcomer to the business. He was staunchly determined (like he had been before when he nabbed Al Capone), to run in the kidnappers of the Lindbergh baby. Irey was not about to let the Treasury Department shed its responsibilities.

After the meeting, the Great Aviator decided to tell Colonel Breckinridge the truth. To his surprise, Breckinridge told him he knew what was going on. "He suspected something was amiss when Condon joined the inner circle." Lindbergh told him of his dilemma. "Charlie was sick and needed someone to devote a lot of attention to him and he simply did not have the time." Breckinridge was saddened by the news of the baby's death and he offered his condolences to the Great Aviator. He told him that what was most important now was to follow the operation through, the way they had planned. He would do his best to assist as he had done all along. He told the Great Aviator that he understood his dilemma and that he knew about the baby's afflictions. Despite the admission that his son was disabled, Lindbergh was relieved.

For Condon, things were getting stressful, but the one thing the old man felt good about was that his new housemate was also on board as a teammate. Colonel Breckinridge told Condon as well that since he was the Great Aviator's friend, confidante, and counselor, he would secretly help to finally bring an end to the kidnapping fiasco. Breckinridge, like so many others before him had been manipulated by the Great Aviator. But like so many others before him, he was still in awe of the national hero. With the other Colonel now assisting in formulating the kidnapping strategy, they both agreed the best thing to do as they waited, was to keep the communication and correspondence going. On April first, Condon sent another ransom note saying in essence that if they were ready to make the payoff, they should go ahead and say so in the American. With the ransom money now all bundled and marked, the time was drawing near. It finally came on the same day when Lindbergh finally agreed to make the payoff with marked bills. The Great Aviator had no other recourse, he told Condon to send in the ad to the American. They would meet the Germans at the old dock near the swamps of Throg's Neck on Saturday night and pay them off. On Saturday morning April 2nd the ad finally ran. It said: *"YES EVERYTHING O.K."* Condon had created a fake rendezvous in St. Raymond's Cemetery just down the road from Throg's Neck when in reality they would never step foot in the cemetery. He would include elaborate details of the so-called pay off with 'Cemetery John', a fictitious man cut from the cloth of all the principle characters involved. And the old man could play it up for all that it was worth, with himself on center stage trying to desperately do something noble for America's hero and for the nation as a whole. It would be a perfect script for any thespian, especially a conniving one. To insure the final act of the play got off without a hitch, the Great Aviator arranged for all law enforcement people to stay clear of the southeast side of the Bronx on Saturday night April 2nd. It would make it real convenient for the two manipulators to get their business done on Throg's Neck.

CHAPTER THIRTY-SIX
READY FOR A PAYOFF

That Saturday evening, Doc Condon claimed to have received another note with the trademark signature from the kidnappers with further instructions about the payoff. He said it was again dropped off by a cab driver, but not the same cab driver who dropped off the note once before. He even convinced his daughter Myra, that she too saw the cab driver race down the street after dropping it off. In the note the kidnappers had arranged another rendezvous in a cemetery, this one St. Raymonds. With most of law enforcement under the impression that the payoff was going to take place there, the diversion would allow them to meet at the old dock at Throg's Neck with no interference. His new note said:

> *Dear Sir: take a care and follow Tremont Ave to the east until you reach the number 3225 east Tremont Ave. It is a nursery. Bergen Greenhauses Florist there is a table standing outside right on the door, you find a letter undernead the table covert with a stone, read and follow instructions.*

On the reverse side of the note, Condon added further instructions:

> *don't speak to anyone on the way. If there is a ratio alarm for policecar, we warn you, we have the same equipment. have the money in one bundle. We give you 3/4 of a houer to reach place.*

Condon took out the note that Hauptmann had written and sent with the sleeping gown. He would say he found it under the stone that he mentioned in the new ransom note.

The new notes would serve as Lindbergh and Condon's phony itinerary for the evening. Lindbergh felt he had to meet the Germans in person and explain to them that he tried to keep the money clean. He didn't want Condon's friend Al Reich anywhere near Throg's Neck when they dropped off the money. Reich graciously allowed the Great Aviator to borrow his Ford. With Lindbergh behind the wheel, the two men would speed off in the direction of Saint Raymond's Cemetery. When they got out of sight of Condon's house they would make a u-turn and head toward the swamps of Throg's Neck.

CHAPTER THIRTY-SEVEN
THE PAYOFF AND THE SEARCH

T hrog's Neck was dark and chilly. There was not a car to be found. Not only did the police stay away, they made sure everyone else did as well. The swamps had not yet reeked of the rank, foul smells of summer. The early spring had been cool and the smell of salt was drifting in on April's first wind. The three Germans, Hauptmann, Fisch and Schleser were anxious. Hauptmann strategically backed his Dodge in front of some scrub trees. He was in position to easily see any car lights traveling down the sandy road. All three men were packing pistols just in case things turned ugly, but the three men felt confident that the Great Aviator and his coy assistant Doctor Condon would not double-cross them. They wanted their money, and they hoped Lindbergh was able to keep the money clean.

At a few minutes past nine, circular lights bounced up, and then down, and from left to right along the curvy road. This was it. Finally, after a month of waiting they were going to get their money. The black Ford was traveling fast. As it got closer, they could see the Great Aviator behind the wheel and the white haired, mustached man peering out from behind the dashboard. He pulled up closely alongside Hauptmann's Dodge. When the Great Aviator got out, they could see that he too was packing. A black gun handle jutted up from his shoulder strap.

"Gentlemen, gentlemen. We finally get to close this deal." As usual, Condon had to speak first. "I'm afraid however, that although you will get the money that we agreed on, we were unable to keep the money clean."

"Fellas, I am sorry," replied the Great Aviator. "I tried to do everything in my powers to keep the money clean. The T-men were totally unwilling to cooperate with me. I don't know what else I could have done. Fisch responded first.

"Well, that smells like a rat. What the hell are we supposed to do with marked money?"

"Colonel Lindbergh couldn't you pay us with something other than gold certificates?" asked Charlie Schleser. "I mean, my wife and I went through a helluva lot, taking care of your baby, what should I tell her?" Condon interrupted.

"Look, the Colonel did everything possible for you boys. But I'm telling you right here and now that if you spend this money, you run the risk of messing everything up." Condon handed over the wooden box with the money. As he reached down to break the string that was tied around it, he sliced his finger on the metal clasp. His finger started bleeding profusely and the old man kept flicking the blood down into the sand. The Great Aviator handed him his handkerchief, and he tied it around the third finger on his right hand. It slowed the bleeding down, but the blood was dripping onto the first few packs of ransom money. Uninterested and unsympathetic to Condon's minor injury, the men resumed their business.

"There is fifty thousand dollars here," said Lindbergh. "I can only suggest to you that you take it and divide it up, and then bury it somewhere. Maybe in ten years you might be able to use it, I don't know. There are fives, tens and twenties. I tried to keep the denominations as low as possible, but I'm not sure what good that will do. Now it was Hauptmann's turn to speak.

"Ten years? Ve need this money now. Ve did our part for you Colonel and ve did as Doktor Condon said. Are you sure ve vould be caught if ve spend it?"

"Truthfully, I can't say you would be caught right away but over time yes, you would be caught, and what would you say if you got caught? I mean there is so much at stake here.

"But Colonel," said Hauptmann "ve all need das money. Vat vould happen if ve get caught?

"You can't take that chance. Really, Richard what would you do if you were caught? Would you rat us all out? Would you do that to all of us? That is the risk you take, and instead of one of us going to the chair we would all burn. I hope you wouldn't want that. You wouldn't do that to us would you? You just can't get something from nothing. The only option you have beside getting caught and I hope that is not an option, is to bury the money, or burn it, but you need to do something right away. And remember there is nothing I can do for you boys if you get caught spending ransom money. I am sorry. I don't know what else to say." Lindbergh's words for once were honest. He tried to hold up his end of the bargain. Richard Hauptmann said nothing.

"I don't care about all that, Colonel Lindbergh, but it just doesn't seem fair that we did our part and have nothing to show for it." Isadore Fisch had made sense with his statement. There wasn't anything to show but $50,000 dollars of marked ransom money. The Germans were at a loss. What were they to do with it? There simply wasn't any solution to the problem.

There were no handshakes, no other comments. Lindbergh and Condon got back into Al Reich's Ford and drove off. The three Germans divided up the money. They were angry but said little; they knew that Lindbergh had tried. After all it was a month later. If he had been able to keep the money clean, the baby might not have died and Isadore Fisch would be in Germany by now waiting for the baby and the Schlesers.

On the trip back up Jerome toward Decatur, Condon placed a black leather bag on the floorboard of the car. It contained $20,000.00 in marked $50.00 bills that Elmer Irey thought would be the easiest way to catch the kidnappers. Irey believed that it would be easy to remember someone who passed a fifty-dollar gold certificate. Condon however, had demanded in the ransom notes to pay with lower bills. And Lindbergh argued with the T-men that he had to pay according to the kidnappers demands. But Irey believing the ransom was $70,000.00 thought they could slip the extra $20,000.00 in fifties hoping to catch the kidnappers. With Irey unaware of what was really going on, Condon could boast to everyone that he saved Colonel Lindbergh $20,000.00 with his hardnosed negotiating tactics. This gave the Germans a better chance of not getting caught if they only had fives, tens, and twenties although Lindbergh clearly warned them not to spend the money. Condon and Lindbergh had agreed on March 1ˢᵗ that if they increased the ransom $20,000, they had a better chance of keeping some of the money clean or at least keep the denominations down. But it didn't work out. Breckinridge agreed with Lindbergh and Condon, and was well aware of the fact that the old man was going to return with the 400 fifty-dollar bills saving Lindbergh $20,000. The Great Aviator's attempt at holding up his end of the bargain just didn't work out.

Riding back to his house Doc Condon pulled out his last note. With it was Hauptmann's directional note. Hauptmann's note that he sent with the sleeping suit fit perfectly with Condon's rendezvous at St. Raymonds. It said:

cross the street and walk to the next corner and follow whittmore Ave. to the

soud take the money with you. come alone and walk I will meet you.

In addition, he had concocted yet another phony communication that he would tell everyone he received in exchange for the money. In his elaborate meeting with 'Cemetery John' in St. Raymond's Cemetery, Condon would detail the exchange for the police, and stick to his original description of the kidnapper being a Scandinavian. The note that he wrote said:

The boy is on the Boad Nelly. It is a small boad 28 feet long. Two per-
son are on the Boad. The are innosent. You will find the Boad between
Horseneck Beach and gay Head near Elizabeth Island.

When they returned to Condon's house, they placed the black bag, along with another extra one they used for transporting some of the other money in the parlor. They informed everyone including the law enforcement people who were present that the payoff had been completed. They had sealed the deal. The old man was already bragging how he saved his friend $20,000. After about fifteen minutes, Condon, Breckinridge, and the Great Aviator asked Al Reich to drive them to Mrs. Morrow's apartment on East 72nd Street in Manhattan, where many of the top dogs of law enforcement had assembled. On the way out, Breckinridge grabbed the bag with the four hundred $50.00 bills. At Mrs. Morrow's apartment, they would meet up with some of Jimmy Finn's NYPD and Elmer Irey's Treasury guys. Lindbergh seemed very relaxed for a distraught father still waiting on the return of his kidnapped son. Before they went into the meeting, he remarked to Condon and Breckinridge that he couldn't wait to see the reaction on Elmer Irey's face when the old man told him he saved him $20,000 in marked fifty-dollar bills. Throughout the whole payoff, he never mentioned his son's death. It seemed he was more interested in successfully deceiving law enforcement. When they entered the apartment everyone asked where the baby was. Condon handed over the note that said the boy was on a boat off the coast. To the surprise of those that were present, he quickly changed the subject.

"I saved the Colonel $20,000" Condon said, immediately upon entering the apart-ment. "A good day's work I call it." Without hesitation Elmer Irey hit the roof.

"You did what?"

"I talked him out of $20,000."

"What?"

"You are kidding me, right?"

"No sir, I am not kidding you. Condon went to the black bag they had brought in and pulled out the four hundred $50.00 bills.

"Gentlemen, I saved the honorable Colonel Lindbergh $20,000. Look." He handed Lindbergh's money to one of the FBI agents who was present. The lead agent from the bureau Leon Turreau was astounded. He kept shaking his head in disbelief.

"Colonel Lindbergh and his wife need every bit of that $20,000 dollars," said Condon.

"Jesus Christ," muttered Irey. "We wasted all that time planning." One of the other agents remarked that "Condon was taking a big gamble fooling around with that much money without being armed, he must be crazy." The old man reached into his overcoat and produced two antique horse pistols he carried with him to the payoff. Irey not impressed with the old man, turned to Lindbergh.

"I hope we can find your son out there in the water Colonel. We will need to get on that right away."

Lindbergh took over the conversation and said he would arrange an all out search for the Nellie with the U.S. Navy and the Coast Guard immediately. He also would arrange to charter a Sikorsky aircraft and scour the area of the Elizabeth Islands where everyone presumed the Nellie was located. Essentially, it meant they would fly over the area from Long Island Sound all the way up to Cape Cod, Massachusetts. Irey asked if he could go along for the flight and Lindbergh said that he could. Doc Condon had also claimed a seat on the plane ride and not wanting to feel isolated, Lindbergh's advisor Henry Breckinridge decided to go along for the ride as well. But only Elmer Irey would be looking for the Lindbergh baby. Before they would embark on their search, Doc Condon had laid out as many details of 'Cemetery John' that he could and the police were already out scouring the streets looking for the mysterious Scandinavian. At least for the time being he was a Scandinavian. In the morning, Colonel Breckinridge, the new minister of propaganda, planned to hold a press conference explaining the payoff. He would state to everyone that they were intensely searching the shores of Long Island hoping to find the missing child.

Three men kept the charade going during the bumpy plane ride over the New England coast. Only Elmer Irey was out of the loop. He was sincere and determined to find the Lindbergh baby; the other three men knew the child was dead. For the Great Aviator, it was an opportunity to show off his aviation prowess. For Condon and Breckinridge, it was a one in a lifetime chance to go flying with the Great Aviator. But Condon was nervous and edgy. Unlike his personality when safely planted on Bronx ground, he was not so sure of himself. He was trying to counter his fear by reciting lines from Hamlet. Although the optimistic Irey was annoyed with Condon's blatant nonchalance during the search, he said nothing because Lindbergh and Breckinridge were silent as well. Still, despite the intense hum of the Sikorsky aircraft, the voice of the vociferous Dr. Condon reached his own annoyingly high level of decibels.

For six hours, from six in the morning to noon, Lindbergh manned the control panel flying over the area that Condon mentioned in the note. Horseneck Beach and Gay Head were part of the Elizabeth Islands, and the Great Aviator circled and buzzed those areas several times. Elmer Irey searched from above, hoping he would spot the Nelly. They landed in Buzzards Bay, ate lunch, and resumed the search, but by late afternoon the search for the Nelly proved unsuccessful, and the Great Aviator admitted to Irey that he thought they had been double-crossed. They landed in the prearranged landing strip on Long Island where big Al Reich was waiting to drive them back to the city. The Navy and the Coast Guard were equally unsuccessful.

During the next few days the optimism Anne and her mother might have experienced with the payoff was quickly dashed as the Great Aviator, realizing that the fiasco was coming to end, related to his wife as well, that he thought the kidnappers double-crossed them and the only hope was to continue searching the coastline from Massachusetts to Virginia. Lindbergh was going to spend time down in the coastal town of Cape May, New Jersey pursuing some "new leads", and using every possible means including planes and boats to find his lost son. It was a great chance for the Great Aviator to get away from the continuing hustle of the farm at Sorrel Hill, and do what he liked best, flying and spending time around the water.

CHAPTER THIRTY-EIGHT
VIOLET'S STRUGGLES

I t was now April. The Great Aviator had depended on Betty to get the word out to Violet that Red Johnson was being sent back to Norway. He was leaving through Ellis Island. Without saying anything to her since the kidnapping, Lindbergh thought it would be better if Betty leaked the information, and Violet found out through the grapevine. Lindbergh wanted her to know that she could no longer depend on Red to help her out. With him gone, any disclosure about the kidnapping would only serve to implicate her and send her to prison. Violet struggled with so many things at one time. The unknown whereabouts of the baby, her relationship with Red, Betty's relationship with Red, her sister's departure, the Newark detectives who insinuated she had something to do with the kidnapping; it all made her feel so alone.

The distraught woman had found out through Emily, another server, about Red's departure. Violet felt her heart pumping madly. Her eyes quickly filled with tears, and she placed her hand onto her forehead; then cupped her eyes to hide her tears. With another revelation about Red and Betty, she felt like someone had just kicked her in the back displacing her oxygen. Emily claimed Betty was upset as well, because she and Red had been lovers. Red had lied to Violet. He denied that they were intimate, and it angered her. With the tears rolling steadily downward, she wondered when her misery was going to end. She covered her mouth with a trembling hand. Her eyes shouted her pain. She looked at herself in the mirror and stared ahead, stunned. She couldn't believe the person staring back at her; she had lost so much weight. It couldn't be the same twenty-eight year old Violet Sharpe she was staring at in the mirror. She looked so old. "Where was Violet Sharpe, the young lady with so much personality? Where did she go? It had to be someone else. She wasn't even a shadow of herself". Violet was thinking aloud. It was obvious her depression was getting worse now that she had been dealt yet another blow.

The Great Aviator was aware that she was having health concerns, exasperated by emotional problems stemming from Red and the phony kidnapping. He would wait patiently to see how it would play out. If he had to, he would figure a way to silence her. He could say she was unstable and suffered from a 'case of nerves'. He could have her committed and destroy her credibility. He knew with several different relationships going on at one time, she really didn't have much credibility anyway. The staff at Next Day Hill sensed something was wrong with her, but doubted she had anything to do with the kidnapping. Some members suspected Red and Violet had been getting too close before the kidnapping, especially with their giddy behavior, but both Red and Violet were outgoing, had gregarious personalities, and were well liked by most of the staff. The staff preferred to stay out of their personal relationship. Violet however grew paranoid and neurotic, and she worried that someone would find out about her and Red, and their role in the kidnapping. She was fighting a throat infection, and gargling with peroxide wasn't working. Her health was a major concern, and now she had to face up to the reality that she would never see Red Johnson again. Fortunately, she had been smart enough to give the $600 that Red had given her to her sister Emily, when she sailed back to England. In case she had to go to the hospital, she did not want anyone to find it in her room. When the time was right, she would write her sister, and tell her about the Great Aviator's kidnapping hoax.

Two weeks later on April 13th Inspector Harry Walsh of the Jersey City Police Department gave her another interrogation but like before, she was coy and evaded the questions. She recalled no names, and could not tell him where she had gone on the night of March 1st. Walsh was perturbed by her attitude; he was sure she knew more than she was leading on. He vowed to get to the bottom of Violet Sharpe's involvement in the kidnapping.

With her health steadily declining, and under doctor's orders, she checked into the hospital. On May 10th Violet had her tonsils removed. The infected tonsils were a complication of a weak immune system. Removing them meant getting the infection out of her body. The doctors however, were more concerned about her weight loss. They suspected it had more to do with emotion than disease. But Violet knew what it was. She wasn't eating because her mind was preoccupied with Red and little Charlie. Her brain stopped producing the chemicals needed to trigger her appetite. She was depressed. She had not seen Red or Charlie since the night of the kidnapping. Little did she know; her nightmare was not quite over.

CHAPTER THIRTY-NINE
A BABY'S BODY IS FOUND—MAY 12, 1932

A light but silent rain was falling, when the rugged, logging truck pulled off to the side of the road. Its exhaust pipe choked on a puff of bluish gray smoke. The rain like little teardrops rolled off the truck's windshield. The passenger door opened and a lean black man hurried to relieve himself. The driver Orville Wilson sat patiently as his companion William Allen tried to get away from the road just in case there was a passing car. The old truck, laden with heavy tree trunks and limbs had struggled around the Sourland Mountain turns on Mt. Rose Road, and was taking advantage of the brief respite. Less than four miles to the northwest was Sorrel Hill and the Lindbergh estate. Besides Allen answering nature's call, the pair agreed that it would be a good idea to give the worn truck a rest, even if for only a few minutes. Within minutes, Wilson's co-worker came running up from the slanted ground. He tripped as he tried to pull his overalls up and attach the shoulder strap. After picking up his floppy cap, he made it back to the truck. He was out of breath and shaking.

"My God, there's a dead child over there." William Allen took a deep breath before he spoke again. "I could tell it was a baby, there was some clothing around it."

"Where, where is it?" asked the middle aged white man; his voice in a high pitch.

"Right over there, only a few feet or so off the road." The two men ran to where the body lay. It was half covered with leaves and blackened from decay, but on the front side there was a spindly foot twisting out. The other foot and leg were gone and part of an arm was missing. The corpse had been there for a while because the body was badly decomposed. Not far from it was the burlap bag. Wilson and Allen stared down at it, seeking reassurance that it really was a child's body. They eye-balled each other then ran back to the truck.

The pair leaned on different sides of the truck's hood facing each other. Wilson pulled his fedora back and scratched at his scalp.

"What the hell are we going to do?" he asked. Allen was excited.

"We have to get to West Trenton or Lambertville where the state police barracks are. Or at least we need to get to a telephone. I know for sure there is a state police barracks down by the river in West Trenton."

"Wait, William! Better yet, let's go see the constable down in Hopewell. You know, I bet that baby might be the Lindbergh baby."

"Jesus, Mary, and Joseph! I can't believe this."

"Let's get going," said Orville Wilson. Before the two men rushed off, William Allen turned and then stretched his neck 180 degrees to each side. He wanted to check out where he was and make sure he knew the exact location of the body. The two men jumped into the truck and took off up the steep incline and then down in the direction of Hopewell. For a while, they were too stunned to say anything else. They both agreed to drive down into Hopewell and notify the police there, instead of going to Trenton. Driving down Main Street, the duo noticed a police car in front of the local barbershop. Through the front plate glass window they saw an officer getting a haircut. Quickly, they rushed through the door and told him of their gruesome discovery. The officer identified himself as Constable Charles Williamson. He had been one of the first officers called to the scene of the kidnapping on the night of March 1st. His suspicions were immediate. Without waiting for the barber to dismiss him as being finished, he leapt from the barber chair and led the two men to the outside. They walked over to the police station where Williamson informed the chief what was going on. The two policemen got into a patrol car and had Allen and Wilson lead them up to Mt. Rose Road to view a child's body.

The two truck drivers led the police to the exact spot. The four men stared down at the body. Neither of the officers had much experience in dealing with dead bodies. They all were wondering the same thing, whether or not this was the kidnapped child. After only one half hour, the word had gotten out, and other town folk were making their way up to view the body. Williamson left the other three men behind, and raced to the Lindbergh estate where he would tell everyone at the command center in the Lindbergh garage of his find. Soon, the word would be out among law enforcement. The state police barracks at Trenton and Lambertville were notified immediately, and each sent out a group of troopers. Other local officers raced up the roads to Mt. Rose. Even Jersey City Inspector Harry Walsh who was at the Lindbergh estate, joined a covey of lawmen and snaked his way down to the site to see the body that they presumed was the Lindbergh baby. Men gawked as they offered their theories about the find.

"It was a group of cold hearted cowards." "They were gangsters looking to cash in." "It was one cold calculating killer." A lot of theories but none knew the truth except a group of ten people who were nowhere near Hopewell. One person, the father was sailing off the coast of southern New Jersey leading law enforcement and others on a wild goose chase looking for kidnappers. He would have to be notified immediately.

As the crowd toyed with the truth, Harry Walsh took it upon himself to move the body over. Without any previous experience dealing with such a badly decomposed body, the overzealous Walsh prodded the corpse with a stick, trying to turn it over. In an act of pure ineptitude he inadvertently poked a hole through the back of the skull. It was as if a group of first grade boys had stumbled upon a dead animal. There was very little reverence or concern given to the child's body. And once again a potential vein of evidence had been compromised. Determined but desperate lawmen paid to solve crimes, had only complicated the case even more. As in any murder case, the body should have been a source of key information but because of inexperience, it was not. And that would only serve to assist the Great Aviator in his deception.

When the call came into the New Jersey State Police in Trenton, they too immediately relayed the call over to the headquarters at Sorrel Hill. Colonel Schwarzkopf was already en-route to the spot on Mt. Rose. He wanted to see the body before he contacted the Lindbergh family. He had his driver take him to the spot, a mere four miles from the estate. After viewing the body, he felt certain it was the Lindbergh baby's body. They would drive back to the farmhouse and inform Anne and her mother. It would finally close the damper on the hopes of Anne Lindbergh and Mrs. Morrow. Scharzkopf entered the house on the garage side. He meandered around to the living room where Mrs. Morrow was reading.

"Mrs. Morrow, do we know when Colonel Lindbergh will be returning from Cape May?" Schwarzkopf knew she did not. He knew he was still off the coast of southern New Jersey rubbing elbows with some underground characters, trying to locate the baby. But Schwarzkopf knew he had to tell the mother. Fortunately, Anne's mother was there to consul her. The superintendent of the New Jersey Police did not want his announcement to sound so matter of fact and lacking in empathy. Before he became the bearer of bad news he turned around and poked his head into the servant's quarters where Betty Gow was working.

"Betty, do you remember exactly what the baby was wearing when he disappeared?"

"Why, yes I do Colonel, he was wearing a flannel nightshirt that I made for him in addition to his sleeping suit. He also had two diapers and plastic training pants." Betty provided him with all the details of the baby's clothing, and also showed him a remnant piece of flannel and blue thread that she had used to sew the nightshirt for the baby. Schwarzkopf was scared and nervous. He decided instead of saying anything to Anne or her mother, he was going to go back to the woods where the body was found. He wanted to be sure before he said anything. He needed to verify that the flannel was the same. A large group of police officers were doing their best to keep back all the thrill seekers. Schwarzkopf went right to the corpse. Looking down, he noticed that the badly decomposed body was covered in the same flannel material that Betty showed him. There was no doubting that, but there were no diapers and no plastic pants. The superintendent made no connection and drove back to the Lindbergh estate. He should have realized that the baby was missing certain clothing, clothing that had been removed by Mrs. Schleser soon after they arrived at the cabin. Schwarzkopf returned to the house and went straight inside the front door, through the foyer. Directly in front of him was Mrs. Morrow. She was still sitting in the living room.

"I hate to disturb you again Mrs. Morrow but is Mrs. Lindbergh upstairs?" Mrs. Morrow replied softly.

"Yes, Colonel Schwarzkopf, do you want me to get her?"

"That would be appreciated Mrs. Morrow. I guess it would be best if we told you first however, so you may help break the news to her. We believe we have found Charlie's body." The matriarch of the Morrow family placed her hand over her mouth as tears welled up in her eyes.

"Oh, no," she said softly, barely audible.

"I am sorry Mrs. Morrow." The staid leader of the New Jersey State Police could not fight back the emotion that overwhelmed him as well. Mrs. Morrow signaled Colonel Schwarzkopf to follow her up to the master bedroom, to break the news to her daughter. Together, they struggled up the stairwell.

Mrs. Morrow gently called to her daughter. "Anne, Colonel Schwarzkopf would like a word with you." Within seconds the neatly dressed young woman came to the doorway. "Anne, Charlie is with Daddy now." Anne didn't know what to say.

"Mrs. Lindbergh" said Colonel Schwarzkopf. "We have found the body of a young child not far from the Hopewell estate. We believe it is the baby because of the flannel he was wearing. We will need Colonel Lindbergh to make an identification." Mrs. Morrow placed her arms around her daughter. They sobbed together. Anne couldn't speak. Her mother's voice quivered.

"Colonel Schwarzkopf, I don't know when my son in-law is coming home, but I think we should be able to contact him. He has left a contact number."

"I thought it best if we send two troopers down to inform him of this development."

"That would be great, Colonel," said Anne regaining her composure. "You know I thought from the very first night that someone killed my baby. We are sure it is him right Colonel? Are we sure it is Charlie?"

"Yes, ma'am. I feel certain it is because of the clothing. We must still wait however, for a positive identification. We must wait for Colonel Lindbergh to return from Cape May. As soon as he returns, we will go down to Trenton to the morgue. I think they will take him to where the coroner works, at the Swayze and Margerum Funeral Home down by the train station."

"Do you think it would be okay if Betty examined the corpse to see if she could make a positive identification?" After some hesitation, Mrs. Morrow answered quickly for her daughter.

"Colonel, we should talk this over with the baby's father first and I am sure you will have to ask Betty if she would be willing to look at the body. If everyone is in agreement, then I suppose that would be the best thing to do at this time."

"Okay I will be in the garage headquarters. I will be waiting with everyone else for the Colonel's return. Thank you Mrs. Morrow, and Mrs. Lindbergh I am truly sorry you must go through this. It is a senseless travesty."

"Thank you for everything you have done, Colonel Schwarzkopf," replied the tearful young mother.

CHAPTER FORTY
A FATHER EXAMINES HIS SON'S BODY

The Great Aviator relished getting away from his farmhouse in Hopewell because things were just too hectic and complicated. He miscalculated how extensive the investigation would be and the amount of time it would take for things to return to normalcy. The New Jersey State Police had been pursuing every possible lead, though every one of them seemed to vaporize in the end. The garage command center was constantly inundated with investigators and troopers. Cars clogged the entrance in front of the house and also the area to the right beside the garage. Inside, there was little privacy. Since the garage connected to the kitchen and the serving quarters, and there were no doors in between, that end of the house stayed crowded. Lindbergh seemed unconcerned that his wife was stuck there, while he was out flying and sailing along the beautiful, southern New Jersey coastline. It was okay. She was with her mother who was providing her with the comfort and companionship she needed. Spending time alone on a friend's sailboat the Cachalot, and socializing with idol stalking extortionists who claimed to know the kidnappers, proved to be an avenue of entertainment for the Great Aviator. He was thrilled by the adventure. But he really enjoyed spending time doing the things he loved most, flying and sailing, even if it meant playing the role of a distraught father searching for his lost child. Being away however, did not resolve two dark clouds hanging over his head. One was, he worried that the Germans would get stupid and spend the ransom money. The second was there would come a time when someone would inevitably and haplessly stumble upon the remains of his son. Unbeknownst to him Richard Hauptmann had already spent a few of the marked bills. And on May 12th he got the notification he hoped would never come. Two of Colonel Schwarzkopf's troopers informed him that they had discovered the body of a young child, just four miles from his estate in Hopewell. With Hauptmann circulating marked ransom money there wasn't anything he could about that. With the discovery of the body, it was imperative that he took care of things quickly. He would return to Hopewell immediately, and get rid of the body as fast as he could. Hopefully, it would bring an end to the ordeal. It also meant he would have to resume his life at home, and go back to his research in New York City. There was a good chance he wouldn't be making any quick little jaunts over to Throg's Neck anytime soon.

With Lindbergh's okay, Betty Gow reluctantly agreed to be driven down to Trenton to see if it was the Lindbergh baby that the two truckers had stumbled upon. Walter Swayze, the owner of the funeral parlor and also the Mercer County Coroner, led her to the embalming room where the corpse was laying on a table, its smell lifting from the table. Without hesitation, the Scottish nursemaid nodded to Swayze that it was indeed little Charlie. She could tell by the two overlapping toes and the child's protruding eyeteeth. She showed little emotion when she said, "That's him." Also on hand was Dr. Phillip Van Ingen the baby's pediatrician who wasn't as confident as Betty that it was Charlie, but after some thought gave a positive identification. The identifications did not last but a few minutes. Betty Gow wasn't in the mood to hang around for too long; she exited out the door as fast as she had entered. It was probable the baby's father would analyze the remains the next day.

Lindbergh did not arrive home until the following morning at two o'clock. He said nothing and showed no emotion as his wife struggled with her sleep. He sat in a chair in the bedroom wondering which hurdle he would have to jump next.

The next morning was Friday, May the thirteenth. The Great Aviator had made up his mind to examine the corpse. With a crowd gathered outside the funeral home on Greenwood Avenue, he had to sneak in through the back door. Greeting him was Walter Swayze and also Dr. Charles H. Mitchell who was to perform the autopsy. By New Jersey law an autopsy was required since it was assumed the child met a violent death.

Lindbergh did not flinch and did not grimace when he stared down at the decaying body of his son. The odor had progressed from the fetidness of death to the advanced stages of decay, but was still pungent. He watched as Walter Swayze took over the task of examining the body from the elderly Dr. Mitchell who was totally unable because of age and arthritis to steady a hand that could render a medically efficient autopsy. After they probed the dried out corpse several times and lifted it on its side, the Great Aviator was sure that it was his son. He nodded at the overlapping toes. Swayze carefully placed the body face up. The dark, crystallized fluid that used to be Charlies' eyes stared right up at his father.

In an unexpected move, Lindbergh asked for one of the probing instruments and a pair of forceps from the balding Swayze. He held the probe on the chin of the corpse and tried to lift back the brittle skin beneath the nose to get a better look at the teeth. Taking the forceps and without flinching, he deliberately snapped the blackened tissue breaking the child's crumbling face in half. The old physician Mitchell jumped momentarily. The coroner winced in disbelief; the Great Aviator was unfazed. With the boy's face now in half, the four quadrants of primary teeth were now exposed. Lindbergh tossed the instruments down on the table. "This is my son," he replied. He moved away from the table, the odor of rotted skin overpowering. "We need to get this body cremated immediately."

The coroner in a dual role as undertaker knew exactly where to take the baby's body for cremation. Within minutes, they had placed the little corpse in a small oak casket and placed it in the back of a hearse. Outside the crowd grew larger. There amongst the gawking crowd was Lindbergh's cohort Doc Condon. He had positioned himself across the street so he could watch the Great Aviator escort his son's body to the car. As the car slowly reversed out of the drive and then lunged forward, Condon nodded to his cohort. They sped off east on Greenwood Avenue past Chambers Street and Quinton Avenue, the streets that bordered the sprawling expanse of Trenton Central High School. They turned up Olden Avenue, and headed northward so they could hook up to Route One. In about seventy minutes they would be in Linden, at the Rose Hill Crematory.

It took less than two hours to reach Linden, and less than ten minutes to cremate little Charlie's body. For ten minutes, Charles Lindbergh peered in at his son's body. A child of twenty months now totally consumed by bitter flames; the Great Aviator mesmerized by the science and the energy of its white flame. Emotionless, he turned away when the remaining bits of dried flesh vanished into a miniscule clump of white dust. The small pile sat alone upon the glowing sheet of stainless steel, absent of human spirit. His eternal spirit had now departed, gone to a place that was free of pain and anguish, a place where he didn't have to depend on anyone, a place where his soul was free. All that remained on the tray was the dust of a child, a child that had lived a very short life on earth. And there wasn't much left for the Great Aviator as his work was now complete. Hopefully, he would be able to resume his life as the Great Aviator without bearing the responsibilities of a father with a needy child. But he still was concerned about some others. There were ten people who knew the truth about the kidnapping.

CHAPTER FORTY-ONE
THAYER WANTS THE TRUTH

——————◼——————

With the news of the Lindbergh baby being found murdered, media people clamored for the immediate arrest of the evil monsters that were responsible. Within an hour, the news had been disseminated among all the newspapers, local and national. A perturbed Bobby Thayer thought it was time to question his friend and fellow lawyer Henry Breckinridge about a few things. Now that the search was over, Breckinridge was more accessible. He called the Colonel and asked him to pencil him in for a few morning minutes. It took him just a few minutes to travel the short distance from Donovan's law firm to Breckinridge's Manhattan office. Thayer wasted no time on small talk. He went right to the heart of the matter, to the Lindbergh kidnapping.

"Colonel, it seems the Lindberghs are more at ease now that the child's body has been found. The Colonel is amazing. I don't think I ever saw him shed any tears over all of this."

"What are you trying to say Bobby?"

"Well Henry, I am going to cut right to the chase. I think it is rather strange that Lindbergh seemed so cool through all of this. Even now, with the death of his son, he is still doing practical jokes, he still eats like the Minnesota farm-boy that he is, and I haven't seen him comfort his wife one time through all of this."

"Yes. So what? That is his way. He has always been like that."

"Henry, come on. You are smarter than that. That old man Condon, Lindbergh knew him before the baby was kidnapped."

"How do you know that, Bobby?"

"Because I was there when they met the first time. Colonel Lindbergh and I would get away from the office on occasion and head down to the beaches.

Condon would hang around Throg's Neck when the weather got cold. He was always down there pontificating to everybody ranting and raving about nothing at all. The man is nothing more than a big blowhard. He is friends with some of the immigrants down there. I think they used to work for him doing odd jobs to make a few dollars. All of a sudden this guy is working for Charles Lindbergh, the Great Aviator? C'mon Henry you know, tell me the truth."

Breckinridge snapped. "What do you want me to tell you Bobby? Are you saying Lindbergh was responsible for all of this?"

"No, no. . . . I'm not saying that Henry. But things are queer, they just don't add up. Henry, you know Colonel Lindbergh as well as anyone. What is the story with 'Jafsie the mystery man'? I know you know."

"You can't demand answers from me Bobby, I am his attorney and friend." Thayer was not intimidated.

"Fuck that stuff Henry. A child has been murdered."

"He was not murdered!" Breckinridge could not stop himself. Without saying so, he had admitted he knew more than he was saying.

"Colonel Lindbergh wanted to send his son to Europe, where he could get treatment for his condition. He couldn't do that here in America, the papers would be all over him. The child was not murdered; he died of pneumonia about ten days after he was taken.

"I'll be a son of a bitch. Where did he go? Who took him?"

"Some of those German friends of Doctor Condon took him. Lindbergh paid them to take the boy to Germany where he would get special attention. Bobby, the boy couldn't hear and he had not yet walked because of weak bones. I know that, I saw him that weekend right before he was taken. Anne was not aware of the kidnapping plan, as far as I know, she still doesn't know about it. It took so long because the Treasury men wouldn't allow the Colonel to pay with clean money. You know that. You saw how Lindbergh kept trying to keep the money clean. That meant they couldn't get out of the country fast enough and the boy died. Apparently his cold worsened, and he was too weak to fight off an infection." Thayer was shaking his head in disbelief.

"Henry, for God's sake, a child has died because of one man's selfishness and ego. He should have admitted his son was sick and sought proper care and help. My God this is an absolute travesty. Who else knows about this Henry?"

"I suspect that detective Walsh from Jersey City knows something, he seems condescending to everyone and he certainly doesn't trust Doc Condon. He has also made a few comments that were not too flattering toward Colonel Lindbergh. He and Schwarzkopf are going after Violet Sharpe, one of the maids from Next Day Hill. I think they suspect several of the staff."

"Yes, I know who Violet is. Is she involved?"

"She was tricked by Red Johnson, Betty's boyfriend."

"So Betty is in on it, too, I guess."

"You got it right. There were several people involved. I think there are about nine or ten people who know. There were three German men, and the wife of one of them. Betty, Red, and Violet all were in on it, although like I said, Violet was tricked into the role she played. Betty supported the plan because she wanted what was best for the boy. She got Red to trick Violet, and Condon had his boys pick up the baby and hold him until the time came when they could exit the country."

"I knew it, I knew it," responded Thayer. I figured Betty had to know something and I knew Anne was too naïve to realize anything was going on. How do we know somebody won't say something? Especially Condon, I don't trust that dirty old bastard. What about that?"

"If anyone says anything, they might be in trouble. Lindbergh made that point perfectly clear."

"Hell, Henry. What's he going to do—kill them?"

"Bobby you don't know him. He made a deal. He expects them to do the same. Doc Condon is sure they will not say a word."

"Dammit, I just knew that old man was up to no good. Well let me tell you Henry I want out of all this bullshit; I want no part of it. I cannot attach my name to this. The 'Lone Eagle' is no damn hero; that's for sure. It appears to me that he is nothing but a self-centered conman."

"Well, what do you want Bobby? You can't say a word of this to anyone. I know you are a great lawyer I'd hate for you to jeopardize your career over this.'

"What do you mean by that Henry?"

"Well, you understand attorney-client privilege. I am his attorney; I should not even be discussing this with you. Look Lindbergh is a powerful man; people are not going to believe all this. He would turn it around on everyone else especially the Germans. And besides, Lindbergh was really trying to help his son."

"Henry, Charlie was his only child. Sending him off to another country was trying to help him? I thought I was his friend as well, I did not look at him as a client."

"Well, I do, that's the way it is. You and I cannot compromise anything here."

"You know what, Henry? I feel like I have been used here. I spent a whole month working on this, answering those goddamn telephones and trying to find that child, and all you fellas knew what was going on." Breckinridge cut him off.

"I didn't know until March 16th after the baby died. I was not in on it until the Colonel felt like he had to tell me the truth. And now I have an obligation to protect my client."

"Henry, I thought I was a friend of both of you. Why didn't you tell me the truth?"

"I can't answer that for him but there were already too many people involved in this. No one thought that it would end up this way. The hope was for Charlie to be safe in a home in Germany with competent caregivers, and the attention surrounding the kidnapping would settle down. I really did not know how you would react to all of this if I did tell you. Obviously, you are not happy. I don't know what else to tell you."

"Happy? You have got to be kidding me. Does Colonel Donovan know about all this?"

"No, and don't tell him. As you know he has a political career ahead of him, and if this comes out, and he was working as an attorney on the case like yourself, it would ruin the both of you."

"Look, Henry, you've already said enough. I just want to leave and go home. I need to be alone for a while. Unlike some people, it bothers the hell out of me that a little child has died because of all of this. I do appreciate you being honest with me and I do understand your position, but I am beginning to hate America's big hero. And tell the son of a bitch I said that!"

"Just don't say anything to anyone! You got that?"

"I am not going to say a word to anyone, believe me. I have too much respect for Colonel Donovan. I would not want him to be hurt by all of this." Bobby Thayer had enough; he couldn't believe his ears, but he suspected all along that something was amiss. He headed back to his home in Manhattan.

After Bobby's abrupt departure, Colonel Breckinridge knew he had to talk to the Great Aviator to let him know that Bobby Thayer knew the truth. Since the New Jersey Police had access to the phone conversations, Breckinridge did not want to discuss the issue over the phone. He decided to take the afternoon off and drive over to Next Day Hill where the Great Aviator was now spending much of his time. He would take his wife for a ride along the Palisades to the Morrow estate.

At Next Day Hill the Lindberghs were given more space, as they were trying to deal with the death of their child. Even though there was a cloud of suspicion around the staff, Lindbergh had kept his promise and kept the police from hounding them to death. When Henry Breckinridge arrived, the Great Aviator was glad to see him. Henry's wife Aida immediately went down the hall to talk to Anne, and to see how the pregnant mother was doing. The Great Aviator waved Breckinridge into the study and shut the door. They were alone.

"How is Anne holding up, Colonel?"

"Henry, I honestly believe that Anne feels better knowing this thing is over."

"Well, I thought you should know Thayer knows the truth."

"What? How did he find out?"

"You know him Colonel; he's very smart and perceptive. He approached me with his suspicions especially about Condon and asked a boatload of questions. I tried to keep the truth from him but he wouldn't stop. I had to tell him."

"What was his response?"

"He was angry. He felt we should have let him know the truth. He thinks he was used." Lindbergh was calm. He liked and trusted Bobby Thayer. Maybe Bobby would understand if he explained to him the situation with the baby's illness.

A few days later, Thayer asked Breckinridge if he could use his connections to get him a government job somewhere away from the hustle and bustle of New York, maybe even something in the military. Colonel Henry Breckinridge told him he respected him, and would do whatever he could to help the young attorney out. "Come see me when all this stuff blows over," he told the young attorney.

CHAPTER FORTY-TWO
VIOLET'S SHORT HOSPITAL STAY

W hen the word came to the hospital that they had found the remains of the Lindbergh baby, Violet Sharpe became emotionally unstable. She was angry. How could a father allow that to happen, regardless of his intentions? She wanted to go home but where was home? Her sister Emily had returned to England. Could she do the same? Was Next Day Hill really her home? Where on earth could she go? She certainly couldn't run to Red.

Violet wanted to tell someone what she knew, but if she did they would just say she was crazy, and she'd end up spending the rest of her life in some rubber-walled sanitarium. One thing was sure, she wanted out of the hospital. It was making her feel worse. She told the doctor she wanted to go home, but he would not comply with her wishes. Without his knowledge, she dressed and left the hospital. She called Septimus Banks and told him she was given the okay to leave, and he sent Henry the chauffer to pick her up. As they pulled into Next Day Hill, she thought of the detectives. She figured they would return. Two interrogations were not enough. She was not forthcoming with information the first two times; it was inevitable they would return. They had made it quite obvious that they were suspicious. They even said they would be back.

Septimus and Marguerite Junge helped her to her room. It felt good to be back in her own bed, but it didn't take long for her mind to start racing again. She laid there wondering about everything. Not only did she feel abandoned by the man she was madly in love with, now there was a chance she might be implicated in the kidnapping and murder of the Lindbergh child. She felt so sad for the boy, and she couldn't help feeling sorry for herself as well. She felt like there was nothing left in her life. The man she loved was gone and now there was a possibility she could end up in prison somewhere. She thought about going home to England. Emily did it, but she really didn't feel comfortable anymore back in England. She needed to talk to her sister, but she wondered if she was suspicious of her as well. What would Emily think now that they found the body? Besides, she thought, Emily was busy with her own life now.

Violet had always battled depression, but now it seemed the emotion monster had reared its ugly head again. Violet fell deeper into her self-pity and depression. She closed her eyes, but could not sleep. She kept replaying the events again and again in her mind.

Why would Red do this to her? "He said he loved me, he told me that more than once." She cried again, sobbing out of control. She now hated her life and started thinking of ways to get away. She knew if she was to leave however, she would have nowhere to go. She repeated the questions in her mind. Where in the world would she go? Why did Red do this? Her mind shifted back to the baby. She thought of little Charlie's body left on the side of some mountain by the very people who were supposed to be protecting him. Her heart ached with the thought. Now, those detectives would be back and ready to blame her for the kidnapping. She was sure that Lindbergh would buy everyone off. He was such a powerful person everybody would believe him no matter what he said. Or maybe he would blame her and those two German immigrants Hauptmann and Fisch for kidnapping his son. Violet's stomach ached from her problems. She had no reason to think that things would get better. She continued to spiral downward into her depression.

Septimus Banks gently knocked on the door of Violet's room. He was worried about her. She was too weak to open the door and told him to enter.

"Violet, you need to go back to the hospital. Let Henry Ellerson take you back to the doctor." She could barely lift herself off the edge of her bed. Septimus leaned over to help her. "Are you sure the doctor gave you permission to return home?" Violet told him he did and that she was fine. "Okay if there is anything I can do, please let me know." The butler shrugged his shoulders, and gently closed the door. The English servant drifted off into an uneasy sleep.

For the next two weeks, Violet struggled but slowly acclimated back to work. Mrs. Morrow was understanding, and allowed her to lie down when she didn't feel up to her job. Depression was mangling her mind and body. On May 21st, Inspector Walsh returned to ask Violet more questions. He was determined to find out who Ernie was. She had told him earlier, she dated a man named Ernie on the night of the kidnapping. And like the last time, Violet was not forthcoming with information.

Inspector Walsh went right after her, asking the same questions as last time. Immediately, Violet began shaking and acting as if she was on the verge of convulsions. After a few minutes, she acted comatose. The interview only lasted for six minutes, when two police physicians called off the interrogation. Walsh was incensed; he thought she was feigning ill. He vowed to return and get to the bottom of the kidnapping and murder. He suspected Violet had information to tell, but what it was exactly, he did not know. He thought Violet may have tipped off the kidnappers to the fact that the Lindberghs were staying in Hopewell on the night of the kidnapping. And he also suspected there were other people in the house that night that were equally deceptive. Somebody around Next Day Hill knew the truth, and he was determined to find out who it was. Two days later, he interrogated her again. He asked her several times about someone named Ernie Brinkert but didn't get anywhere. She gave him conflicting answers about the afternoon of March 1st. He showed her a photograph of the man. When asked if he was the guy she went out with on the night of the kidnapping, she replied. "It looks like him."

CHAPTER FORTY-THREE
VIOLET'S DEATH

O n June 9th, Walsh had returned for yet another round of questioning. Again, he only became more frustrated as Violet continued her evasiveness. Walsh had questioned a man named Ernest Brinkert about the kidnapping. He had found his name on a card in Violet's room the last time he was at Next Day Hill. He had searched her room without her knowledge and found the business card. In discussions with Brinkert, he was unable to get definitive information. Brinkert said he did not know Violet, and had nothing to do with the kidnapping. Walsh wanted Violet to tell him about her relationship with Brinkert. But the trembling servant had had enough of the interrogations, and was no help to the red faced Walsh. Violet had made up her mind by the end of the interrogation that it was the last time. When the doctor suggested that Violet had enough questions for the day, the persistent Walsh said he would return the next day. But Violet Sharpe was not going to answer any more questions; she had other plans.

That night, Violet stared at the ceiling in her room. She cried hard and then stopped. She smiled and then remembered the cyanide in her medicine chest. Quickly her smile vanished, for she just couldn't go on with things the way they were. She closed her eyes and tried hard to make these new problems go away. Her thoughts turned back to Red, maybe she would meet up with him one day. She loved him and he had told her the same. Finally she fell asleep, a sleep that was dominated by her uneasiness. Her dreams came to her like waves, crashing in on her, one after another. Sweet waves of elation and then the painful waves of guilt tumbled over and over. The good times with Red came in on wisps of fluffy sea foam, and then the bitter salt and sand would crash in with her break-up and the decomposing body of the Lindbergh baby lying helpless on the beach. The terrorizing dreams went on. Her night was a struggle. Her body ached; her mind throbbed from emotional distress.

Violet rose early on June 10th. Poor sleep exacerbated her body's pains. For the last eight hours, all her thoughts were centered on Red and little Charlie. She checked her clock it was 9:00 am. When she went downstairs she saw that Mrs. Morrow was not around, she was alone. Once again guilt overcame her. She cried, and headed back up the stairs when she heard the phone ring. In another room, Arthur Springer, Mrs. Morrow's secretary lifted the receiver. Again, it was Inspector Walsh. The Jersey City detective was persistent.

Violet crouched on the steps and listened. Her intuition had told her who it was. She hated Harry Walsh. He was determined to lay the blame for the baby's death all on her. She was sure of it. She knew what he was saying on the other line.

"This is Inspector Harry Walsh from Jersey City. You need to tell Violet that we would like to take her to Alpine to ask some additional questions. It's nothing really, but we are confused about some of her statements. We will be there within the hour."

Andrew Springer nodded to the man on the other line. "I shall tell her to be prepared for your arrival sir." He hung up the phone. Violet had made up her mind; she was not going to listen to any more intrusive questioning from ruthless investigators. She started to cry again and rushed up the steps. She plopped on her bed and cried some more. She could hear the Great Aviator downstairs asking questions of Springer. He defended her and said she did not need any more questioning. She wanted to think that he was defending her because he cared about her, but she knew if he had cared he would not have tricked her into the part she played. He was only worried that she would tell the truth, and place the blame all on him, the Great Aviator. She waited in her bed; she was staring at the ceiling. After twenty minutes, she heard the doorbell ring. Downstairs, she could hear the detectives enter the parlor. Violet had enough. She entered her room. On her shelf, in a tin can was a container of cyanide chloride. She removed the lid, and mixed it with a glass of water sitting on her nightstand. Without any more thought, she gulped the mixture. Her throat tightened and she began to choke. Within seconds, she could feel her body's response. It was already rejecting it. In a violent spasm, her stomach attempted to throw the poison upward but couldn't. The poison was already speeding through her bloodstream, paralyzing the stomach. Staggering now; she fell to the floor. She crawled on her hands and knees down the hall toward Emily Kempairien the chambermaid. All coherent thoughts had now evaded her. Violet wanted to say something but couldn't. She looked up at Emily, but her eyes rolled backward. Her legs stiffened and folded under her body. She convulsed violently, and then shook, as her body continued to reject the poison. Violet's mind went black as she entered an unconscious world. For sixty more seconds her body twitched uncontrollably, and then went limp. Other members of the staff came running up the steps to see what was going on, but before they could do anything, Violet Sharpe was dead.

CHAPTER FORTY-FOUR
LIVING ON BORROWED TIME

Themes summer of 1932 was fast approaching. The Lindberghs were safely ensconced in their wing at Next Day Hill. Anne prepared for the birth of her second child, and the Great Aviator continued his research with Alexis Carrel in New York City. Both were troubled by the suicide of Violet Sharpe. Anne, who grew to like the English servant, looked at her death as just another roadblock as she tried to move on with her life after Charlie. Violet became a victim in Anne's mind, the pressure of law enforcement, and their desperation to place the blame on someone for little Charlie's death. The Great Aviator also felt that Violet was a victim, and he regretted that he got her involved in the kidnapping. The drastic effect the kidnapping had on everyone worried him. He regretted that he underestimated the aftermath. The overwhelming attention it garnered, the relentless police search for the kidnappers, the loss of Violet, Red Johnson's forced departure, the beginning of what appeared to be a money trail, and the uneasy feeling that the Germans were going to spill the beans caused him great consternation. He worried about getting caught. He knew that a few gold certificates had already surfaced, and it angered him that the Germans had the gall to take the chance and get caught. It also angered him that he had to testify against two con men, who had tried to take advantage of the kidnapping by trying to extort money. No matter what he did to try to shed the kidnapping and resume a semi-normal life, proved to be virtually impossible. Magazines and newspapers continued to write sensational articles about the case. Reporters as well as police, dogged Doc Condon relentlessly. Everyone was highly critical of the negotiations and the payoff. As he approached every corner, the Great Aviator was on pins and needles waiting for something else to go wrong.

On August 16, after a grueling pregnancy affected by the loss of her first son, Anne gave birth to her second child, a healthy boy. His weight was just short of eight pounds. Much to the chagrin of most people involved in the crime, the Great Aviator decided to name the boy Jon. Even though he claimed he did it because of his Scandinavian heritage, he liked the attention it brought because Jon was the supposed name of the kidnapper. He thought of it as a chance to taunt anyone who criticized him for his handling of the kidnapping. Once again, Lindbergh was undaunted by what people thought. It didn't matter to him that his new son had the same name as the man who supposedly stole his baby, Cemetery John. What did matter was that Jon appeared to be a healthy baby boy. He was not about to repeat the events of the past year.

"Let's see what people say about the name. It will be interesting to hear them speculating about where we got it from." Anne never questioned her husband as he continued to flaunt his power.

The Lindberghs debated back and forth on the issue of whether or not they should return to the house in Hopewell. By the end of the summer they were spending more time there, and Anne was growing fond of it again. Betty Gow had remained by her side, and continued playing nursemaid. Anne never suspected she had anything to do with the kidnapping. It was yet another flaunting of the Great Aviator's power.

The Germans were also trying to restore their lives. For the Schlesers, they gave up their share of the marked ransom money for fear of being caught. This allowed Fisch and Hauptmann to split the entire fifty thousand. Charlie Schleser was too smart; he and his wife agreed that spending the money could possibly mean the death penalty. He was more content conning people, and despite his felonious tendencies, he wanted no part of something that could end up in a murder conviction. He knew spending the ransom money meant the electric chair. By the summer, Isadore Fisch and Richard Hauptmann ignored the danger and both were spending ransom money. Hauptmann kept spending more than Fisch, and he believed that there was no way they would be able to track him down in a city the size of New York. Hauptmann, by summer's end, was spending his money on fancy meals, stylish shoes and clothing for both he and Anna, including beautiful dresses, the latest radio equipment, new furniture, and continued investments in the stock market. Fisch was a little more cautious; he maintained the same persona as a typical down on his luck fella, wondering where his next meal was coming from.

For the wily Doctor Condon, he continued to give differing accounts to all the police investigators and that included Jersey City's Harry Walsh. Walsh, like most of the police, was very skeptical of the old man and thought that he was deliberately evading questioning. He even tried to get the old man to admit to being a conspirator by taking him for a walk along the steep palisades of Englewood. The old man's criminal constitution was not shaken. Even Jimmy Finn of the NYPD had his doubts about the old man. It appeared to be obvious to most law enforcement people that the old schoolmaster was hiding something, but Lindbergh and Breckinridge were uncompromising in their defense of the mysterious 'Jafsie'.

By the end of 1932, things had not changed much. The case was unsolved. The Lindberghs were bringing up their second son with much assistance as usual, Richard Hauptmann kept spending ransom money, and he and Fisch continued hustling phony stocks and cheap furs. Charlie Schleser was doing the same with an attorney friend of his named Kurtz, and occasionally Isadore Fisch. Doc Condon was eloquently narrating to anyone who would listen to him, the events that occurred while he was the famous intermediary of the Lindbergh Kidnapping. Betty Gow kept to her story and to her job. Red Johnson was living in Norway trying to make a few dollars doing whatever he could. Violet Sharpe was dead from suicide, and so was little Charlie Lindbergh who would already have celebrated his second birthday.

On July 9, 1933, the Lindbergh's began a new expedition financed with their money, and without an itinerary in place. With a new modified aircraft, they took off toward the northeast with no set time for their return. Their second son Jon was barely 11 months old when they left. He was placed in the care of their respective mothers and without any expected anxiety, nursemaid Betty Gow. For more than five months they toured Canada, Greenland, all of Scandinavia, Estonia, Russia, all of Great Britain, France, Spain, Switzerland, Portugal, the Canary Islands, Cape Verde Islands, across to the east coast of South America, Trinidad, Puerto Rico, Santo Domingo. At one point in early November, Anne had mentioned that she missed her new son and wanted to go home. The Great Aviator's reply was simple and to the point. "My time is my own." They did not return home until December 19th. The Lindberghs were away from their second son for five months and ten days. Jon was now almost 1 1/2 years old, and like his deceased brother, was not quite sure who his parents were.

The New York City Police and its chief investigator Jimmie Finn were hot on the trail of the person or persons who were spending the ransom money, but in a city the size of New York, finding the responsible parties proved difficult. With occasional bills popping up, they had hoped that bank clerks and merchants would have been much more cognizant of the serial numbers. Isadore Fisch, as usual, was shrewd and was careful not to spend too much of the ransom money. Sometimes he would portray himself as a pauper, and other times to impress women he would whip out a wad of cash. He would have a legitimate twenty-dollar bill on the outside, and underneath he would have a roll of twenty-dollar, gold certificates. Some of the people Fisch knew couldn't quite figure him out. With a cough due to the early stages of tuberculosis, he sometimes seemed weak and fragile. Other times he was an energetic conniver who even toted a pistol. He would don pauper attire, get people to feel sorry for him and give him a free meal, and then other times he would dress like a businessman and prey upon people getting them to invest in his many enterprises. He even deceived his friends, the same Germanic people he socialized with, getting them to invest thousands of dollars into his many fake companies. Sometimes he played one against each other, including Schleser and Hauptmann. He and Schleser had agreed that if one of them was caught, they would blame it all on Hauptmann and he didn't mind conducting secret deals with Hauptmann behind Schlesers back. But with Schleser giving up his take of the money and Fisch carefully hiding most of his, it left them in a better position should someone find out something. And they both were aware that Hauptmann was living the good life, spending the ransom money. He and his wife Anna, who was still unaware of her husband's role in the kidnapping, were living high off the hog and they often dressed like they were members of New York City's upper crust. Anna didn't mind showing off her array of fancy dresses. This didn't sit over too well with Fisch and Schleser, but the wiry Fisch maintained his friendship with the German carpenter throughout the next eighteen months as they continued to hustle people, making money at their expense.

In the fall of 1933, Richard Hauptmann's life was about to change. Anna was getting ready to give birth. He knew he would have to seek more legitimate means of making money, including trying to round up more carpentry jobs. But as a new father, he knew it would not be that easy to find work. As Hauptmann prepared for his new life, Isadore Fisch was worried his life was winding down. With his tuberculosis getting worse, he decided that he needed to go back to Germany where he could be in the care of his family. An ailing Fisch announced that he would be heading back to his hometown of Leipzig, Germany. A short time later in the middle of November, he spent over four hundred dollars in gold certificates to pay off the balance for two steamship tickets back to Europe. He figured it didn't matter about the gold certificates once he made it back to Germany. He then asked Hauptmann if he would make a deal with him. In return for two thousand dollars of exchangeable cash, he was willing to give Hauptmann the rest of his inventory of sealskins, and his remaining six thousand dollars of gold certificates. With his tuberculosis compromising his ability to maintain a decent quality of life, he wondered if he would ever be able to return.

CHAPTER FORTY-FIVE
THE MARIONETTE–NOVEMBER 1933

ichard Hauptmann was anxious to pick up his wife and newborn son. It was already ten days since Manfred's birth. The drive over to Misericordia Hospital on 86th Street wouldn't take him that long, just a short trip south from his home on 222nd Street. He was familiar with the area having spent time down on 86th street trading stocks at Steiner-Rouse, and enjoying playing cards and eating fine German cuisine at the Yorkville Boerse, a favorite meeting place for many New York City Germans. The drive from the hospital was a quick one. Richard Hauptmann wanted to get the baby home as fast as he could. Since his car was unheated, he didn't want the baby to develop a cough from the chilly weather. He seemed almost paranoid, when thoughts of the Lindbergh child's death in the cold cabin kept drifting in and out of his mind. He drove fast; he wanted Manfred out of the cold as soon as possible. The new parents were giddy and excited with their newborn son. Hauptmann was ecstatic, when the infant crawled beneath his mother's chin and fell fast asleep. He doted on both mom and child, and Anna was overjoyed with her husband as he embraced his new responsibilities.

With Anna and Manfred fast asleep on the sofa, Hauptmann was puttering around the baby's nursery. He looked down at the wooden marionette he held with his two hands, and pulled on the waxed strings, lifting the bottom limbs upward. He struggled awhile, as he tried to get all four of the disjointed appendages to move simultaneously. The young carpenter marveled at the German craftsmanship, and wondered if he could duplicate it with his own woodworking skills. The wooden pieces were perfectly carved and the eyelets lined with soft black rubber. They fitted securely into the painted oak trunk of the marionette. As skilled as he might have been as a carpenter, he couldn't quite grasp the method of making the little puppet work. Regardless of how inept he was as a puppeteer, he knew that one day his young son Manfred would be tickled pink watching the little wooden man dance effortlessly in the air, while his proud dad held it up for him to see. A year earlier, he and Anna had talked about having children, and Anna had picked up the marionette from a German woodworker on her visit back to Germany. She was hoping to give it to him for his first Christmas, but he decided to take it out and place it in Manfred's crib, so it would be there when he came home from the hospital. Hauptman was excited about being a father, and he smiled thinking of the expression his young son or daughter would have on his face as he danced the puppet up and down. He knew he had to practice for a while before he could become a good puppeteer.

Hauptmann's smile quickly turned to a frown, when he thought about the Great Aviator's plan to send his son away and how manipulative he was. But he also knew he wasn't forced to involve himself in the kidnapping scheme. He did it because he wanted to make some easy money. And now he had to worry about getting caught for his role in the kidnapping. Even though he wasn't fully responsible for the boy's death, he knew that he could serve serious jail time for driving his Dodge to pick up the boy, and then ten days later dropping his body along that hilly, road between Princeton and Hopewell. He understood that it wasn't what the original plan had called for, but he had no other recourse of action. He felt a blast of emotion as he thought about the little boy's corpse, hastily and recklessly being tossed into the leaf pile. It hurt him now more than ever. He hated the fact that Lindbergh and Condon had proposed such an idea. How could Lindbergh be so callous? The plan had gotten way out of control and he believed the Great Aviator's role in this was more sinister. He tried to justify his own actions by projecting the blame elsewhere. He adamantly believed the reason he involved himself was for financial reasons. He was only trying to make a few dollars for himself and Anna, and if they were going to start a family they would certainly need more money. Decent work was hard to come by. It was 1933, there weren't too many people willing to employ an immigrant carpenter, and if they did, they weren't going to pay a lot of money. When the opportunity arose, he fully used it to his advantage. He had to put food on the table. Anna totally relied on him.

But now things were different. Hauptmann was now a father with unconditional love for his child. He had not experienced that since he was a child in Kamenz. He knew his responsibilities would increase significantly, and he would have to settle down and stop being a hustler. The ransom money wasn't going to last forever, and he still had to be careful not to get caught. He had the skills to be a good successful carpenter; maybe the new president Roosevelt could expand some of his programs to include carpentry and building positions. It was becoming obvious to him that emotions that had been dormant for so many years were now becoming more accessible. He thought about his abusive father, and he knew he had to overcome any bad tendencies that were cast his way. He thought about the Great Aviator and his baby. And he thought about the role he played in his kidnapping. It troubled him.

With Anna's niece Maria helping out, Richard was able to spend more time helping Anna tend to their baby boy. One day after the two had fallen asleep, and Maria had left, he headed down to the garage. He had some business that needed attending to; he needed to hide some more ransom money.

He had mixed feelings when he found out his friend Isadore Fisch had decided to go back to Germany. Hauptmann wondered if he would ever see him again. He knew his partner was very sick, he could see it in his eyes and in his peaked coloring. Fisch had asked him for a big favor. He thought about the deal he had made, trading $2000 cash for the remaining ransom money. It was an offer that Fisch had proposed and he agreed to it. He and Anna were already enjoying the benefits of the ransom money, and since no one seemed to be paying attention, he was willing to spend more, including Fisch's $6.000.00. Even though they were still partners, he could also access the money that he and Fisch had buried in Summit, New Jersey. Back in the late spring when the ground had softened, Hauptmann drove Fisch through the tunnel to the north part of Jersey near Summit. There they found a nice wooded spot in the hills. They did the best they could to mark the area, by counting steps and using a couple large rocks to cover the exact spot. The money was wrapped in waxed paper and placed in two metal lock boxes that were additionally wrapped with cheesecloth on the outside. Each box contained approximately $12,500.00. The two Germans took the remaining twenty-five thousand and again halved it. Richard knew that unlike himself, Fisch had been more careful and was very selective in where he spent his bills. Hauptmann did not know for sure, but he thought Fisch had invested some of his money in a few private enterprises with Charlie Schleser and his lawyer friend Kurtz. But Fisch wanted to take only clean and usable money back to Germany just in case some government person got too nosy. He knew that he had spent over $400.00 in gold certificates to pay off the balance of two steamship tickets he purchased for himself and a friend named Henry Ulig.

Hauptmann could tell Fisch had kept good care of his money. Knowing Fisch the way he is, he thought, he probably kept it beneath his mattress. He counted it out very carefully making sure it was all there. He had counted it once before to make sure Fisch had given him the full six thousand, but now he was count-ing it again. Meticulously, he sorted it. Fisch had indeed been honest and the money was exactly $6000. Hauptmann had already found a nice obscure spot for the exchanged money. He would wrap $2000 of it in newspapers and stash them between two wall joists and then cover them with another board. The rest he placed with his own share, beneath some rags in an old shellac can. Just in case someone stumbled upon it, he stashed another $1000.00, next to his pistol in some bored out holes in a couple two by fours. It would be his mad money. He could use it for any emergency or possibly some new item that Anna had her eyes on. Anna rarely went into the garage and always allowed her husband to take care of the finances. She believed him when he told her the money was coming from his stock investments, and never questioned him about where he got the money to buy that new phonograph or that new dress. It was always money that came from the stock market.

The following March, Isadore Fisch succumbed to tuberculosis. Lindbergh and Condon had found out from some of their contacts at City Island. Neither man expressed any grief. In their eyes he was one less con man they had to worry about. When the word reached Hauptmann, he had mixed emotions. He liked Fisch despite his questionable character. But in some ways Hauptmann knew Fisch was a lot like he was. They both loved the freedoms that America had given them and they both enjoyed reaping the rewards it had to offer, even if some were not on the up and up. He also liked Fisch's strange personality, and the fact that he never seemed intimidated by anyone even the Great Aviator. Now that he was gone he could access his share of the ransom money. He had not spent the additional $6000 from Fisch, it was with his own ransom dollars in his garage, and when the time was right, he would dig up the remaining $25,000 in Summit, New Jersey.

CHAPTER FORTY-SIX
HAUPTMANN GETS CARELESS

———◼———

By the end of the summer of 1934, Richard Hauptmann had spent nearly three thousand of his certificates. In September, after using a ten dollar gold certificate for a fill-up, an observant gas station attendant in the Bronx wrote down his license plate number on the back of the bill. After the money was deposited in the bank, a teller noticed it was Lindbergh ransom money. He also noticed the license plate number and called the police. It was the break the police had been waiting for. They traced the license number to Hauptmann and staked out his Bronx home on East 222nd Street. On the morning of September 19th, a joint task force made up of NYPD, FBI, and the NJSP observed him through binoculars as he entered his garage to get his car. Before he drove too far up Tremont Avenue, they pulled him over. Hauptmann's world came crashing down. The police ran a registration check on his blue Dodge, found out his name, and that he was a German carpenter. In an effort to portray himself as an honest person, Hauptmann started giving the police as much information as he could, but the police were not buying it. Desperate to hide his guilt, the German carpenter vehemently denied any involvement in the kidnapping. Immediately, they suspected that he was not telling the truth. But he informed them he was in the country without the proper papers, and that he was married with a child. He was also quick to tell them that he had reformed his crooked ways. When they found a crisp, unfolded twenty-dollar gold certificate in his wallet, instead of telling them he got it from somewhere else, he didn't know what to say. For the first time since the kidnapping had taken place, Hauptmann was at a loss for words, unable to make things up. He decided to play stupid as if he had no idea what they were talking about. Back at his rented house, the police were impressed with the expensive furniture and stylish wardrobes. After the police were unsuccessful in their quest to find more gold certificates, they dragged him down to the lower West Side police station on Greenwich Street. For the next twenty-four hours, the police tried everything they could to get the German carpenter to give a legitimate explanation for the certificate at the gas station and the one in his wallet. Hauptmann stuck to his plea of ignorance; refusing to budge. He kept repeating that he had nothing to do with the Lindbergh Kidnapping, that they were all wrong. The police refused to buy it. Ruthlessly, they punished him with every possible form of abuse. Cuffed to a chair, they screamed at him and called him derogatory names. When that didn't work, they punished him physically. They turned out the lights, took a hammer and pummeled his body from his head to toe. The abusive behavior continued when they deprived him of sleep and food, while the interrogators took turns working him over.

During the early morning hours, they asked him to give some writing samples. When his writing did not match up with the ransom notes, they had him write misspelled words like boad instead of boat. As Hauptmann tired, they kept on demanding more and more writing samples, and as he wrote the way they wanted, he was implicating himself as the writer of the ransom notes. When daylight came and the interrogation continued, the three law enforcement groups descended upon the Hauptmann house for a second round. This time they headed for the garage. With little care they tore it apart. It would not take them very long to discover the rest of Richard Hauptmann's ransom money.

When the word of their find reached the station, they gave him one more chance to tell the truth before they told him what they found in his garage. When he repeated his innocence, they repeated the intimidation.

"Okay, you son of a bitch. How do you explain over fourteen thousand dollars in ransom money? You going to come clean now, or do we have to knock the shit out of you some more. Tell us the truth Bruno. Do you have any more ransom money?" Jimmie Finn was leading the questioning and enjoyed ruffling Hauptmann's feathers by calling him Bruno.

"Don't call me Bruno. Dats not my name. My name is Richard."

"Tell us, Bruno—you don't have any more gold certificates lying around do you?" Hauptmann remained steadfast but gave up trying to get them to call him Richard.

"Bruno, you are a lying son of a bitch. We found the money in your garage. Are you going to keep on lying to us?" Hauptmann now realized they had found the money. He had to tell them something or they were going to beat him some more. For the first time, he regretted spending the ransom money. The Great Aviator told him not to spend it, but he did not listen. Now, he had to pay the consequences.

"I can explain das money."

"You can? Well, let's hear it, and no lies."

"I got das money from my friend Fisch. He gave it to me ven he left for Germany. It is truth. He went to Germany because he vas sick, he died over dere."

"Repeat that again; we need to the truth; what did you say?"

"I got das money from a friend. It vas in a shoebox. He told me to hold it for him ven he left. I put it in my garage. But Fisch died in Germany so I decided to spend his money. I don't know vher he got money from, he vas a good business-man. Ve vere partners in a fur business."

The police still did not believe him. The next thing the police needed to do before the word got out, was to call Charles Lindbergh and tell him that they caught the no good bastard who killed his young son.

The Lindberghs were staying at Will Roger's ranch in California while he was away, when the Great Aviator got the news from Colonel Norman Schwarzkopf. Lindbergh knew immediately, that he had to get in touch with his old buddy Doc Condon. He found a private room on the ranch, and called him long distance to share the bad news with him. "Doc? Have you heard?"

"Don't tell me that those no good Germans have spent more of the ransom money."

Lindbergh showed no emotion as he told the old man the truth. "Doc, Im afraid it is worse than that. They caught Hauptmann."

"What?"

"They caught Hauptmann, and found part of the ransom money."

"That stupid son of a bitch! Colonel, I'm sorry for my outburst, but he is a hard headed dumkopf. Did the thought ever occur to him that he could get caught passing those certificates?"

"I am afraid not, Doc. Look, I'm sure the police are going to get you to try to identify the stupid bastard today. They will probably ask me as well. We are going to have to continue the run around. We have to try to get him off the hook somehow, or he might rat everybody out. Tell them you are not sure he is Cemetery John. You know, that he does not fit the description. If they ask me to identify the voice I will go in and do the same. I will say that I cannot positively recognize it because it was so long ago." Condon nervously laughed.

"Colonel Lindbergh, I have prepared for this day just in case. I will have them scratching their heads. Sir, please do not worry. Hopefully, if they do not have any other incriminating evidence, he might be able to play stupid and say he got the money from somewhere else."

"Doc, the police told me that Hauptmann said he was given the money from someone in Germany and the man died."

"Fisch?"

"Exactly. He told them that his business partner Fisch had asked him to hold it for him until he returned.

"Colonel–that is not a bad idea. Since Fisch has died, they won't be able to bring him into this. What about the others?"

"Who? You mean Schleser?" The Great Aviator acted as if he almost forgot the rest of the conspirators.

"Yes– Schleser and his wife, but also my girl Betty and the Norwegian. What about them?"

"The police have not said anything about anyone else, I hope the son of a bitch did not rat us out. Now you have me worried, Doc. Listen we're going to have to arrange a meeting somehow with Hauptmann. You are going to have to tell him if he says one word, it will be his son next."

"Yes Colonel, but how do we do that?"

"Let me work on that. The problem is we do not have much time. I want to get the message to him before he does rat everybody out." As Lindbergh paused trying to figure a way to relate the threat to Hauptmann, the ingenious Doctor Condon came up with an answer.

"What I can do, Colonel Lindbergh, is tell them that I need to talk to him in private to see if I recognize his voice from the cemetery. I am not sure however if those conniving police will allow me to speak with him in private because it may imply that I am involved."

"I agree Doc, but that is exactly what you need to do. You can't be obvious. Just do your magic and keep them guessing."

"Yes, Colonel. I will be back in touch with you when I can. We also have to be careful they don't listen in on us. By the way, where is he now?"

"He is at the second precinct jail on Greenwich Street."

"Okay Colonel, we shall be in touch." The old pedagogue slumped in his chair; his hands covered his wrinkled face. What he and the Great Aviator feared most was now happening. And now, Lindbergh left it up to the slick old man to get the word out to Hauptmann, that he better not do something stupid.

A few minutes after getting off the phone with the Great Aviator, Doc Condon got a call from Inspector John Lyons who was now in charge of the interrogations. He asked Condon "if he could come over right away. They think they have apprehended the mysterious Cemetery John. We want you to identify the kidnapper of the Lindbergh baby." Condon was ready to perform his magic. He was going to take the stage in a few minutes, to try to take the heat off the man Charles Lindbergh warned not to spend the money. Old Jafsie knew he had to be careful about how he was going to communicate with Hauptmann. The last thing he wanted to do was cast a shadow of suspicion on himself and the Great Aviator.

Greenwich Street was a stone's throw from Decatur Street. The police had sent a car to pick the old man up. Condon came prancing into the office with all his bravado, immediately turning heads. He was loud and obnoxious until Inspector Lyons asked him to keep it down a bit. It wouldn't take him long to go to work. He walked back and forth in front of the contrived police lineup. He kept looking surprised, even though the lineup was a sham. Hauptmann stood out like a sore thumb amongst the broad shouldered detectives who were clean-shaven and well dressed. Hauptmann was tired, he had been beaten, was denied food and sleep, and he looked suspicious. Condon then took over. He started shouting out orders to everyone and started asking names of everyone in the lineup. "Did you ever see me before?" when they all answered no, Condon got in Hauptmann's face. "Are you sure you never saw me before? You don't remember me-speaking to you?"

"I can't say that I can."

"What is your name?"

"Richard Hauptmann."

"You know 233rd Street?"

"233rd Street? Yes."

"How long have you lived in the Bronx?"

"Nine years."

"Nine years up there; you don't know me?"

"No."

"Why?"

"You didn't speak to me about the baby?"

"No."

Seeing the conversation going nowhere fast, Inspector Lyons interjected a question of his own for Doctor Condon "Would you say that he was the man?"

"I would not say he was the man."

"You are not positive?"

"I am not positive."

"What about the voice, do you recognize the voice?"

"The voice I heard was husky."

Lyons and the rest of the police were obviously frustrated with Condon. He had achieved his objective of confusing everyone, including Richard Hauptmann. He even had Hauptmann read questions that he wrote on paper, covering everything from his mother and his weight, and even asking him his name again. Condon wrote the word kinderlich, a German word for baby, and pointed to Hauptmann. The German carpenter said nothing, not understanding Condon's threat about

Hauptmann's baby. The detectives thought Condon was trying to get Hauptmann to say something about the Lindbergh baby, but what the old man was attempting to do was to get Hauptmann to understand that his baby son could be in danger should he decide to run his mouth. With no response from Hauptmann, Condon went on. He pretended to listen intently, to see if he could recognize Hauptmann's voice when he answered his other written questions. Again, Lyons wanted to know the most important question.

"Is he the man?"

"I couldn't say that he is not the man."

"What? He looks like him?"

"Yes."

"But you cannot identify him?"

"No, I have to be careful. The man's life is in jeopardy. This could mean the electric chair. He has a wife and child." Lyons threw up his hands in frustration. "Well we are going nowhere fast." Hauptmann felt relieved. Condon had given the police the run-around. Before he left, he stared long and hard at his co-conspirator, but was afraid to point back at the word kinderlich, for fear that the police might suspect something and realize Condon was threatening Hauptmann's baby. Even though Hauptmann felt confident that Condon would protect him, he was confused. The old man was equally flustered because he couldn't say anything. He felt he was unsuccessful in relating the threat because of the constant police presence. He wanted to tell Hauptmann to continue pleading ignorance to the kidnapping, and maybe he could get out of the mess he got himself into. The old educator would have to inform the Great Aviator that he would have to try again. A few days later, Charles Lindbergh entered the police station in disguise. He listened while Hauptmann shouted out the words "Hey Doktor" several times. He told Finn, Schwarzkopf and Lyons he could not identify the voice, it was just too long ago.

By now the police had received Hauptmann's rap sheet from Germany. It included hold-ups and burglaries, and they felt confident he was their man. It became apparent that the mob gang theory was out the window. In their custody was a master criminal who could find the Lindbergh estate in the dark, climb a homemade ladder, steal the most popular baby in the world and then murder it, afterward write a dozen ransom notes with a secret code, ask for only fifty thousand dollars and then miraculously make off with the ransom money. Despite the improbability of this heinous accomplishment, some of the police were buying it. Others like Walsh and Schwarzkopf were not ready to let the lone wolf theory take precedent. Both felt strongly that it was an inside job, and the staff was at the center of their suspicion, especially Violet Sharpe. She didn't commit suicide over nothing. They weren't sure if Hauptmann was an extortionist or a cold calculating murderer. But he wasn't forthcoming with information, leading them to think he was involved in the kidnapping. Hauptmann's unwillingness to provide them with information had them leaning toward the idea, that he was part of a group that included members from the inside. Even without Condon's positive identification, law enforcement had enough circumstantial evidence to pursue a murder charge. The N.Y.P.D. had enough on him to nail him for extortion, and the state of New Jersey had something else in mind, they wanted to extradite him for murder. Experts were ready to testify that the handwriting, despite the fact that it was taken when Hauptmann was under duress from the beating, was the same as the kidnap notes. Other so-called experts were claiming that Hauptmann crafted the ladder with boards from his own attic. And New Jersey's young Attorney General, thirty-nine year old David Wilentz had rounded up several witnesses that saw him near the Lindbergh estate. One witness claimed he saw Hauptmann with a ladder in his car. Regarding the ransom money, they had several people who identified Hauptmann as the man who passed the Lindbergh certificates. The state of New Jersey was compiling an impressive mound of evidence, both real and fabricated.

By October, and after some political wrangling, it was becoming obvious that Hauptmann should be sent to New Jersey to face the more serious charge of murder. And not just any murder, it was the kidnapping-murder of the world's most famous baby. On October 19th the papers were signed to extradite Richard Hauptmann to Flemington, New Jersey to stand trial for the murder of the Lindbergh baby. That night under the cover of darkness, a motorcade pulled up to the Flemington jailhouse. Inside one of the cars, Richard Hauptmann wondered what his next step should be. He thought about his future and where all this was heading. "Doc Condon was a shifty character. Was he going to continue his charade and protect him? Did the Great Aviator have a strategy to get him out of this mess or would he testify against him as some of the press was now reporting? Would they seek the death penalty that he was so fearful of? Surely the Great Aviator would not let that happen." But he remembered what the airman told him. "Don't spend the money! Burn it or bury it."

Hauptmann got out of the car. He could hear what sounded like hundreds of people shouting his name through the darkness. "Hauptmann, Hauptmann murderer! Die, you German son of a bitch! Die Hauptmann, you will die! Kill Hauptmann, Kill Hauptmann!" He could see some of the angry faces, illuminated by kerosene torches. They hated him—and wanted him dead! His mind raced. They detested him for something he didn't do. He knew he did not kill the Lindbergh baby; all he did was drive his car. He wished he hadn't owned that car, if he hadn't owned it maybe he would not have gotten involved. He was told not to spend the money. He had made a stupid mistake spending the money, that damn money. He remembered what the Great Aviator had asked him. "Would you rat us all out, Richard? Would you do that to us?" He knew that being a rat would serve no purpose other than dishonoring himself and putting everybody else on trial for murder. A decent and honorable man would not do that. "Dammit!" He knew he should not have spent that money. "That damn money!" ….. Hauptmann needed a way out, but there was none in sight.

With Hauptmann now awaiting trial for murder in New Jersey, Lindbergh and Condon felt another meeting was needed. Attorney General Wilentz was also hoping to get the old schoolmaster to give a positive identification of Hauptmann. The Great Aviator however, was still hoping to relate a threat to Hauptmann. On October 22nd, a second meeting was set up at the Flemington jail. Sitting together on a bench outside Hauptmann's cell, the teacher and the carpenter spoke for nearly an hour. With troopers watching his every move, the old man found it difficult to relate a threat from the man in charge. He had to be careful what he said for fear of incriminating himself.

"You have seen me before?"

"I saw you once, this is the second time."

"What is your name, what does your mother call you?"

"Richard."

Condon wrote down a few words in German. Like he did in New York, he wrote down the word kinderlich. Hauptmann acted surprised, but he recognized the word, which meant baby. He shrugged his shoulders. Condon moved on and wrote down a few more words.

"Do you remember these words, they made trouble for me. The New York Police called me wacky and screwy. Do you know what that means? I have never found it in the dictionary." Again Condon was in a conundrum. He wanted to give some advice to the prisoner but because of the trooper standing alongside of him he couldn't. He found himself rambling, and not making much sense, just like he did the first time. He switched to talking about himself. He explained to Hauptmann that he had traveled the country in search of the baby and now all he wanted was the truth. Hauptmann was perplexed; he wondered what Condon wanted him to say. Hauptmann responded by saying he had nothing to do with the crime. Condon shifted the conversation and mentioned the word higher. Again Hauptmann was confused. Condon reiterated. "Is there someone higher?" …….Capone, Al Capone. Have you heard of him?"

"I don't know any gangsters. I had nothing to do with the kidnapping." Hauptmann stuck to his plan.

"What about the money?" asked Condon.

"I tell you da same as police. My business partner give it to me to hold."

"Tell me about my phone number in your house, how did it get there?"

"I do that all the time I write down numbers." Hauptmann did not know that a writer named Tom Cassidy had written it down as a joke and then the police decided to use it as evidence against him. He remembered during his interrogation; he said he had written it down. He was so tired and frazzled, he admitted to something he didn't do. He assumed someone else wrote it down to make him look guilty. He did not even have a phone in his house! As the conversation went on about nothing, Condon continued to talk about himself until the end of the hour. He pointed his index finger toward the written German words. "Do you know this?" He was more specific, and put his finger on the word kinderlich.

"Baby? Condon looked at Hauptman and whispered, "Yes, the baby."

"I told you I had nothing to do with the baby." Condon nodded his head. The trooper shouted. "It's about time for you to leave Doctor Condon." The old man rose up from the bench. With the trooper distracted as the meeting came to an end, Condon pointed to Hauptmann. "You, yours" and he pointed to the word kinderlich. He turned and walked through the jail gate. Hauptmann had now figured out what he meant and it angered him. He felt like someone just punched him in the stomach, and he knew exactly where the threat came from. It was a little message from the Great Aviator. But he knew they had nothing to worry about; he wasn't going to say a word. "How could I?" he thought. "It wouldn't save me anyway."

David Wilentz wanted to know once and for all what Doc Condon's plans really were. Was he going to testify that Richard Hauptmann was Cemetery John or not? He needed to know before the trial started what the cagey old man was going to do on the stand. He summoned him to his office in New Jersey. A few days before Thanksgiving, Wilentz sent a driver to pick him up.

"Okay, Doctor Condon, are you on the good list or the bad list?" Condon acted surprised.

"With all due respect Mr. Wilentz, I am quite puzzled by your question."

"You know exactly what I am talking about you old codger. We all know you are hiding something here. You continue to play this fucking game and you will find your ass in the slammer as an accomplice."

"Mr. Wilentz, I am quite appalled at your lack of appreciation for the effort that I put forth in trying to place that little child back in his mother's arms."

"Stop the bullshit!" I have had enough! Listen to me Condon, J. Edgar Hoover along with several other lawmen including Inspector Walsh suspect you as an accomplice. Do you understand that? And we know that you are trying to protect his ass. I am not sure what involvement you had in all of this Condon.

I suspect you are trying to protect more than just him, but it will be your ass on the line if you don't give us a positive identification. There is a helluva lot riding on this old man, and our main focus right now is on your buddy Bruno. We want you to identify him as Cemetery John. We are not going to settle for anything less than a conviction of Bruno Richard Hauptmann as the kidnapper and killer of the Lindbergh baby. There is a lot at stake here Condon. Do you understand? You will do as I say! Silence filled the room. Doc Condon had met his match with the politically driven Wilentz. He doubted Wilentz knew anything about the kidnapping, but in order to save himself and the Great Aviator, he would have to point the finger at Richard Hauptmann.

"Mr. Wilentz, I do not believe a word of that spiel you just laid at my feet, but what I was going to inform you when I entered this room sir, is that I believe that Hauptmann is Cemetery John."

"Alright, Condon, remember what I said. I expect when you are called, that you will rise up and identify that German son of a bitch as Cemetery John. Good day, sir."

Doc Condon had nothing else to say, he knew he had been beaten and was visibly shaken by the exchange with Wilentz. He would have to call the Great Aviator, and tell him what was going on. He was uncertain what Wilentz really knew, but things had now changed. Wilentz had an agenda, and he was fiercely determined to follow it through. Condon and Lindbergh would both have to place the blame for everything on Hauptmann. They both knew that David Wilentz was a self-absorbed politician aiming to make a name for himself, in what the press had already dubbed the Trial of the Century. What Condon wasn't sure about however, was whether or not he would come after him, when the trial was over and he had ascertained Hauptmann's conviction. Wilentz emerged as an antithesis to the conspirators and every bit as slippery.

After arriving back in the Bronx, Condon rang up the Great Aviator. He told him about the exchange. The Great Aviator told him there wasn't anything else they could do, except comply. He would tell Wilentz that it was Hauptmann's voice he heard while he waited in the car outside St. Raymond's. The German had no one to blame but himself; he told him not to spend the ransom money. But Lindbergh made it clear to Condon that if Richard Hauptmann implicated him once they identified him, he was going to kill him with his pistol right on the stand for everyone to see, and there wouldn't be one person other than his wife who would say that Richard Hauptmann didn't deserve it. After all, in the opinion of the court, he was the killer of the Lindbergh baby. Condon agreed. He was impressed with the Great Aviator's threat. And he believed him because he knew that Charles Lindbergh loved the power and feared nothing.

One thing that Lindbergh, Condon, and Hauptmann did not know was that Charlie Schleser had been called in for questioning. Some of Wilentz' boys wanted to know what his relationship was with Hauptmann and Fisch. Like the rest of the conspirators, Charlie Schleser was a con man. In an effort to save his ass, he was trying to portray Fisch as a good guy and Richard Hauptmann as a bad guy. Schleser disliked the carpenter, and looked at him as an opportunist newcomer. He thought he was arrogant, and it was blatantly stupid of him to think that he could spend the ransom money and not get caught. Schleser had agreed to help Wilentz get information from Hauptmann's friends by infiltrating their little clique. When Hauptmann's friends discussed the upcoming trial, Schleser listened intently and then dishonestly suggested ways of getting Hauptmann off the hook. The carpenter's friends blamed everything on the deceased Isadore Fisch. Over a period of several weeks, Schleser would check in with them and attempt to extract as much information as he could, so he could pass it on to the Attorney General. Although they knew Hauptmann was a friend of Isadore Fisch, they did not mind ridiculing the dead man for taking their money in his sketchy investment deals. Schleser acted like he had no idea that Fisch was such a con man, and then joined the crowd as an Isadore Fisch hater. Schleser, who had liked Fisch, agreed with them that the sneaky little Jew had set up Hauptmann and was the real kidnapper. But Schleser had a motive. As he penetrated their group, he turned around and gave the information to Wilentz' prosecution team. He knew this would protect him and his wife from being implicated. The more information he could funnel to Wilentz, the better the chances were that the David Wilentz might spare him, should Hauptmann implicate him and his wife. The convicted felon and accomplice in the Lindbergh kidnapping, had essentially become a snitch for the prosecution.

Once the attorneys completed their shuffling of the paper work, and with the media anxiously awaiting the trial, the honorable Judge Thomas W. Trenchard set the date. The trial of Richard Hauptmann would commence on Wednesday, January 3, 1935.

CHAPTER FORTY-SEVEN
THE TRIAL

B y dawn on the morning of the trial, the blanket of snow from the previous weekend was barely visible. As the cars started lining the streets and the masses of people descended upon the little town of Flemington, the remaining snow had been trampled into brown slush and then into nothing. What was once a picturesque scene from Currier and Ives a few days earlier, had now been transformed into P.T. Barnum's Greatest Show on Earth. Hordes of people, from all walks of life were milling around the courthouse. In the past, the modest little courthouse had served its purpose well, but the onslaught of humanity for the upcoming trial had reduced it to a holding pen. Once its doors opened, reporters rushed to get any remaining seat. Some of the privileged media were fortunate enough to get special passes in the front of the courtroom. Out of 500 available seats, which were almost 300 more than the norm, 150 of them were designated press. There were people standing along any available wall. The legal teams and their witnesses filled in the front rows. Law enforcement was seated to the sides. In other designated areas of the courtroom, famous celebrities had also been given privileged seating arrangements. Anyone else fortunate enough to get a seat filled in the remaining spots. Inside the little courtroom, it was loud, stuffy, and crammed, but it was the greatest show on earth and everyone wanted to be there. Had he been alive, P.T. Barnum would have been tantalized by the spectacle.

Shortly before ten o'clock, the crier shouted "Oyez, oyez, oyez, his Honor Justice Trenchard." The seventy-one year old veteran of the court entered from a side door. A few minutes later, Richard Hauptmann neatly dressed in a double-breasted suit, followed and took his seat in the courtroom. As the crowd ogled and gawked, Richard Hauptmann was shocked to see the hundreds of scorn-filled faces twisting to see the murderer of the Lindbergh baby. Some of those were the same professionals paid to uphold justice. Hauptmann's attorney was the flamboyant Edward J. Reilly, who was compensated for his efforts by the Hearst Newspaper Company in return for exclusives. Donned in pinstripes, Reilly strutted across the floor to take his seat alongside his defense team. New Jersey's debonair Attorney General David Wilentz was equally pompous, making sure he and his well-dressed team of prosecutors were clearly visible for all to see. The main draw however, was the Great Aviator, who entered through a side door to avoid the crowd. Accompanying him was the newly mustached Superintendent of the New Jersey State Police, Colonel Norman Schwarzkopf. The Great Aviator had made sure he had the best seat in the house, at the prosecutor's table and just four seats away from the defendant. No one bothered to suggest that sitting with the prosecutorial team might be influential toward the jury. It was obviously unethical to the members of the court. But Lindbergh's ignorance to courtroom ethics didn't seem to matter. What was most important for the Great Aviator was that he had a seat close enough to the front, just in case his co-conspirator Richard Hauptmann decided to spill the beans.

The first day of proceedings dealt with jury selection. On day two the trial got off with a bang. After the jury was seated, Wilentz began his dramatic opening remarks. He worked on the sympathies of everyone as he described the baby as a "delightful little tot that was killed by the gentleman in the custody of the sheriff's guards." Wilentz exploited the jury; he detailed the kidnapping with Hauptmann as the callous perpetrator who stole the Lindbergh baby, and then dropped him to the ground below, when he stretched onto his homemade ladder. Hauptmann then proceeded to toss the "dead package" to the ground. The Attorney General went on to describe the ransom negotiations and the finding of the dead baby. With that image firmly planted in the jury's mind, the baby's mother was called to testify. Anne Morrow was neatly dressed, and conducted herself with an air of class and dignity. She described the last day she spent with her son, and the desperation that ensued when they discovered him missing. She was well rehearsed, and although nervous, spoke clearly for all to hear. Her testimony was designed to evoke the emotion of the jurors. Later that afternoon, the Great Aviator was called to the stand. Knowing that Hauptmann was not going to be called that afternoon, he had removed his gun in the morning. Wilentz had informed him, that he would not ask him to identify Hauptmann until the next day. The trial was essentially over on the third day, when the Attorney General and the Great Aviator decided to drop the bombshell. Lindbergh had re-armed himself with his pistol, only this time it was well concealed. Wilentz had deliberately planned an exchange with Lindbergh. He brought the Great Aviator back to the night of the payoff, and spoke in the first person as if he was Charles Lindbergh.

"I heard a voice coming from the cemetery, to the best of my knowledge calling Doctor Condon. It was a foreign accent, 'Hey, Doctor!'" The Attorney General was going back over the scene one more time, and then he went right to the throat of the accused. "Since that time Colonel Lindbergh, have you heard the same voice?"

"Yes, I have."

"Whose voice was it, Colonel, that you heard in the vicinity of St. Raymond's Cemetery that night, saying 'Hey Doctor'?"

There was a pause and the Great Aviator turned toward Richard Hauptmann. "That was Hauptmann's voice," he declared loudly for the entire courtroom to hear. Lindbergh, as usual was calm and collective. He waited for a response from Richard Hauptmann. He knew there was a possibility that he could turn to him, and point his finger and say for the world to hear, "You had your own son kidnapped, it was your fault".......And when he did, the Great Aviator would be ready. He would swing around toward Hauptmann, and shout for everyone to hear,

"You cold-blooded monster, how dare you to say such a terrible thing!" He would pull out the pistol from his shoulder harness. 'BAM, BAM, BAM!' He would let him have it right there in the courtroom. An angry crowd would immediately support the Great Aviator's impulsive decision to shoot the no good German alien who callously killed the little eaglet. They would say the same thing "How dare he accuse the Great Aviator!" After a brief inquiry by the Grand Jury, the case would be dismissed and Charles Lindbergh would walk away a free man.

The Great Aviator kept waiting for a response from Hauptmann. There was none. He was relieved. He did not have to follow through on his plan to do away with Richard Hauptmann. But he knew he would have to be keenly aware of what was being said during the rest of the trial, just in case Hauptmann felt compelled to tell the truth. The Great Aviator would need to be vigilant, especially when Doc Condon gave his testimony. And he would hold on to that seat next to the prosecution table.

For the next eight days of testimony, the prosecution paraded numerous experts and witnesses to incriminate Hauptmann. Arthur Koehler, a so-called wood expert said the wood from Hauptmann's attic matched the ladder. Albert Osborne, despite confidently denying the ransom notes had been written by Hauptmann when he was detained in New York City, now had changed his mind, and said they were indeed written by him. The state was able to get seven other handwriting experts to support Osborne's claim. Joseph Perrone, the cab driver who really didn't get a good glimpse of Hauptmann when he gave him the note to give to Doc Condon, was now pointing his finger at him. They even used the planted phone number of Doc Condon's that had been written as a joke against him. There were two witnesses from Hopewell, one of whom was a legally blind 87 year-old Prussian immigrant named Amandus Hochmuth. Hochmuth claimed he saw Hauptmann with a ladder in his car. The other man, a dirt poor mountaineer from the Sourlands named Millard Whited initially said he saw nothing unusual, but changed his mind, when the state policeman had told him there was a reward offered. He quickly echoed Hochmuth's claim. Young Benny Lupica said he saw a person with a ladder, but was not sure who the person was. The state gave him a hard time when he also said the car had New Jersey plates. The Great Aviator was worried about the young man. He remembered he had to pull over his car with the ladder protruding out the window when Lupica passed by. However, the state did not spend much time with him; they just wanted an admission that he saw a man who could have been Hauptmann with the ladder.

By the end of week two, it was Doc Condon's turn to implicate Hauptmann. With Wilentz being his set up man, the old codger felt right at home and unleashed his usual array of thespian sputum. When Wilentz asked him who was Cemetery John, the old man rose up from his chair, pointed his finger and slowly bellowed "Bruno….Richard….Hauptmann!" He did this three times during the testimony and although Hauptmann was seething, he said nothing. The Great Aviator was ready to move, but he did not have to brandish his weapon. One time during cross-examination, Condon slipped up. When Reilly asked him if he knew about Johnson's phone call to Betty Gow, he replied, "I knew that the night of the kidnapping." Hauptmann's attorney as usual, failed to exploit the comment, and it was assumed by most that the old man just made a mistake.

With the trial continuing for a few more weeks, Hauptmann had to face up to the realization that he was the scapegoat. The dilemma was not just that he had to decide to either tell the truth or accept a guilty verdict, but he felt there was no one to talk to or confide in. He did not trust Reilly his lawyer; and the two main conspirators Lindbergh and Hauptmann were now his enemies. But he believed that the Great Aviator would do everything he could, to save him from electrocution. He knew he made a mistake by spending the ransom money, but did that deserve a death sentence? Hauptmann didn't think so. What he did not realize was that the Great Aviator now wanted him dead. He didn't want to spend the rest of his life worrying that Hauptmann would rat him out. Soon, his fate would be in the hands of the jury, and the way things were going, Richard Hauptmann's future looked bleak at best. The mounting evidence and the prevailing attitude from the judge on down to the jury seemed to be that Hauptmann was guilty. There were three points of evidence that overwhelmingly pointed the finger at him being at the least an extortionist. The fact that he had the ransom money in his house was indefensible. Condon's testimony that he negotiated and gave the money to Hauptmann was convincing. And although it might have seemed minor in comparison with the other evidence, the Great Aviator's identification of Hauptmann's voice at St. Raymond's put a final nail in his coffin. All this was devastating to his claim of innocence. Essentially, the case was over once the iconic Lindbergh indicted the German carpenter on the stand.

As the case against him grew stronger, Hauptmann's frustration became evident on two occasions. One time he stood up and went after Special Agent Thomas Sisk, one of the men who searched his garage and had stated that the money had been there longer than Hauptmann had said. He shouted, "Mister, Mister you stop lying. The other time there was a heated exchange between him and Wilentz about Condon's phone number written in the closet. It was the same number that journalist Tom Cassidy had written. Hauptmann had admitted in the Bronx that he wrote the number, and now he was saying he did not. He didn't remember, "Putting them numbers on. I'm positively sure I wouldn't write anything on the inside of a closet." Wilentz thought Hauptmann was getting too comfortable.

"You think you are a big shot, don't you?

"No," replied Hauptmann. "Should I cry?"

"No, certainly you shouldn't. You think you are bigger than everybody, don't you?"

"No, but I know I am innocent."

"Lying, when you swear to God that you will tell the truth! Telling lies doesn't mean anything."

"Stop that!" shouted Hauptmann

On one occasion Hauptmann aroused the courtroom crowd with his comments about the ladder. Ed Reilly asked him "How many years have you been a carpenter?"

"About ten years."

"Did you build that ladder?" The German carpenter smirked.

"I am a carpenter!" Later the courtroom erupted in laughter when Hauptmann claimed the ladder looked like a musical instrument. David Wilentz did not like it one bit, and continued to try to break him down and portray him as a callous and arrogant murderer.

The trial went on with more experts and more witnesses. After twenty-nine days of actual testimony, the prosecution had rested. By now the newspapers were calling Hauptmann's attorney Death House Reilly. But he was impressive in his closing remarks. "Judge not, lest ye be judged." Quoting St. Matthew, he wanted the jury to use their conscience in rendering their decision. He explained how difficult it would be for one person to pull off the kidnapping. He went on to accuse the police of falsifying evidence. He asked them to "do their duty under the law and under the evidence." David Wilentz spent over four hours hammering away at the jury going over the evidence. Seemingly desperate to further his career, he gave up any sense of dignity when he went into a vicious attack on Hauptmann lambasting him with disgraceful insults.

"He was an egomaniac.....he had ice water in his veins.....the filthiest and vilest snake that ever crept through the grass....an animal lower than the lowest form in the animal kingdom....Public Enemy Number One of this world!"

The next day Judge Trenchard informed the jury of their obligations, gave them a few hints of his own leaning of guilt and sent them off for deliberations. After one full day of discussion, they were ready to announce the verdict. At 10:45 on the thirteenth of February 1935, the jury foreman Charles Walton shook as he read the verdict:

"We the jury, find the defendant guilty of murder in the first degree." Anna Hauptmann clasped her head in her hands and sobbed uncontrollably. Outside in the old tower, a large bell tolled slowly informing the community of the jury's decision. A distraught Richard Hauptmann was led back to his cell, collapsed onto his cot, and wept incessantly. The Trial of the Century was now over. Trenchard set the execution date at March 18th. Unless they were able to get an appeal, Richard Hauptmann had a little more than a month to live. Outside, reminiscent of an ancient coliseum crowd, the masses cheered and chanted "Death to the Lindbergh kidnapper!" Richard Hauptmann was transferred to the death house at Trenton State Prison. He became Prisoner No. 17400 and would occupy cell nine.

The Great Aviator went back to his volunteer position at the Rockefeller Institute working with Alexis Carrel. It would not take long before they picked up their conversation where they left off. Both were still trying to figure out a way to preserve the smartest and strongest members of society and eliminate the weakest. Doc Condon found enjoyment in a new career as a Lindbergh Kidnapping expert, emoting and acting out his role as the intermediary. Charlie Schleser went back to his shady business enterprises looking for old people to prey upon. Red Johnson was back in Norway selling fruit and battling alcoholism. Betty Gow was back in Scotland and refused to comment on the case. Violet Sharpe and Isadore Fisch had met their deaths while Richard Hauptmann was awaiting his.

Once the appeal process started, the first date of execution was pushed back. On May 10th Lloyd Fischer who replaced Ed Reilly as Hauptmann's counsel, filed for a new trial. He cited several reasons. The Great Aviator's presence at the trial was prejudicial, Judge Trenchard's instructions were biased toward the state, and the extensive pre-trial publicity along with the circus atmosphere had unfairly influenced the jury. All these factors had denied Hauptmann of a fair trial according to the fourteenth amendment.

Richard Hauptmann was adapting to prison life even if he was in Trenton's death house. He was situated in the last cell alongside the electrocution room. It was as if they deliberately put him there so he could watch the other doomed prisoners shuffle their last few steps of life on the way to their execution. Maybe it would make him finally talk and tell the truth. But the German remained stubbornly undaunted to his new life inside Trenton's granite walls. He was friendly with the guards, ate well and exercised to keep in shape. Without a real understanding of the judicial system, he mistakenly believed that the new Governor of New Jersey, Harold Hoffman would keep him alive. It was Hoffman who gave him a thirty-day reprieve, and was pushing for a new investigation into the kidnapping. He had openly announced his doubt that one man could pull off the crime. But Hoffman could not change the court's verdict by himself, there would have to be a hearing. And it was becoming apparent that he was one of a few lone dissenters. David Wilentz and his prosecution team, along with New Jersey's masses were outraged at the republican governor for what they thought was a usurping of the judicial system. Hoffman's political affiliation did not help him, since Wilentz and most of the state government was democratically controlled.

CHAPTER FORTY-EIGHT
ARTHUR JONES

———————————————————————

Every morning, Richard Hauptmann reluctantly checked off another day on his calendar. The new execution date was set for August. Since he was still alive, he continued to believe that the state of New Jersey was going to spare him his life. Inside the prison, people were nice to him. Sometimes the warden, Colonel Mark Kimberling would stop down to the death house and talk with him. Waiting for their destiny were several other prisoners on death row. Hauptmann was able to play chess through the bars and on rare occasions he would get the opportunity to talk to his cellmates. Two of his death-row comrades had become quite friendly. John Favorito was a cold, callous murderer who had shot a gas station operator over four dollars. He often started conversations with Hauptmann, mostly about trivial things. Hauptmann wasn't really comfortable with Favorito and limited the conversation to small talk. The other convict was a young man named Arthur James Jones. Jones was a young semi-literate Negro who Hauptmann hit it off with right away. It was an odd relationship since Hauptmann had never really befriended a Negro person before. Hauptmann really liked Jones because he seemed oblivious to the kidnapping. He was shy and not intrusive. Jones was awaiting an appeal hearing in September on a Newark, N.J. murder conviction. Hauptmann got the impression that Jones was a scapegoat like himself, and had been vilified simply because he was a Negro. From talking to him, he could discern that Jones didn't have any family support, and had been in the wrong place at the wrong time. It was as if both men were on the outside looking in. Their relationship grew out of that commonality. They both felt they were being railroaded. In their minds, America was becoming a place where you were not innocent until proven guilty but automatically deemed guilty if you were an illegal German immigrant or a Negro. Richard Hauptmann was willing to take the punishment for the crime he committed but not for the crime of murder. Arthur Jones knew he was no angel, but he was confident his appeal would grant him a new trial. He didn't read much, but he was perceptive for an uneducated, twenty-five year old convict.

In a very short time, the two had become good friends. Hauptmann even had Anna put a little money in his prison account in case he won his appeal and was given his freedom. It was Arthur Jones who Hauptmann finally found, as someone he could confide in. The two men would talk as often as they could. One day in March, Jones uncharacteristically asked Hauptmann about the kidnapping. Hauptmann told him that he knew what really happened that night, but did not provide him with any details. After further discussions, Hauptmann started giving Jones little hints of his involvement. Realizing that Jones didn't really know much about the kidnapping because he didn't read much, and didn't run with a crowd that would even discuss it, he added more information. Hauptmann liked that Arthur Jones did not make such a big deal about it.

After a month's worth of short snippets detailing the kidnapping, Richard Hauptmann had divulged yet another secret. He told Arthur Jones he was tired of being the fall guy for the two masterminds of the Lindbergh Kidnapping. Without telling anyone else, Hauptmann told Jones he was going to talk. But then, without anyone knowing, Governor Hoffman visited the German prisoner during the early hours of April 2nd. Hoffman told Hauptmann he knew that there were others involved, but that he did not want Hauptmann to say anything until he sorted everything out. He told Hauptmann that he had one of the best detectives in New Jersey, Ellis Parker working on finding out the truth. Until he was finished his investigation, he wanted Hauptmann to remain quiet.

Over a period of six months, Hauptmann fed Arthur Jones enough information about the kidnapping to explain how it happened, with the Great Aviator calling the shots. Jones did not know much about Charles Lindbergh, other than the fact that he flew across the Atlantic. Finding out that Lindbergh was responsible for the kidnapping came as a surprise to him. During the six months of their relationship, the two men had used every possible means of communicating without anyone knowing what they were talking about. Since the shower room was across and directly in line with Jones' cell, they were able to talk on bath days. The guards often stayed clear of the shower room. Other times, Hauptmann would write down information in code. Using each letter of the alphabet for a number, such as A for 1, B for 2, C for 3, the two men pretended as if Hauptmann was teaching Jones Arithmetic. When the opportunity arose, Hauptmann would pass pieces of paper inside books that they pretended to share. Richard Hauptmann had made up his mind to tell Arthur Jones the whole story, so long as Jones maintained the secrecy.

Governor Hoffman made another impromptu visit to Hauptmann. The prisoner was surprised when Hoffman told him he knew who was involved but that he did not think they could prove it, even if Hauptmann came forward and told what he knew. He thought that without concrete proof no one would believe him and it was still best if he kept quiet. Hauptmann followed the governor's request, but did not seem to mind updating Arthur Jones. He knew he did not always make the right decisions but there was something about Arthur Jones that he liked. He confided in him and trusted him and he liked the fact that Jones did not talk much to the other prisoners. In August, John Favorito was executed and for the next month Hauptmann would only talk to Jones. During their time together, a friendship developed that provided Hauptmann with some comfort as he waited for his fate to be decided by the politicians. After every conversation, Jones would add the new information to the kidnapping story that Hauptmann had already given him. He would write it all down on paper and then tear it up. Out of loyalty to Hauptmann and to prevent guards from finding out about their conversations, Jones tore up the papers into tiny pieces and flushed them down the toilet. He found that by writing it down, he could remember the details better. At one point after a visit from his spiritual advisor Reverend Matthiesen, Hauptmann told Jones that he was torn between keeping silent and telling the truth. Matthiesen wanted him to come clean, but the governor was still telling him to keep quiet. Richard Hauptmann told the young man that if he died, he could speak the truth for him. He could let the world in on the big secret. He even told him he could make money off it. "Take it to the New York newspapers and they vill pay you for it." Hauptmann believed that Arthur Jones could be the one to tell the world the truth about the Great Aviator and his manipulative sidekick Doctor Condon. The two masterminds would have to finally own up to the kidnapping.

New Jersey's Court of Errors and Appeals was analyzing the legal arguments from both sides, to see if Richard Hauptmann had been denied a fair trial. Hauptmann's execution for now was again on hold. In September, Arthur Jones was given a new lease on life when he was granted a new trial. Before he left on the morning of September 11th, the guards allowed him to speak with Richard Hauptmann for almost thirty minutes.

"Arthur, I vant you to promise me three things."

"Richard I will do whatever you want me to do."

"First I vant you to promise me you vill learn to read and write. Get as good an education as you can in das prison system." Arthur Jones nodded his head as the famous prisoner went on.

"Secondly, Arthur I vant you to remember evryding I told you about the kidnapping. When I die I vant you to let the truth be told. I vant Condon and Lindbergh to own up to their role and evryvon must know how they sent a man who is innocent of murder to death. They must pay for that."

"Yes sir, I will do that for you."

"The last ding I vant you to do Arthur is to promise me you vill never try to get something from noting". Hauptmann took out a pencil and a piece of paper. He wrote down a three and a zero.

"Remember you can get two from three, you can get one from two, and you can get one from one. But you can't get anyding from zero. Arthur, don't ever try to get something from noting.

"I won't Richard, I promise."

"I vill die for ten people. Maybe vun day they vill know the truth." Richard Hauptmann smiled at the young man as he rose from the bench.

"Goodbye, Richard. Maybe I will see you on the other side." Arthur Jones headed upstairs to catch his ride up to Essex County.

As the courts were trying to figure out if Hauptmann was given a fair trial, Anna Hauptmann was pounding the pavement in the German American communities gathering support for her husband. In order to pay the legal fees for the appeal, she needed to get donations. Many of Hauptmann's friends were instrumental in collecting the money. Charlie Schleser however was not one of them. After the trial ended, he was of no use to the prosecutors and went back to his phony real estate business hustling people. Hauptmann's circle of friends no longer served a purpose for him, and he was nowhere to be found when they went looking for support.

On October 9, 1935, the fourteen judges of the N.J. Court of Errors and Appeals issued a forty-five-page decision that upheld the murder conviction. Lloyd Fisher then appealed to the United States Supreme Court, but in December they announced they would not review the case. Judge Trenchard again set a date for execution. It was now slated for January 17, 1936. Without Richard Hauptmann's knowledge, and despite the denials of the higher courts, Governor Hoffman was still trying to get to the bottom of the Lindbergh Kidnapping. He was continuing the investigation based on some new evidence that he had received. Right before the Supreme Court had turned down the appeal, the newspapers reported that Governor Hoffman had been conducting his own investigation since the court case began. Hoffman was planning on breaking the case wide open because he felt the floorboards from Hauptmann's attic were not the same as the ladder, and that the entire ladder evidence had been nothing but a fabrication. In his mind, that evidence along with Doc Condon's phone number found in Hauptmann's house, and Koehler's forced opinion that Hauptmann wrote the ransom notes, was just part of a scam. The police and the Attorney General's office were in cahoots together to force a conviction of the German carpenter. When word reached the Great Aviator of Hoffman's intentions, he immediately told his wife Anne to "be ready to leave the country in twenty-four hours". Without her knowledge, he had secretly applied and received passports for himself, his wife and the baby. Citing a fabricated increase in threats, he thought that he and his family would be safer in Sweden or England. What he did not tell his wife was that he was worried that Hoffman would uncover evidence, implicating him for his role in the kidnapping. A few days later, Doc Condon purchased steamer tickets to Panama. On December 21st, the Great Aviator took his wife and son and fled to England where he would seek permanent residence. On December 23rd Lloyd Fisher filed for a final appeal with the N.J. Court of Pardons of which Governor Hoffman was a member. The Great Aviator, Anne and Jon were on the high seas, where they would spend their Christmas. The following week before the year ended, with the courts and the governor still working on finding out the truth, Doc Condon was also traveling the high seas. Leaving his wife behind, he talked his daughter Myra into accompanying him for an extended vacation in Panama. They would celebrate News Years Day at sea.

On January the 11th, the New Jersey Court of Pardons completed their hearing. In a seven to one decision they voted to uphold Hauptmann's death sentence. The lone dissenter was Harold Hoffman. The Governor of New Jersey was fast becoming an unpopular governor. The majority of New Jersey citizens criticized him for wasting the court's time and money. Most Americans were disgusted that he would support the murderer of the Lindbergh baby. His political career was now in jeopardy. Some New Jersey residents started calling for his impeachment. Shortly after the decision, Hoffman visited Hauptmann yet again. The newspapers had found out about this visit and hanged him in the court of public opinion. Hoffman told Richard Hauptmann that his investigation went up in smoke, when his investigator coerced another man to sign a twenty-five-page confession that he was the kidnapper. When it came out that the man was beaten and physically forced to confess, whatever credibility the governor had left was destroyed along with his career. The only thing he could do for him was to grant him a thirty-day reprieve. Harold Hoffman's political career was in ruins because he did the right thing and sought the truth, but the majority of people did not see it that way. Giving the impression that he was trying to get Hauptmann to talk when he visited him, he did just the opposite. He told Richard Hauptmann to remain quiet. He told Hauptmann that he had a strong hunch who was responsible, but that there wasn't much he could do about it. Even if he talked, he was still going to die because people would not believe him over the Great Aviator and his masterful manipulator Doc Condon. In addition, Hoffman told him that if he did decide to sing, there was a possibility that his wife and child would be in danger. As usual, the Great Aviator had exercised his power and won. Governor Hoffman told him that his wife and child would be taken care of, and that he should use the thirty days to find his peace with God. There wasn't anything else he could do.

After one more final appeal was shot down, the execution date was set for April 3, 1936. Richard Hauptmann wrote a final statement and gave it to his lawyer Lloyd Fisher. He reiterated that he was not guilty of murder and had nothing else to say. With the world anxious for him to tell what he knew about the Lindbergh Kidnapping, he disappointed everyone because he had made a deal with the governor. With no more political maneuvering, and satisfied that he was at peace with his God, Richard Hauptmann took the short walk to the death room next door, faced his executioner, and was electrocuted.

CHAPTER FORTY-NINE
LIVING EVER AFTER

———————————————————

W hen the word came that Bruno Richard Hauptmann was executed, Isadore Fisch and Violet Sharpe were dead. Betty Gow had already moved back to Scotland where she would live out the rest of her life unmarried. Red Johnson's life in Norway turned into one of struggle as he battled alcoholism and a failed marriage. Charlie Schleser continued to hustle people but found a way to stay out of jail. His wife remained with him until he died. Henry Breckinridge parted ways with the Great Aviator, and dealt with his own marital problems. With the war looming in Europe, he would focus all his energy on politics and strategies for dealing with Nazi Germany. Bobby Thayer did the same, and later took a job with the C.I.A. where he spent most of his time overseas. Neither talked to the Great Aviator again except when Lindbergh accused Breckinridge of defaulting on a $20,000.00 loan. They never discussed the Lindbergh Kidnapping case. Doc Condon lived into his early eighties and never changed. He savored any opportunity to talk about his contribution to the Lindbergh Kidnapping case until his death ten years later.

In the late 1930s, the Great Aviator found himself embroiled in controversy over his anti-Semitic views, and his cozy relationship with the Nazi government. He gave anti-Semitic speeches and refused to give his Nazi Flying Cross back to Herman Goering. He and Anne went on to have four more children after Jon. Although the media portrayed them as the perfect couple, they both struggled to hold on to the marriage, both having various extramarital affairs. Lindbergh continued to travel, often away from his family for long periods of time. In 2003, the world found out that the Great Aviator had fathered six other children with three different women in Europe. He never told anyone of those relationships. Most of his time was spent away from his family, only occasionally dropping in to see them. On those rare occasions, the family often had to deal with the conflict and tension that seemed to emanate from his ascorbic and unpredictable personality. In 1974, after a battle with cancer, the Great Aviator died on the island of Maui where he spent most of his time alone. His family stood by him and comforted him through his illness. He was buried on the island in a wooden coffin, in a simple plot of farmland that overlooked beautiful Kipahulu Bay, not far from spiritual aura of the Seven Sacred Pools. In 1978 his <u>Autobiography of Values</u> was published. It contained provocative theories on procreation. Anne lived on into her nineties and died in 2001. She spent most of her life surrounded by her family.

On his tombstone The Great Aviator requested this phrase from the 139th psalm: "IF I TAKE THE WINGS OF THE MORNING AND DWELL INTO THE UTTERMOST PARTS OF THE SEA.... He failed to complete the phrase which reads: EVEN THERE WOULD THY HAND LEAD ME/ AND THY RIGHT HAND WOULD HOLD ME."

CHAPTER FIFTY
1999/THE NOTE

T he middle aged man struggled as he went through his Dad's belongings. His father's untimely death was more a result of hospital negligence than pulmonary emboli. A person can never really prepare for the finality of losing a loved one. But such responsibilities often accompany a loved one's death. After his wife Elizabeth had died in 1994, Nick had spent many a lonely day listening to the Sinatra songs that he and his wife had danced to back in the 1950s. He often struggled with the memories of his life with her; the pain of losing her had aged him and expedited their reunion. Going through all those precious things that had been left took up a great deal of his time. Now it was his son who was going over his Dad's things, including an extensive collection of baseball cards that had kept him busy during those lonely days. He kept his cards meticulously organized by teams, and years, and in binders and boxes. Besides cards, there were other possessions. In another drawer, there were a few pieces of jewelry, a ring, a couple watches. Stuffed in the back of his dresser drawer was the same envelope that was given to him by Arthur Jones in 1950. It had been almost fifty years since the young prison guard was given the note, and for those fifty years it lay there in the drawer. Occasionally, his youngest son would go in there and read the note, intrigued by its contents, and then place it back in the envelope, and back in the drawer.

"Hey Dad, where did you say you got this from?"

"Ah, some inmate gave it to me when I worked at the prison."

It's amazing how fast life comes and goes; at the time of his death Nick's five children had grown into middle-aged adults with kids of their own. Going through a person's belongings after death is hard, especially when it's a parent. But his son couldn't help but reminisce about the days of playing catch with his Dad, the first time he took him to Connie Mack Stadium and the times he came to watch him play baseball. He also remembered the first time he asked him if he could read the note that detailed the Lindbergh Kidnapping. He wondered who the author was and whether he was telling the truth. His youngest son took the note with the approval of his siblings and placed it in his shirt pocket. He would put it in his own drawer, but only temporarily. In 2001, he pulled it out and started writing a book about the Lindbergh Kidnapping.

The following is the exact unedited Arthur Jones account given to Nick the prison guard in 1950.

"DID JUSTICE TRIUMPH"

There have been tones of copies written about the Lindbergh Kidnaping, but out of the few billions of words printed, only a few have been factual. I happen to know that there are at least five people alive today who know all the facts of this case. I myself, know some of the facts. . .

There are a few things I don't know about the kidnapping that are Unimportant. But could be important if you are one to want the whole story complete and in detail. However, here is what I know about Lindbergh Kidnaping that can proven! To begin with, Bruno Hauptman did not kidnap the Lindbergh baby! The baby was actually kidnapped by Violet Sharpe. Betty Gow, who was the baby's nurse, was placed in the Lindbergh home by the kidnapers for the sole purpose of setting the baby in the proper spot for the convenience of the kidnapers when the time came.

Doc Condon had the final say in the choice of a nurse for the Lindbergh baby, and he chose Betty Gow. But that isn't surprising; Doc Condon and Betty Gow along with Red Johnson, Isadore Fisch and Charlie—comprised a regular kidnap ring. Doc Condon picked for him- by Charles Lindbergh himself. Charles Lindbergh actually paid Doc Condon $20,000, to take away the child, The money was handed over in three payments. And the records will show , in the banking accounts of both Charles Lindbergh and Doc Condon between the dates on their accounts you will find that Lindbergh withdrew $20,000, and that Condon deposited $14,000. This is the first of many things that should have been looked into. But for some reason, was not, and it can still be known at this late date. Another thing that can be readily proved, is that an all important meeting took place on March, 1932, in which Lindbergh met with Doc Condon, Red Johnson, Isadore Fisch and Hauptman. They spent four hours of that eventful afternoon working out the details which were climaxed with the finding of the Lindbergh baby —dead.

When the meeting broke up on the afternoon of March 1st, 1932, Lindbergh placed in the rear of his car a two piece extension ladder given him by Hauptman, and was driven away by a woman. Less than a hour after Lindbergh arrived at his home the baby was taken by Violet Sharpe and handed to Isadore Fisch who was waiting at the front door and was wisked away in a car driven by Hauptman. . . .

The next night Red Johnson delivered to the Lindbergh home the first ransom note which was dated March 4th. The ransom note, written by Doc Condon, as were xxxxxxxxxxxxx the others received by the Lindbergh, these note had a peculiar mark that Doc Condon used habitually in all his writings and in his classes as illustrations. The mark,, sign or signature could be easily recognized by those who attended his classes, if brought to their attention... Violet

Sharpe, who was unaware that she was being promoted for the part she was to play in the kidnapping. Had she known that Betty and Red Johnson were living together she would have been far removed from the Lindbergh estate. But as it was, she remained at Reds' beck and call and didn't hesitate when told to pick up the baby and deliver it to the car...

Upon reaching downtown Princeton, Miss. Sharpe was dropped off in front of a theatre, and the car with Hauptman, Fisch, and the baby continued to the outskirts of town to the house occupied by Charlie. And his wife.(I can't remember this Charlie's last

      page 1

name)..

The child died about ten days later the kidnapers thought pneumonia to be the cause of death. Bruno Hauptman drove the boy body where it was eventually found... death for the boy was not included in the deal. When the ransom money was paid the kidnapers were to leave for Germany and take the boy with them. Isadore Fisch left for Germany right away to await the others and his part of the ransom money, Hauptman, Red Johnson, Betty Gow along with Charlie and his wife were to follow and wait until Doc Condon had lined up another kidnap job for them. But the trip to Germany fell through for them when they found out that the ransom money was marked and could not be used for the expenses the trip back home would entail. The reason it took so long to pay the money, is because Lindbergh did not want to pay the marked money. He wanted to give good money so as to keep up his end of the deal.

Here are the answers to some questions that have been raised many times: The muddy footprints in and around the baby's room: Betty Gow, using a pair Charles Lindbergh's shoes spread those prints around. This was an after thought and was not included in the plans of the kidnapers. It was thought that Betty Gow did a bad job with those footprints.............

Second was the blood stains on the ransom money; it was Doc Condon's blood .xxxxxxxxxxxx It got on the money when he cut the third finger on his right hand breakin; the string that bound the money immediately before giving it to Bruno Hauptman.......................

Third, who washed, pressed and returned the sleeping gown worn by the baby when kidnapped. Charlie's wife, the woman who took care of the baby until it died, laundered the sleeping gown and had it return through Miss. Gow...............

The reason behind the story that Lindbergh hired the kidnapers to take the boy is that the boy was abnormal. Betty Gow reported to Hauptman that the boy would never learn to walk, nor would he ever be able to talk well enough to be understood. The baby was nineteen months old when taken and hadn't walked a step nor uttered a word. I don't know if that's true or not, but that is the way it was it was told to me Bruno Hauptman. This can easily be proven, did anybody ever see the boy walk, or hear him talk. Someone would surely know if the child was normalxx.

Doc Condon was never investigated because Lindbergh and his friends said it was unthinkable... and they did not want to insult him...But Bruno Hauptman swore that Doc Condon and the rest would be exposed. When the time drew near and he was being readed up for the chair, Bruno Hauptman was ready to talk. He told me that he was going to burn alone. He worried about the welfare of his wife and child. Then Governor Hoffman visited Hauptman in his cell in the Deathhouse and changed his mind. When Governor Hoffman left his cell, Hauptman told me that his wife and child would be supported for the rest of their lives, and that he was going to die without talking. He repeatedly told me how he was dying for ten people and that if it wasn't for Governor Hoffman some of them would burn with him............

I guess the most important questions at this time, is, how do I know these things? Where did I get this story from, Bruno Hauptman himself, and I put it down here as I remember it...... I was in the Death house long before Hauptman was arrested, tried and convicted. When he was brought in he would not talk to anyone but me for weeks. Death house guards can verify this. We became good friends in the next few months. He would order things from the prison store for me, and would have his wife and lawyers leave money in my account

continued from page #2

in the front office.... As soon as I was granted a new trial Bruno began telling me this story and I will swear it is true... I know that if it wasn't for his wife and child, and the visit from Governor Hoffman he would have talked... Hauptman and I would talk for about five minutes every bath day. The shower was in front and right in line with his cell... One day he told me we could talk without anyone knowing what we were saying. He had a code a child could understand, but we used it and here is how it worked...............

he was supposed to be teaching me arithmatic so that no one would know we were using the figures for conversation. For instance, he would say, add these figures and give me the answers.

9	11	20	25	14	3	2	8	23
____	14	8	15	15	15	1	5	9
	15	1	21	20	13	3	18	12
	23	20	____	____	5	11	5	12
____	____			____	____	____	____	

These figures equaled this message: I know that you will not come back here.

We used the figures 1 to 26 to equal the number of letters in the alphabet. 1 for A 11 for K 23 for W and so on. After about seven months of this along with our weekly talks, and a few notes passed in books, Hauptman told me this story. I wrote what he told me on pieces of papers and added to it every day. I read it and reread it until I could not forget it...

Bruno Hauptman insisted that I memorize the story until I got out and suggestd how I could do it. I have followed his instructions since I left the deathhouse. Every month or so I rewrite the whole story, and then tear it up. I don't always use the same words but it always the same story. Hauptman told me that when I got out of Prison I am to go to the New York Daily News and give them this story just as he told it to me; and that they would pay me for it. He told me that when they xxxxxxxx investigate this story they would find it to be true and factual. He said that if those ten people are still alive when this story comes out they will admit that they owe everything to Gov. Hoffman. He told me that he didn't hold anything against Charles Lindbergh because of the marked bills. Hauptman was told the bills were marked and also told not to try and use them. But the money he got from Doc Condon wasn't the amount xhe wished to take back to Germany when he left. The morning I left the deathouse the officer permitted me to speak to Hauptman while waiting for the Sheriff to take me back to Essex County to be retried. I spoke to him for about twenty-five minutes, from 11:am to almost 11:30. As I was leaving he told me to always remember on thing, when I asked what it was, he took a pencil and paper and wrote down a 3 and an 0, he said, you can get two from three, and you can get one from two, but you can't anything from zero. So remember you can't get something from nothing, so don't try it. He made me promise that I would never try to get something from nothing; and he told me that he would die. I did not believe that he would, but he knew. He knew that he would die for ten people, because he had made a deal with the Governor.

EPILOGUE

A s Arthur Jones stated in his 1950 account, there are millions of words printed about the Lindbergh Kidnapping. There are hundreds of theories. The more you research it the more complex it gets. As I told Mark Falzini, the Lindbergh Kidnapping archivist who oversees the artifacts and the innumerous pages of evidence at the N. J. State Police Museum in West Trenton, "The more I read about the case and the more I research it, the more confusing it becomes." He agreed and smiled as he said, "I love my job!" No wonder there has never been any viable theory presented that perfectly matches up with the outcome. In my opinion, there was no way one man could have pulled off the kidnapping by himself. To think that he could have climbed such a shaky ladder, entered the baby's nursery and descended the ladder without anyone hearing or seeing him is ludicrous. The nursery was above the library and there was a downstairs window as well. The ladder only weighed thirty-seven pounds and did not reach the actual windowsill. As a young man most of my summers were spent painting houses. Even after I started teaching, I tried to supplement my income hustling paint jobs. I learned keeping a ladder against a house on a windy day is nearly impossible. A thirty-seven pound ladder would have blown in the wind like a twig. Also if a ladder does not reach, and you have to extend the bottom outward, climbing it is like walking a tightrope. To prevent that, you can place it alongside the window. I have tried to enter a window by going in through the side. An agile person with moderate difficulty can grasp the sill and climb onto the window ledge, and noisily enter a room. But there is absolutely no way you can climb out of the window carrying thirty pounds in one hand, with a stiff wind blowing at your back, grasp a thirty-seven pound ladder and then quietly descend it without knocking it over or have someone hear you in the process. Too many variables make it highly improbable. The ladder would swing; you would lose your balance almost immediately and then haplessly crash to the ground. I do not believe the ladder had any true relevance in taking the baby out of the house. If there were two people involved, a person who entered the window and then handed the baby off to a confederate waiting at the top of the ladder, they would have been visible and noisy. The ladder had to be a ruse. Examining it one would question the craftsmanship, but because of its unique telescoping features it appears to have been built by someone who had an engineering aptitude. In the early thirties Charles Lindbergh had built a small telescoping ladder for his plane the Sirius. He also had an engineering aptitude. I believe he built the kidnap ladder.

When I visited the house, the first thing I wanted to look at was the proximity of the staircase with the nursery. It was as I assumed. When you enter the house the staircase is directly to the left. At the top of the stairs, directly to the left, is Betty Gow's room. If you turn right and take one step, you enter the nursery. It would have been quite easy to climb the stairs, grab the baby, descend the stairs and head right back out the front door. This could be done in approximately thirty seconds. Because of the house design, people on the right side of the house by the kitchen and pantry would not have heard the kidnapper, especially with a strong wind blowing. If Anne had been working at her corner desk in the living room like she claimed at eight o'clock, she would have had her back to the doorway and would not have seen the kidnapper. In my mind it is without question, that the baby went right out that front door.

Some theorists believe Richard Hauptmann used the ladder and dropped the baby to the ground (without anyone hearing him) and the baby died almost immediately. Standing beneath the nursery window, I was amazed at how short the window actually was from the ground. Unless the baby hit his head, I sincerely doubt he would have died immediately especially in three layers of clothing. Children that age can also be resilient because of the flexibility of their bones. Unless he took a fatal blow to the head, he would have screamed loud enough for everyone inside to hear him.

If we conclude the baby died, and Hauptmann took the body to the spot where he was found, then where were the baby's rubber pants? The FBI report claims the baby was wearing rubber pants. Where did they go? This point was never discussed, but I believe it to be extremely important. Rubber pants aren't biodegradable, at least not in two months. Did Hauptmann take the sleeping suit off the body along with the rubber pants, and leave the outer layer of clothing that Betty Gow had made for him? That garment was found on the baby. Why would he do that? What did he do with the rubber pants?

Would he have the courage to continue to try to extort money after killing the child? He would have to be psychopathic, without a conscience. Although he was a criminal, I don't believe he was a psychopath. It is well documented that during his incarceration at Trenton State Prison, when he was alone in his cell, he was often heard sobbing. Not typical behavior for a sociopath.

Arthur Koehler initially said the ransom notes had not been written by Hauptmann. He suddenly changed his mind to appease the police and the prosecution. If Hauptmann had carefully planned the kidnapping for a long time, why would he write ransom notes with a German accent and set himself up to be caught?

Why would he write down Doc Condon's phone number in his closet when he did not even have a telephone in the house?

If we look at the theory that Lindbergh accidentally dropped his baby, would a grieving father be so callous to wrap him in burlap and cast him into the woods so forest animals could eat away at his body? He could if he too was a psychopath lacking a conscience. That would suggest that Lindbergh didn't really feel much emotion toward the child or his wife My opinion of Lindbergh is that he did not have much of a conscience, but I can't believe that he would continue to orchestrate a one month kidnap plan that included a ransom payoff with a totally unknown stranger named Doc Condon just for the fun of it. The whole scenario is too unrealistic. There was more to the story.

In every biography of Charles Lindbergh, his strange behaviors as a young man have never been fully explained nor defended. Placing a poisonous snake in someone's bed and replacing a water-filled pitcher with kerosene, is not typical behavior for a young man. Only overzealous Hauptmann defenders from the various Lindbergh websites question him on these behaviors. Without a doubt, he should be held accountable because these behaviors go beyond maliciousness. In both cases they could have resulted in murder charges against him.

One of the strangest aspects of this case is indeed the role that Doctor Condon assumed. There is evidence suggesting he was accused of molesting young girls, and that immediately throws up a red flag, suggesting he has criminal tendencies. Why would Lindbergh allow this stranger to become the intermediary after only speaking with him for one hour? That same night he let him sleep on the floor of his missing son's room! How could normal parents even if they were distraught and irrational, allow something like that to happen?

Hauptmann was found with the ransom money. If he was just trying to extort money he would have said so instead of facing execution. He said on more than one occasion that he was not guilty of the crime they have charged him with. This implies however that he was guilty of something. What was it then? I believe

Richard Hauptmann was an accomplice to the crime. As I have stated, there was no doubting that he was a criminal, as was Isadore Fisch and Charlie Schleser. Not one of the three men saw anything wrong with robbing or bilking people, including their own friends. Fisch, by all accounts seemed to be a masterful con-man. Red Johnson and Betty Gow had to know something about the kidnapping, as did Violet Sharpe. The phone calls, their jobs, and the suicide are at the least suspicious. I believe Violet felt guilty for the baby's death, and then allowed that guilt to get the best of her. Regarding Henry Breckinridge, why would such a polished professional spend so much time with Doc Condon including sleeping at his house for days? This is suspicious behavior as well. And why wasn't Bobby Thayer called to testify when he was such an integral person in the early days of the investigation? After the baby was found, he disappears from the picture. I believe he found out something about the kidnapping and wanted to recuse himself for fear of being implicated in some way.

Regarding Arthur Jones, he also was a criminal and there is no doubting the fact that criminals can be creative. But the account he wrote contains information that a criminal who could barely read would not know about. For example, he says the person who took care of the baby was Charlie….. and Charlie's wife. He did not know Charlie's last name. Where did Jones get the name Charlie from? He didn't just make it up. Charlie Schleser and his wife were right in the middle of all the business operations that Isadore Fisch was involved in. It is also a fact that Schleser did provide David Wilentz with information during December of 1935 that helped him plan his case. Jones would not know this information un-less Hauptmann brought it up. The account that Jones wrote did not appear that farfetched, once I started putting everything together. The methods that Jones and Hauptmann used to exchange information were definitely possible at Trenton State Prison in 1935. And the fact that he admitted that the "facts might not have been always the same but the story is," suggests he was not making things up. When Jeff Newman recalled his interview with him, he spoke about how philosophical Jones was and how important it was for him to get the truth out before he died. Jones had recalled how Hauptmann was forced to go to the electric chair four times before they finally turned the voltage wheel, and that Arthur Jones was empathetic. Newman said, "There was something about him, that you knew he was telling the truth." If Jeff Newman had said to me, "I think the man was a conman or a liar," I would have abandoned this project. Newman is a very credible person. During the fifties, sixties and seventies, Arthur Jones sent letters to NJ governors asking them to look at his information and they declined any communication with him. And what would Arthur Jones have to gain by coming forward on his deathbed in 1976, to describe the same story forty years later? Distinguished journalist and attorney Jeff Newman certainly had nothing to gain by telling me he believed Arthur Jones. It is truly astounding that almost eighty years after the Lindbergh Kidnapping was committed, the event is still surrounded by such amazing intrigue, maybe more than ever before.

The end

ACKNOWLEDGEMENTS

Special thanks to:

My wife Pam for her continued support of this project

Hal Hammond–Editing

Mark Falzini–NJSP Archives

Jeff Newman—Author and attorney

For being nice and helpful along the way:

Bobby Barnes—<u>St. Augustine Record</u>

Lisa Calvert, St. John's County Library

Harry Camisa—Author, <u>Inside Out</u>

Peter Ellis—<u>St. Augustine Record</u>

Lloyd Gardner—Author, <u>The Case That Never Dies</u>

Paul Carluccio, Cleophix Hendrix, Sharon Lauchaire–Highfields NJ Boys Home

Eileen Morales–Princeton Historical Society

Matthew Schuman—NJ Prison System

Special thanks to Thelma Miller

All the many authors who have written about Charles Lindbergh and the kidnapping

An unlikely trio of encouragement: Ken Davenport, Leigh Ann Frazier, Gayle Horton

Ellen and Annie for their unknowing encouragement

Daulton and Quinn for their editing and consultation

Made in the USA
Lexington, KY
05 March 2011